FRENCH PREPOSITIONS

Forms and Usage

Trudie Maria Booth

University Press of America,® Inc.
Lanham · Boulder · New York · Toronto · Oxford

University Press of America,® Inc.
4501 Forbes Boulevard
Suite 200
Lanham, Maryland 20706
UPA Acquisitions Department (301) 459-3366

PO Box 317
Oxford
OX2 9RU, UK

Printed in the United States of America
British Library Cataloging in Publication Information Available

ISBN 0-7618-2611-4 (paperback : alk. ppr.)

™ The paper used in this publication meets the minimum requirements of American National Standard for Information Sciences—Permanence of Paper for Printed Library Materials, ANSI Z39.48—1984

Contents

Preface

French Prepositions is an in-depth study of the forms and usage of simple and compound prepositions in the French language of today. Its goal is to be as comprehensive as possible in the coverage of these small, yet ever so important words, and to provide a reliable source of information about an aspect of French grammar that is often neglected. While it can be used as a manual in intermediate and advanced French courses, the book is primarily intended to serve as a reference tool for both teachers and students of French. Since the use of French prepositions is compared with the use of prepositions in English throughout the text, it also offers valuable information about the English language to French natives.

The book is divided into ten chapters. After presenting an inventory of the French prepositions and indicating their presence in a wide variety of contexts, the manual proceeds to an analysis of the use of these words between verbs and their noun complements, between conjugated verbs and infinitives, and between nouns as well as adjectives and verb objects, always emphasizing the difference between English and French. Verbs and expressions that can be used with different prepositions before a following noun or infinitive and may change their meaning depending on which preposition (if any) follows them, are described at the end of chapters six and seven (e.g. *servir qn/qch, servir **à** qch, servir **de** qn/qch*; *venir* + infinitive, *venir **de*** + infinitive, *venir **à*** + infinitive). The last chapter is devoted to geographical names (cities, continents, countries, islands, regions, French regions, provinces and departments, American states and Canadian provinces), and shows how to use *en, au, aux, dans le, dans la, dans les, de, du* and *des* correctly to indicate location, destination and origin.

Throughout the book, sections entitled 'Mistakes to avoid' point out frequent errors made by anglophone speakers and show how to correct them (e.g. *Incorrect*: Je cherche ~~pour~~ mon chien. *Correct*: Je cherche mon chien.).

The material treated under the headings 'Translation Difficulties' calls the attention of the reader to those prepositions that cannot be translated literally into French and points out idiomatic usage (e.g. ***in** the picture* = ***sur** la photo; **on** Sunday = dimanche*; *I have waited **for** three hours.* = *J'attends **depuis** trois heures.*). It also includes a detailed description of the numerous French equivalents of the English word 'about'.

Many sections end with a list of proverbs, sayings and idiomatic expressions containing the prepositions covered in them. Most examples are alphabetized to enable the user to find the answer to a question as quickly as possible, and all examples (which include useful modern vocabulary and, whenever possible, cultural information about France) are translated into English for comparison purposes.

Inspired by my students and the result of many years of research and teaching experience, *French Prepositions* was written with the intention of giving a clear and thorough description of an aspect of the French language which is treated only superficially in most grammar books. When learning a foreign language, the mastery of prepositions is one of the most difficult tasks. If the present book facilitates this task, leads to a better understanding of the French language, and contributes to the reader's ability to express himself with native accuracy, its goal will have been achieved.

Abbreviations used in this book are

adj. *adjective*

e.g. *for example*

fam. *familiar, informal language*

f *feminine*
m *masculine*

fig. *figuratively*

i.e. *id est (= that is)*

inf. *infinitive*

lit. *literally* (indicating the literal translation of a French expression or sentence)

qn *quelqu'un (= somebody)*
qch *quelque chose (= something)*

sb *somebody*
sth *something*

vs *versus*

Symbols used are

a slash / (to indicate an alternative)

round brackets ( ) (to indicate an optional addition)

Chapter 1

The Forms of French Prepositions

Prepositions establish a relationship between two words. They are invariable. There are simple prepositions (consisting of one word only), and compound prepositions (consisting of two or more words).

A. Simple prepositions

à	*to, at, in*
après	*after*
avant	*before*
avec	*with*
chez	*at/to the house of, in the work of*
concernant	*concerning, regarding, relating to*
contre	*against*
dans	*in*
de	*from, of*
depuis	*since* [+ time point], *for* [+ time period], *from* [+ place] *on*
derrière	*behind*
dès	*from...on, as early as, starting*
devant	*in front of*
durant	*during*
en	*in*
entre	*between*
envers	*towards* [+ person]
excepté (= sauf)	*except, apart from*
hormis	*except for*
hors	*out of, outside*
jusque	*until*
malgré	*in spite of*
moyennant	*for, with*
outre	*besides, in addition to*
par	*by, through, per*
parmi	*among*

passé	*past*
pendant	*during, for* [+ time period]
pour	*for, in order to*
sans	*without*
sauf (= excepté)	*except, apart from*
selon (= suivant)	*according to*
sous	*under*
suivant	*according to*
sur	*on*
vers	*toward*
vu	*due to, given*

Rien en ce monde n'est certain, **excepté** la mort et les impôts.	*Nothing in this world is certain, except for death and taxes.* (Franklin)
Le distributeur est **hors** service.	*The vending machine is out of order.*
Beaucoup d'enfants naissent **hors** mariage.	*Many children are born out of wedlock.*
Outre le français, il parle trois langues.	*Besides French, he speaks three languages.*
Passé dix heures, il ne faut pas faire de bruit.	*After ten o'clock, one must not make any noise.*
Selon (= d'après) la météo, il va neiger.	*According to the weather forecast, it is going to snow.*
Agissez **suivant** mes conseils.	*Act according to my advice.*

Sayings and expressions

balayer **devant** sa porte	*to put one's house in order before criticizing other people*
Le pire est **derrière** nous.	*The worst is over (= behind us).*
selon toute probabilité	***in** all likelihood*

Note:

1. Some expressions contain a combination of two simple prepositions.

Il a divorcé **d'avec** sa femme.	*He divorced his wife.*
Cette bague vient **de chez** vous.	*This ring comes from your store.*
deux **d'entre** eux	*two of them*

2. When several complements are present, the prepositions **à, de** and **en** must be repeated before each word they govern.

Bonjour **à** tous et **à** toutes.	*Hello everybody.*
J'irai **à** Paris et **à** Rome.	*I will go to Paris and Rome.*[1]
Bonne Année et bonne santé **à** toi et **à** toute ta famille.	*Happy New Year and good health to you and your entire family.*
Il est fier **de** sa maison et **de** son jardin.	*He is proud of his house and garden.*
Nous allons **en** France et **en** Italie.	*We go to France and Italy.*
On peut y aller **en** train ou **en** avion.	*One can go there by train or plane.*
Elle a traduit le passage **en** anglais et **en** espagnol.	*She translated the passage into English and Spanish.*

Except when

- the words making up the complements are part of a fixed expression, designate the same person, or form a unit

l'Ecole **des** Arts et Métiers	*the School of Arts and Crafts*
Je parle **à** mon ami et collègue David.	*I speak to my friend and collegue David.*
C'est le fils **de** Monsieur et Madame Dubois.	*He is the son of Mr. and Mrs. Dubois.*
à vos risques et périls	*at your own risk*
à court et moyen terme	*in the short and medium term*

- the complements are numerals combined by '*ou*'

une lettre **de** deux *ou* trois pages	*a two or three page letter*
La Tour Eiffel s'élève **à** 300 *ou* 310 mètres.	*The Eiffel Tower rises to 300 or 310 meters.*
Je peux faire ça **en** cinq *ou* six minutes.	*I can do that within five or six minutes.*

The other simple prepositions do not have to be repeated before each complement.

Il est venu **avec** son père et sa mère.	*He came with his father and mother.*
Elle vit **chez** sa tante et son oncle.	*She lives with her aunt and uncle.*
Nous sommes partis **malgré** la neige et le verglas.	*We left in spite of the snow and ice.*

By repeating one of these prepositions, each element of the complement is emphasized, as is the case in the following fixed expressions.

pour une raison ou **pour** une autre	*for one reason or another*
C'est **pour** aujourd'hui ou **pour** demain?	*Come on, we haven't got all day!*

---

1. Note that English does not repeat prepositions.

B. Compound prepositions[1]

à cause de[2] (= en raison de)	*because of, due to*
à condition de	*on the condition that*
à côté de	*next to, beside*
à droite de	*on/to the right of*
à gauche de	*on/to the left of*
afin de	*so that, in order to*
à force de	*by dint of, through, by (means of)*
à l'aide de	*with the help of*
à l'arrière de	*in the back of*
à la place de	*instead of*
à la suite de	*following, as a result of*
à l'avant de	*in the front of*
à l'écart de	*away from*
à l'égard de	*with regard to, regarding*
à l'exception de	*with the exception of*
à l'extérieur de	*outside*
à l'extrémité de	*at the far end of*
à l'instar de	*following the example of, like*
à l'insu de	*unknown to, without the knowledge of*
à l'intention de	*(intended) for*
à l'intérieur de	*inside*
à l'inverse de	*contrary to*
à l'opposé de	*in contrast to*
à moins de	*unless*
à part	*aside from, apart from, except for*
à partir de	*from...onwards, starting*
à propos de (= au sujet de)	*about, regarding, on the subject of*
à proximité de	*near, close to, in the vicinity of*
à raison de	*at the rate of*
à titre de	*in the capacity of, by virtue of, as*
à travers	*across, through*
au bord de	*by, alongside*
au bout de	*after, at the bottom of, at the end of*
au centre de	*in the center of*
au coin de	*at the corner of*
au cours de	*in the course of, during*

---

1. Most compound prepositions end in **à** or **de**. Note that the end prepositions **à** or **de** of these compound prepositions contract with the definite articles **le** and **les**:
   à + le = **au** à + les = **aux** de + le = **du** de + les = **des**
   grâce **aux** professeurs — *thanks to the teachers*
   à côté **du** tableau — *next to the blackboard*
2. Do not confuse the preposition **à cause de** (because **of**) with the conjunction **parce que** (because) [See p. 165-166].

au-delà de	*beyond*
au-dessous de	*below, underneath*
au-dessus de	*above, over*
au fond de	*at the bottom of, at the end of, in the rear of*
au lieu de	*instead of*
au long de	*throughout*
au milieu de	*in the middle of*
au moyen de	*by means of*
au nom de	*in the name of, on behalf of*
au pied de	*at the foot of*
au prix de	*at the price of*
au risque de	*at the risk of*
au sommet de	*at the top of*
auprès de	*next to, close to, with, to, near*
au sujet de (= à propos de)	*about, concerning*
autour de	*around*
aux alentours de (= aux environs de)	*around, (at) approximately*
aux dépens de	*at the expense of*
avant de	*before*
comparé à	*compared to*
d'après (= selon, suivant)	*according to, (to be named) after*
de crainte de (= de peur de)	*for fear of*
de façon à	*so as to, so that*
de la part de	*on behalf of, from (a person)*
de manière à	*so as to, so that*
de peur de (= de crainte de)	*for fear of*
du côté de	*in the vicinity of, in the direction of, toward*
du haut de	*(down) from*
en amont de	*upstream from*
en attendant de	*while waiting for, until*
en aval de	*downstream from*
en bas de	*at the bottom of*
en comparaison de	*compared to, by comparison with*
en dehors de	*outside, apart from*
en dépit de (= malgré)	*in spite of*
en dessous de	*below*
en échange de	*in exchange for*
en face de	*opposite, across from*
en fonction de	*according to, depending on*
en haut de	*on the top of*
en plus de	*besides*
en présence de	*in the presence of*
en raison de (= à cause de)	*because of, on account of*

en tant que	*as, in the capacity of*
face à	*faced with, given, opposite, facing*
faute de	*for lack of*
grâce à	*thanks to*
hors de	*out of, outside of*
jusqu'à	*until, as far as*
loin de	*far from*
le long de	*along*
lors de	*at the time of*
par-dessous	*under*
par-dessus	*over*
par manque de	*for lack of*
par rapport à	*in relation to, in comparison with*
par suite de	*as a consequence of*
pour cause de	*because of, on account of*
près de	*close to, near*
quant à	*as for*
suite à	*following, with reference to*
vis-à-vis de	*opposite, next to, towards, compared to*
y compris	*including*

A force de bavarder, on n'a pas vu le temps passer.	*By dint of chatting, time passed quickly.*
A force de réflexion, il a trouvé la solution.	*He found the solution through thinking.*
Je voudrais un café **à la place d'**un thé.	*I would like coffee instead of tea.*
A la suite de cet accident, on lui a retiré le permis.	*Following this accident, they took his licence away.*
à l'arrière de l'avion	*in the back of the plane*
à l'avant de la voiture	*in the front of the car*
Il est parti **à l'insu de** son fils.	*He left without his son knowing it.*
à l'instar de son copain	*following the example of his friend*
La quête fut organisée **à l'intention des** enfants martyrs.	*The collection was organized for the abused children.*
Vous trouverez le mode d'emploi **à l'intérieur de** la boîte.	*You will find the instructions for use inside the box.*
A part ça, pas grand-chose de nouveau.	*Besides that nothing much is new.*

A part Yves, personne n'est venu.	*Except for Yves, nobody came.*
Il vend les bananes **à raison de** deux euros le kilo.	*He sells the bananas at the rate of two euros per kilogram.*
Il a été gracié **en raison de** son âge.	*He was pardoned because of his age.*
Le magasin est fermé **pour cause de** décès.	*The store is closed on account of a death.*
Ils ont marché **à travers** le champ.	*They walked across the field.*
au-delà de la mer	*beyond the ocean*
Les enfants **au-dessous de** sept ans paient demi-tarif.	*Children below the age of seven pay half-price.*
vivre **au-dessous/en dessous du** seuil de pauvreté	*to live below the poverty line*
L'avion vole **au-dessus** des nuages.	*The plane flies above the clouds.*
vivre **au-dessus de** ses moyens	*to live above one's means*
à l'étage **au-dessus**	*on the floor above*
J'ai trouvé les clés **au fond de** mon sac.	*I found the keys at the bottom of my bag.*
Les toilettes sont **au fond du** couloir à droite.	*The restrooms are at the end of the hallway on the right.*
au fond de la salle	*in the back of the room*
tout **au long de** la journée	*throughout the entire day*
Il s'est évadé **au moyen d'**une corde.	*He escaped by means of a rope.*
Ils sont partis **au milieu de** la nuit.	*They left in the middle of the night.*
Excusez-vous **auprès du** professeur.	*Apologize to the teacher.*
Pour en savoir plus, renseignez-vous **auprès de** votre agence de voyages.	*For further information, inquire with your travel agency.*
Il a bonne réputation **auprès de** ses chefs.	*He has a good reputation with his bosses.*
Je me suis plaint **auprès d'**elle.	*I complained to her.*
Nous nous sommes disputés **au sujet de** sa soeur.	*We quarrelled about his/her sister.*
La terre tourne **autour du** soleil.	*The earth turns around the sun.*
aux alentours de trois heures	*around three o'clock*

Il doit avoir **aux alentours de** cinquante ans.	*He must be in his fifties.*
La robe est vendue **aux alentours de** 100 euros.	*The dress sells for approximately 100 euros.*
d'après la légende	*according to the legend*
d'après ce que j'ai entendu dire	*according to what I heard*
d'après ce qu'on dit	*according to what they say, as the story goes*
Je vous souhaite la bienvenue **de la part de** toute l'équipe.	*I welcome you on behalf of the entire team.*
Il a sauté **du haut de** la Tour Eiffel.	*He jumped from the Eiffel Tower.*
Bonn est situé **en amont de** Cologne.	*Bonn is located upstream from Cologne.*
Le Pont Neuf est situé **en aval de** l'Ile-de-la-Cité.	*The Pont Neuf is located downstream from the Ile-de-la-Cité.*
en bas/en haut de la page	*on the bottom/on the top of the page*
En dehors du tennis, quels sont vos passe-temps favoris?	*Apart from tennis, what are your favorite pastimes?*
Ils ont fait un voyage **en dehors des** Etats-Unis.	*They took a trip outside the United States.*
Faute de temps, je n'ai pas pu lui écrire.	*I couldn't write to him for lack of time.*
Faute d'argent, je ne peux rien acheter.	*I cannot buy anything for lack of money.*
C'est **hors de** question.	*That is out of the question.*
Le patient est **hors de** danger.	*The patient is out of danger.*
Elle est **hors d'**haleine.	*She is out of breath.*
Ils se sont promenés **le long de** la Seine.	*They walked along the Seine.*
Il a regardé **par-dessus** ses lunettes.	*He looked over his eyeglasses.*
Saute **par-dessus** la palissade.	*Jump over the fence.*
La mairie est **près de** la gare.	*The townhall is close to the train-station.*

Quant à moi, je reste.	*As far as I am concerned, I am staying.*
Suite à notre entretien téléphonique, je voudrais...	*Following our telephone conversation, I would like...*
Vos problèmes ne sont rien **vis-à-vis des** miens.	*Your problems are nothing compared to mine.*
Sa conduite **vis-à-vis de** ses parents a été très mauvaise.	*His behavior toward his parents was very bad.*
Il a tout cassé, **y compris** mon vase préféré.	*He broke everything, including my favorite vase.*

Proverbs, sayings, and idioms

loin des yeux, **loin du** cœur	*out of sight, out of mind*
tourner **autour du** pot	*to beat about the bush*
être **hors de** soi	*to be beside oneself*
hors de prix	*outrageously expensive*
hors **des** sentiers battus	*off the beaten track*
par-dessus le marché	*on top of it all*
Ce que j'aime **par-dessus** tout, c'est voyager.	*What I like best of all is travelling.*
J'en ai **par-dessus** la tête.	*I have had it up to here.*

Note:

The final **à** or **de** of a compound preposition is always repeated before each word it refers to.

grâce **à** son charme et **à** son talent	*thanks to his charm and talent*
faute **d'**argent et **de** temps	*for lack of money and time*
à côté **de** la poste et **de** la banque	*next to the post office and the bank*
Elle était assise près **de** son père et **de** sa mère.	*She was sitting next to her father and mother.*

Chapter 2

Prepositions and other Word Categories

Some prepositions are also used as other parts of speech, i.e. their form is identical with that of past participles, present participles or adverbs. As prepositions, these words *precede* their complement and are invariable.

- The following prepositions are also **past participles**

à l'**insu** de	*without the knowledge of*
excepté	*except*
passé	*after*
vu	*due to, given*
y **compris**	*including*

- The following prepositions are also **present participles**

concernant	*concerning*
durant	*during*
suivant	*according to*

- Many prepositions are also **adverbs** (**après**, **avant**, **devant**, **à côté**, **contre**, **pour**, **près**, etc.). A preposition becomes an adverb when it is *not* followed by a complement. When compound prepositions are used as adverbs, the final **de** disappears.

Les toilettes sont **à gauche de** la sortie. *(preposition)*	*The restroom is on the left of the exit.*
En Angleterre, on roule **à gauche**. *(adverb)*	*In England, one drives on the left.*
Il se tient **à l'écart de** la politique. *(preposition)*	*He keeps away from politics.*
Il vit **à l'écart**. *(adverb)*	*He lives isolated/keeps to himself.*

A part cela, je ne lui reproche rien. *(preposition)*	*Apart from that, I reproach him nothing.*
Tout le monde est d'accord, **à part** toi. *(preposition)*	*Everyone agrees except for you.*
Plaisanterie **à** part. *(adverb)*	*Joking aside.*
Il m'a pris **à part** pour me dire cela. *(adverb)*	*He took me aside to tell me that.*
après le dîner *(preposition)*	*after dinner*
Je te le raconterai **après**. *(adverb)*	*I'll tell you later (on).*
Ils se disputent **à propos de** tout. *(preposition)*	*They quarrel about everything.*
La lettre est arrivée (mal) **à propos**. *(adverb)*	*The letter arrived at the right (wrong) moment.*
A propos, où est votre frère? *(adverb)*	*By the way, where is your brother?*
avant cinq heures *(preposition)*	*before 5 o'clock*
Est-ce qu'on place l'adjectif **avant** le nom *(preposition)* ou **après**? *(adverb)*	*Does one place the adjective before the noun or after?*
Il fallait me le dire **avant**. *(adverb)*	*You should have told me before.*
Avez-vous un remède **contre** la grippe? *(preposition)*	*Do you have a remedy against the flu?*
Etes-vous pour les uniformes? - Moi, je suis **contre**. *(adverb)*	*Are you for uniforms? - I am against.*
Depuis ce jour-là, tout va bien. *(preposition)*	*Since that day, everything goes well.*
Il est parti à Noël et je ne l'ai plus revu **depuis**. *(adverb)*	*He left at Christmas and I haven't seen him since.*
Il y a un jardin **derrière** la maison. *(preposition)*	*There is a garden behind the house.*
Il marche **derrière**. *(adverb)*	*He walks behind.*
Il y a un grand arbre **devant** l'église. *(preposition)*	*There is a big tree in front of the church.*
Je passe **devant**. *(adverb)*	*I'll go first.*
On va se mettre **devant** pour mieux voir. *(adverb)*	*Let's sit in front to see better.*

Note:

The preposition **avec** occurs as adverb only in informal French.

La petite fille joue **avec** sa poupée. *(preposition)*	*The little girl plays with her doll.*
Elle a pris sa poupée et est partie **avec**. *(adverb)*	*She took her doll and left with it.*
Je bois du vin blanc **avec** le repas. *(preposition)*	*I drink white wine with the meal.*
C'est un plat léger. Il faut boire du Chablis **avec**. *(adverb)*	*That is a light dish. One must drink a Chablis wine with it.*
Il va falloir faire **avec**. *(adverb)*	*We'll have to make do with it.*
Il faut vivre **avec**. *(adverb)*	*One has to live with it.*

Chapter 3

The Place and Objects of Prepositions

Whereas in English some prepositions can be placed at the end of the sentence, in French a preposition must always *precede* its complement, i.e. the word it relates to.

Compare:

D'où viens-tu?	*Where are you coming* ***from****?*
A quoi penses-tu?	*What are you thinking* ***about****?*
De quoi parlez-vous?	*What are you talking* ***about****?*
Pour qui travaillez-vous?	*Whom are you working* ***for****?*
Avec quoi écrivez-vous?	*What are you writing* ***with****?*
De quoi as-tu peur?	*What are you afraid* ***of****?*

The object of a preposition can be

- a noun

  Ils sont rentrés **après** *le spectacle.* — *They went home after the show.*

- an adverb

  Téléphone-moi **avant** *demain.* — *Call me before tomorrow.*
  Hors d'*ici*! — *Get out of here!*
  Depuis *quand* es-tu ici? — *Since when have you been here?*

- an adjective

  Il passe **pour** *intelligent.* — *He is considered intelligent.*

- a clause

  D'après *ce qu'on m'a dit.* — *According to what I have been told.*
  J'ai peur **de** *ce qu'il va faire.* — *I am afraid of what he is going to do.*

- an infinitive

Il travaille **pour** *gagner* de l'argent.	*He works in order to earn money.*

- a relative, interrogative or personal (= disjunctive) pronoun*

Ce sont des amis **sur** *lesquels* on peut compter.	*They are friends whom one can count on.*
Chez *qui* habite-t-il?	*With whom does he live?*
Il est sorti **sans** *moi.*	*He went out without me.*

Idioms

En *quoi* puis-je vous être utile?	*How can I help you?*
A *quoi* bon?	*What's the use?*

* *Note:*

Some compound prepositions are never followed by a personal pronoun but use a possessive adjective instead.

à l'égard de

à **leur** égard	*with regard to them*

à l'instar de

à **son** instar	*following his/her example*

à l'insu de

à **mon / son** insu	*without my/his knowledge*

à l'intention de

J'ai acheté un cadeau à **leur** intention.	*I bought a gift for them.*

au sujet de

à **son** sujet	*about him/her*

de la part de

Dites-lui bonjour de **ma** part.	*Tell him/her hello from me.*
Ce n'est pas très gentil de **ta** part.	*That's not very nice of you.*
Ce n'est pas surprenant de **leur** part.	*That's not surprising of them.*

Chapter 4

Prepositions and Verbs

Some prepositions can be followed by a verb. If this is the case, the verb is in the (present or past) infinitive[1] except after 'en' which is followed by the present participle.

Si on allait au cinéma **au lieu de** *regarder* la télévision?	*What if we went to the movies instead of watching*[1] *television?*
Il est parti **sans** *dire* au revoir.	*He left without saying good bye.*
Venez me voir **avant de** *partir.*	*Come and see me before leaving.*
Il est trop tôt **pour** le *dire.*	*It is too early to say.*
A force de *lire* dans l'obscurité, il s'est abîmé les yeux.	*By dint of reading in the dark, he ruined his eyes.*
Faute de *connaître* l'italien, je n'ai pas compris le film.	*Since I don't know Italian, I didn't understand the movie.*
Il parle lentement **de façon/de manière à** *être compris* par tout le monde.	*He speaks slowly so as to be understood by everyone.*
Elle ne manque jamais l'école, **à moins d'***être* malade.	*She never misses school, unless she is ill.*
L'eau peut être utilisée **à condition de** la *faire* bouillir.	*The water can be used on the condition that it is boiled.*
Je fais des économies **afin de** *pouvoir* voyager.	*I save money in order to be able to travel.*
Je n'ai pas osé venir, **de peur de** vous *déranger.*	*I did not dare to come, for fear of disturbing you.*
En attendant de *déjeuner*, nous allons boire un apéritif.	*While waiting for (having) lunch, we are going to drink an aperitif.*
La statue est **loin d'***être terminée.*	*The statue is far from being finished.*

1. Note that English generally uses a present participle (= ...*ing*) after a preposition.

Je suis bien **loin de** *partager* votre avis.	*I am quite far from sharing your opinion.*
Ils ont fait la grève **au risque de** *perdre* leur emploi.	*They went on strike at the risk of losing their jobs.*

But:

En vous **penchant** sur la droite, vous verrez un beau château.	*By leaning to the right, you will see a beautiful castle.*
On résout souvent des problèmes **en dormant**.	*One often solves problems while sleeping.*
On réussit **en persévérant**.	*One succeeds by persevering.*

Note:

1. When a verb follows the preposition **après**, it is always in the *past infinitive,* which consists of the present infinitve of *avoir* or *être* followed by the *past participle* of the verb.

après **avoir fait**...	*after doing...*
après **être parti**(e)(s)...	*after leaving...*
après **s'être couché**(e)(s)...	*after going to bed...*

Mistakes to avoid

Incorrect	*Correct*
Après ~~que j'ai mangé~~[1], je suis allé à l'école.	Après **avoir mangé**, je suis allé à l'école.

2. The preposition '**près de**' changes its meaning when followed by an infinitive. It is then always combined with 'être' and is mostly used in its negative form.

être **près de** + inf.	*to be about to*
J'étais **près de** *pleurer*.	*I was about to cry.*
ne pas être **près de** + inf.	*to not...so quickly, not to be about (= likely) to*
Je ne suis pas **près d'**y *retourner*.	*I am not about to return there.*
Elle n'est pas **près d'***oublier* cette histoire.	*She is not going to forget this story so quickly.*

---

1. Do not use the conjunction 'après que' when the subject of the main clause is the same as the subject of the subordinate clause (here: 'je'). Use the preposition 'après' + past infinitive.

Chapter 5

The Use of Certain Prepositions

A. The preposition à

1. à introduces an ***indirect noun object*** (English: *to*)

J'ai donné un cadeau **à** mon frère.	*I gave a gift* ***to*** *my brother.* or: *I gave my brother a gift.*[1]
Elle a prêté la voiture **à** sa fille.	*She lent the car* ***to*** *her daughter.* or: *She lent her daughter the car.*
Je dois de l'argent **au**[2] dentiste.	*I owe money* ***to*** *the dentist.* or: *I owe the dentist money.*
Tu as écrit une lettre **aux**[2] enfants.	*You wrote a letter* ***to*** *the children.* or: *You wrote the children a letter.*

2. à indicates the *place* where one is or to which one goes

- **à** (without article) expresses 'in' and 'to' before **names of cities,* islands** and **countries** that are *not* preceded by an article

L'avion atterrit **à** Londres.	*The plane lands* ***in*** *London.*
Je vais **à** Paris.	*I am going* ***to*** *Paris.*

* But when the name of the city is modified, or when 'in' is not a simple statement of location but expresses 'inside', one uses **dans** instead of ***à*** before the city name.[3]

dans le vieux Paris	***in*** *old Paris*
dans la vibrante Barcelone	***in*** *vibrating Barcelona*
Il est impossible de se garer **dans** Paris.	*It is impossible to park* ***in****(side of) Paris.*

---

1. Note that in English, 'to' can be omitted. In French, **à** *always* precedes an **in**direct noun object.
2. Note that **à** contracts with the definite articles *le* and *les*: à + le = **au**, à + les = **aux**.
3. See also p. 122.

Elle arrive **à** Cuba.	*She arrives **in** Cuba.*
Il vit **à** Hawaï.	*He lives **in** Hawaii.*
Nous retournons **à** Tahiti.	*We return **to** Tahiti.*
Ils ont passé l'été **à** Monaco.	*They spent the summer **in** Monaco.*

- **à** (+ definite article) expresses 'in/on' and 'to' before *masculine singular* and *plural countries*, some *masculine American states*[1], most *Canadian provinces*[2], as well as with some *islands.*
[For a detailed list of masculine and feminine place names, see p. 283-302]

Je suis né **au** Canada.	*I was born **in** Canada.*
Depuis quand êtes-vous **aux** Etats-Unis?	*Since when have you been **in** the United States?*
Es-tu déjà allé **aux** Pays-Bas?	*Have you ever been **to** the Netherlands?*
Nous allons **au** Texas et **au** Nouveau Mexique.	*We are going **to** Texas and New Mexico.*
Elle voyage[3] **au** Québec.	*She travels **in** Quebec.*
aux Philippines	***in/to** the Philippines*
au Nouveau Brunswick	***in/to** New Brunswick*
à la Réunion	***on/to** Reunion Island*
à la Martinique	***on/to** Martinique*
à la Guadeloupe	***on/to** Guadeloupe*
aux Bermudes	***on/to** the Bermudas*
aux Nouvelles Hebrides	***on/to** the New Hebrides*

---

1. But **dans le** is used before *most* masculine American States to express 'in' and 'to' (see p. 123 and p. 301).
2. Except when the masculine country, American state or Canadian province starts with a vowel or 'mute h':
en Afghanistan, **en** Iran, **en** Iraq, **en** Israël, **en** Haïti, **en** Oregon, **en** Alberta
3. Note that with the verb **voyager**, ***au*** followed by a place name expresses 'in' only, *not* 'to'. To express '*to travel **to***' one uses ***aller***.
Elle **va** *au* Québec. *She **travels to** Quebec.*

3. **à** expresses 'in', 'on', 'at', and 'to' with many other localities

à cet endroit (= **dans** ce lieu)	*in this place*
à quel endroit?	*in which place? where?*
à certains/divers endroits	*in some/various places*
à domicile	*at/to someone's home*
livrer **à** domicile	*to make home deliveries*
à ma montre, il est...	*on my watch, it is...*
à table	*at the table*
au balcon	*on/to the balcony*
au bureau	*at/to the office*
au café	*at/to the coffee shop*
au centre commercial	*at/to the shopping center*
au chevet de	*at the bedside of*
au ciel[1]	*in/to heaven*
au cimetière	*at/to the cemetery*
au cinéma	*at/to the movies*
au coin de la rue	*at the streetcorner*
au combat	*in combat*
au concert	*at/to the concert*
au courrier	*in the mail*
au premier (deuxième...) étage	*on/to the second (third...) floor*
au four	*in the oven*
au frais	*in a cool place*
au grand air	*(at the) outdoors*
au grenier	*in/to the attic*
au gymnase	*in/to the gymnasium*
au jardin (= **dans** le jardin)	*in/to the garden*
au laboratoire	*in/to the laboratory*
au lit	*in/to bed*
au lycée	*at/to (the) highschool*
au magasin	*at/to the store*
au même endroit	*at the same place*
au menu	*on the menu*
au monde[2]	*in/to the world*

---

1. But: **dans** le ciel *in the sky* **en** enfer ***in/to** hell*
2. In expressions such as
   venir **au** monde *to be born* (lit.: *to come to the world*)
   mettre **au** monde *to give birth to* (lit.: *to put in the world*)
   but:
   dans le monde entier ***in** the whole world*
   dans le Nouveau Monde ***in** the New World*

au mur	*on the wall*
au musée	*in/to the museum*
au nord	*to the north*
au paradis	*in/to paradise*
au parc (= **dans** le parc)	*in/to the park*
au péage	*at/to the tollbooth*
au plafond	*on the ceiling*
au premier plan	*in the foreground*
au pressing	*at/to the dry cleaner's*
au purgatoire	*in/to purgatory*
au premier (deuxième...dernier) rang	*in the first (second...last) row*
au rayon (des) chaussures	*in/to the shoe department*
au rayon alimentation	*in/to the food section*
au rayon de la parfumerie	*in/to the cosmetics department*
au recto	*on the front (of a sheet of paper)*
au restaurant	*in/to the restaurant*
au resto-U	*at/to the university cafeteria*
au rez-de-chaussée	*on/to the first floor*
au salon	*in/to the living room*
au sol	*on the ground*
au soleil	*in the sun*
au stade	*at/to the stadium*
au sud	*to the south*
au supermarché	*at/to the supermarket*
au tableau	*on/to the blackboard*
au téléphone	*on the phone*
au théâtre	*at/to the theatre*
au travail	*at/to work*
au verso	*on the back (of a sheet of paper)*
au village	*in/to the village*
au virage	*in the curve*
au volant	*at the steering wheel*
au zoo	*at/to the zoo*

Mon appartement est **au** 3e étage.	*My apartment is **on** the 4th floor.*
Il écrit les mots **au** tableau.	*He writes the words **on** the board.*
J'aime aller **au** théâtre.	*I like to go **to** the theatre.*
En Amérique, on peut aller **au** magasin à minuit.	*In America, one can go **to** the store at midnight.*
Le médecin m'a dit de rester **au** lit.	*The doctor told me to stay **in** bed.*
Ils sont morts **au** combat.	*They died **in** combat.*
Il a mis le vin **au frais**.	*He put the wine **in** a cool place.*

Mistakes to avoid

Incorrect	*Correct*
J'ai parlé avec elle ~~sur le~~ téléphone.	J'ai parlé avec elle **au** téléphone.

à la banque	*at/to the bank*
à la bibliothèque	*in/to the library*
à la boulangerie	*at/to the bakery*
à la campagne	*in/to the country*
à la cave	*in/to the cellar*
(travailler) **à la** chaîne	*(to work) on the assembly line*
à la charcuterie	*at/to the deli/pork butcher's*
à la cité universitaire	*in/to the college dorm complex*
(passer) **à la** douane	*(to go) through customs*
à la fac	*at/to the university*
à la gare	*at/to the train station*
(mourir) **à la** guerre	*(to die) in the war*
à la librairie	*in/to the bookstore*
à la main	*in one's hand*
à la maison	*at home, home*
à la mer	*on/to the ocean*
à la messe	*at/to mass*
à la montagne	*in/to the mountains*
à la pâtisserie	*in/to the pastry shop*
à la pharmacie	*at/to the pharmacy*
à la piscine	*at/to the swimming pool*
à la page trois	*on page three*
à la plage	*on/to the beach*
à la poste	*at/to the post office*
à la poubelle	*in the garbage can*
à la quincaillerie	*in/to the hardware store*
à la radio	*on the radio*
à la résidence universitaire	*at/to the college dorm*
à la réunion	*at/to the meeting*
à la télévision	*on television*
à la terrasse	*on/to the terrace*
à la une	*on the front page* (of a newspaper)

Elle a jeté la lettre **à la** poubelle.	*She threw the letter* ***in*** *the garbage.*
Je vais **à la** maison (= chez moi).	*I am going home.*
Je suis/reste **à la** maison.	*I am/stay* ***at*** *home.*

Il doit aller **à la** banque.	*He must go **to** the bank.*
Je l'ai vu **à** une réunion.	*I saw him **at** a meeting.*
Nous allons **à la** messe de minuit.	*We go **to** midnight mass.*
Mes parents habitent **à la** campagne.	*My parents live **in** the country.*
Il tient/a un stylo **à la** main.[1]	*He holds/has a pen **in** his hand.*

Mistakes to avoid

Incorrect	*Correct*
J'ai vu le film ~~sur~~ la télévision.	J'ai vu le film **à** la télévision.[2]
Elle travaille ~~dans~~ la bibliothèque.	Elle travaille **à** la bibliothèque.
Je vais à ~~ma~~ maison.	Je vais à **la** maison.

à l'aéroport	*at/to the airport*
à l'ambassade	*at/to the embassy*
à l'angle de (= **au** coin de) la rue	*at/to the street corner*
(être) **à l'**appareil	*(to be) on the phone*
à l'arrêt d'autobus	*at/to the bus-stop*
à l'arrière	*in the back*
à l'arrière-plan	*in the background*
à l'autre bout de	*on the other end of*
à l'avant	*in the front*
à l'école	*at/to school*
à l'église	*in/to church*
à l'épicerie	*in/to the grocery store*
à l'est[3]	*to the east*
à l'étage	*upstairs*
à l'étranger	*abroad*
à l'examen	*on the exam*
à l'hôpital	*in/to the hospital*
à l'horizon	*at the horizon*
à l'hôtel	*at/to the hotel*

---

1. But:

J'ai une pièce d'argent **dans** la main.	*I have a coin **in** (= inside) my hand.*
Vous êtes **entre** de bonnes mains.	*You are **in** good hands.*

2. But:

J'ai vu le film **sur** la deux / **sur** Canal Plus.	*I saw the movie **on** channel two / **on** Canal Plus.*

3. For the difference between **à** + cardinal point and **dans** + cardinal point see p.123.

à l'ombrc	*in the shade*
à l'opéra	*at/to the opera*
à l'ouest	*to the west*
à l'université	*at/to the university*
à l'usine	*at/to the factory*

Nous allons **à l'**église le dimanche.	*We go* ***to*** *church on Sundays.*
On va se mettre **à l'**ombre.	*We are going to go* ***in*** *the shade.*
L'Hôtel de Cluny se trouve **à l'**angle du Boulevard St. Michel et du Boulevard St. Germain.	*The Hôtel de Cluny is located* ***on*** *the corner of St. Michel Boulevard and of St. Germain Boulevard.*
Strasbourg est **à l'**est de Paris.	*Strasbourg is* ***to*** *the east of Paris.*
Ils sont descendus/ont logé **à l'**hôtel.	*They stayed* ***at*** *the hotel.*
J'ai déposé mes parents **à l'**aéroport.	*I dropped my parents off* ***at*** *the airport.*

aux abords de	*in the area around*
aux informations	*on the news*
aux obsèques	*at/to the funeral*
aux ordures	*in the garbage*
aux toilettes	*in/to the restroom*
aux urgences	*in/to the emergency room*
(aller) **aux** urnes	*(to go) to the polls*

aux abords de l'aéroport	***in*** *the area around the airport*
C'était **aux** informations de dix heures.	*It was* ***on*** *the ten o'clock news.*
Les Français vont **aux** urnes tous les cinq ans pour élire leur président.	*The French go* ***to*** *the polls every five years to elect their president.*

Sayings and idioms

Je suis **au** septième ciel.	*I am on cloud nine.*
(coucher, dormir) **à la** belle étoile	*(to sleep) in the open air, outdoors*
Qui est **à l'**appareil?	*Who's calling?* [on the phone]
aux quatre coins de...	*all over...*
aux quatre coins de la France	*all over France*

4. **à** combines two nouns or a noun and an infinitive indicating the *use* or *purpose* of the modified noun (English uses a compound noun)

- noun + **à** + noun

une armoire **à** linge	*a linen closet*
une armoire **à** pharmacie	*a medicine cabinet*
les bagages **à** main	*the hand luggage*
une boîte **aux** lettres	*a mailbox*
une boîte **à** gants	*a glove compartment*
une boîte **à** médicaments	*a pillbox*
une bombe **à** retardement	*a time bomb*
un bonnet **à** douche	*a shower cap*
une brosse **à** dents	*a toothbrush*
une brosse **à** cheveux	*a hairbrush*
une corbeille **à** papier	*a wastepaper basket*
une corde **à** linge	*a clothes line*
une cuiller **à** thé	*a teaspoon*
une cuiller **à** soupe	*a soupspoon, a tablespoon*
une épingle **à** cheveux	*a hairpin*
le fil **à** couper le beurre	*the cheese wire*
un filet **à** provisions	*a shopping bag/net*
un frein **à** main	*a hand brake*
un kiosque **à** journaux	*a newsstand*
une lime **à** ongles	*a nail file*
une machine **à** café	*a coffee maker*
la machine **à** traitement de texte	*the word processor*
une machine **à** sous	*a slot machine*
le marché **aux** puces	*the flea market*
un moulin **à** café	*a coffee grinder*
un moulin **à** vent	*a windmill*
du papier **à** lettres	*stationery*
des parcs **à** huîtres	*oyster beds*
des patins **à** glace	*ice skates*
des patins **à** roulettes	*roller skates*
un piège **à** souris	*a mousetrap*
la pince **à** linge	*the clothes pin*
une plaque **à** biscuits	*a cookie sheet*
une pompe **à** essence	*a gas pump*
le rouge **à** lèvres	*the lipstick*
un sac **à** bandoulière	*a shoulderbag*
un sac **à** dos	*a backpack*

un sac **à** main	*a handbag*
une tasse **à** café[1]	*a coffee cup*
une tondeuse **à** gazon	*a lawnmower*
le vernis **à** ongles	*the nail polish*
verre **à** vin[2]	*a wine glass*

- noun + **à** + infinitive

du bois **à** brûler	*firewood*
des cartes **à** jouer	*playing cards*
la chambre **à** coucher	*the bedroom*
un fer **à** repasser	*an iron (for pressing clothes)*
une machine **à** coudre	*a sewing machine*
une machine **à** écrire	*a typewriter*
une machine **à** laver	*a washing machine*
une machine **à** photocopier	*a photocopy machine*
de la pâte **à** modeler	*playdough*
une pince **à** épiler	*tweezers*
des plats **à** emporter	*food to go*
une poêle **à** frire	*a frying pan*
une salle **à** manger	*a dining room*
un terrain **à** bâtir	*a lot (= piece of land to build on)*

5. **à** between two nouns frequently indicates that the second noun is an *ingredient* or *characteristic feature* of the first noun (English often uses a compound noun)

- **à** + definite article + noun gives the *ingredient(s) of food items*

des bonbons **à la** menthe	*peppermint candy*
le café **au** lait	*the coffee with milk*
le canard **à l'**orange	*the orange duck*
des cookies **aux** pépites de chocolat	*chocolate chip cookies*
du coq **au** vin	*chicken in wine sauce*
une crêpe **à la** confiture	*a crepe with jam*
un croissant **au** beurre	*a butter croissant* (= made with butter)
un gâteau **au** chocolat	*a chocolate cake*
de la glace **à la** vanille/**à la** fraise/ **au** café/**à la** pistache	*vanilla/strawberry/coffee/pistachio ice cream*

---

1. But: une tasse **de** café *a cup **of** coffee*
2. But: un verre **de** vin *a glass **of** wine*

une mousse **au** chocolat	*a chocolate mousse*
des œufs brouillés **aux** truffes	*scrambled eggs with truffles*
une omelette **aux** champignons	*a mushroom omelette*
une pizza **au** fromage et **aux** anchois	*a cheese and anchovy pizza*
un potage **aux** légumes	*a vegetable soup*
un sandwich **au** jambon	*a ham sandwich*
la soupe **à l'**oignon/**au** poulet	*the onion/chicken soup*
le steak **au** poivre	*the pepper steak*
une tarte **aux** fraises	*a strawberry tart*
du thé **au** citron	*tea with lemon*

- **à** with (or without) definite article + noun gives the *characteristic feature* of something or someone

une alerte/un attentat **à la** bombe	*a bomb threat/attack*
une arme **à** feu	*a gun, a fire arm*
un autobus **à** deux étages	*a double-decker bus*
une avenue **aux** larges trottoirs	*an avenue with wide sidewalks*
un avion **à** réaction	*a jet plane*
une barbe **à** papa	*a cotton candy*
une bombe **à** retardement	*a time bomb*
une chaise/un fauteuil **à** bascule	*a rocking chair*
une chambre **à** deux lits	*a double room*
une chasse **à l'**homme/**au** trésor	*a man/treasure hunt*
des chaussures **à** talons hauts/bas	*high-heeled/flat shoes*
une chemise **à** manches courtes/longues	*a shirt with short/long sleeves*
un chemisier **à** carreaux/**à** pois	*a checkered/polka-dotted blouse*
le compte **à** rebours	*the countdown*
un dîner **aux** chandelles	*a candle-light dinner*
un emploi **à** mi-temps/**à** plein temps	*a part-time/full-time job*
une femme **au** foyer	*a housewife*
un film **à** suspense	*a thriller*
un fils **à** papa	*a spoiled (teenage) son*
la fosse **aux** lions	*the lion's den*
le four **à** micro-ondes	*the microwave oven*
un instrument **à** cordes	*a string instrument*
un lit **à** baldaquin	*a bed with a canopy*
des lunettes **à** double foyer	*bifocals*

des lunettes **à** verres fumés	*spectacles with tinted glasses*
une maison **à** colombages	*a half-timbered house*
une maison **à** deux étages	*a two storey house*
le marché **aux** puces/fleurs	*the flea/flower market*
un moulin **à** paroles	*a big talker*
un oeuf **à la** coque	*a soft-boiled egg*
une opération **à** cœur ouvert	*open heart surgery*
un pantalon **à** rayures	*a pair of pants with stripes*
la pêche **à la** ligne	*fishing*
une planche **à** roulettes	*a skateboard*
une peinture **à l'**huile	*an oil painting*
un piano **à** queue	*a grand piano*
la presse **à** scandale/**à** sensation	*the tabloid/sensational(ized) press*
un pull **à** col roulé	*a turtle neck sweater*
des questions **à** choix multiple	*multiple choice questions*
une robe **à** volants	*a flounced dress*
une route **à** quatre voies	*a four-lane highway*
le saut **à l'**élastique	*bungee jumping*
un téléphone **à** touches	*a touchtone phone*
une vente **aux** enchères	*an auction*
le vol **à l'**étalage	*shoplifting*
le vol **à** main armée	*armed robbery*
le voleur **à la** tire	*the pickpocket*

- **à** + definite article + part(s) of the body (or clothes) indicates a *distinguishing (physical) feature* of a *person* (English: *with*)

La femme **aux** yeux bleus est ma mère.	*The woman* ***with*** *the blue eyes is my mother.*
C'était un garçon **au** nez long et **aux** cheveux courts.	*He was a boy* ***with*** *a long nose and short hair.*
Je ne connais pas le monsieur **à la** moustache.	*I don't know the man* ***with*** *the mustache.*
Qui est la personne **aux** pieds nus?	*Who is the person* ***with*** *the bare feet?*
le garçon **à la** casquette rouge	*the boy* ***with*** *the red cap*
l'homme **au** chapeau de paille	*the man* ***with*** *the straw hat*
la vieille dame **aux** (or: **à**) lunettes	*the old lady* ***with*** *the glasses*

6. **à** indicates the *location of a pain* or *injury* with parts of the body after expressions such as *avoir mal, (se) faire mal* and *se blesser*

avoir mal **à** la tête	*to have a headache*
avoir mal **à** l'estomac	*to have a stomachache*
avoir mal **au** dos	*to have a backache*
avoir mal **aux** dents	*to have a toothache*
se couper **au** doigt	*to cut one's finger*
Il s'est fait mal **au** genou.	*He hurt his knee.*
Elle s'est blessée **au** bras droit.	*She injured her right arm.*

7. **à** indicates a *precise moment of time* or a *time period* in the following expressions

à midi	*at noon*
à minuit	*at midnight*
à deux heures[1]	*at two o'clock*
à sa mort	*at his death*
à (l'âge de) quatre-vingt-un ans	*at (the age of) eighty-one years*
à ce moment-là	*at that time, at that moment*
à un moment donné	*somewhere along the line*
au moment de sa nomination	*at the time of his nomination*
à tout moment	*at any moment*
à cette époque-là	*in those days*
à notre époque	*nowadays*
à une heure pareille	*at such a (clock) time*
à marée basse/haute	*at low/high tide*
à Pâques et **à** Noël (dernier)	*at Easter and (last) Christmas*

à l'âge de	*in the age of*
à l'Age de Pierre	*in the Stone Age*
à l'aller	*going, on the way there*
à l'arrivée	*at the arrival*
à l'atterrissage	*during landing*
à l'aube	*at (the) dawn*
à l'aube du troisième millénaire	*at the dawn of the third millenium*
à l'avenir[2]	*in the future*
à l'entracte	*during intermission*
à l'époque	*at the time, at that time*
à l'époque de	*at the time of*

---

1. Also: **à** quelle heure? *at what time?*
2. But: **dans un** avenir proche/lointain *in the near/distant future*

à l'heure actuelle	*at the present time*
à l'heure du coucher	*at bedtime*
à l'heure du déjeuner/dîner	*at lunch/dinner time*
à l'instant	*at this very moment*
à la fin[1] (de l'année/du mois)	*at the end (of the year/month)*
à la même heure	*at the same (clock) time*
à la mi-janvier	*mid-January*
à la mi-journée	*at midday*
à la pause café	*at coffee break*
à la tombée de la nuit	*at nightfall*
à la veille de	*on the eve of, just before*
au bon/mauvais moment	*at the right/wrong time*
au bon vieux temps	*in the good old days*
au coucher du soleil	*at sunset*
au crépuscule	*at dusk*
au début[2] (= **au** commencement)	*at the beginning*
au décollage	*at take-off*
au petit déjeuner	*at breakfast*
au déjeuner	*at lunch*
au dîner	*at dinner*
au départ	*at the beginning, initially*
au fil des années/des mois	*over the years/months*
au fil de la journée/du temps	*as the day/time goes/went by*
au lever du jour	*at daybreak*
au lever du soleil	*at sunrise*
au matin	*in the morning*
au petit matin	*in the early morning*
au mois de janvier/février	*in the month of January/February*
au point du jour	*at daybreak, in the early hours*
au printemps	*in spring*
au retour	*upon returning, coming back*
au soir	*in the evening*
au temps de (= **à l'**époque de) Molière	*at the time of Molière*
au vingt et unième siècle	*in the twenty-first century*
au siècle dernier	*in the last century*
au tournant du siècle	*at the turn of the century*

---

1. But *no* preposition is used before 'fin' when the name of a month follows
   fin août/septembre *at the end of August/September*
2. But *no* preposition is used before 'début' when the name of a month follows
   début juin/juillet *at the beginning of June/July*

aux heures creuses	*during the off-peak periods*
aux heures de pointe/d'affluence	*during rush hour*

Mistakes to avoid

Incorrect	*Correct*	*English meaning*
~~dans le~~ seizième siècle	**au** seizième siècle	***in** the 16th century*

8. à expresses 'until' in time expressions such as

à (très) bientôt	*see you (very) soon*
à demain	*see you (= until) tomorrow*
à tout à l'heure	*see you in a little while*
à la prochaine	*see you next time*
à ce soir	*see you tonight*
à tout de suite	*see you in a moment*
à lundi	*see you Monday*
à la semaine prochaine	*see you next week*
à plus tard	*see you later*
à un de ces jours	*see you one of these days*
Also in:	
au revoir	*good bye (= until I see you again)*

9. à is used to indicate *means of transportation* on which one travels

à bicyclette	*by bicycle*
à cheval	*on horseback*
à dos d'âne	*on a donkey*
à dos de chameau	*on a camel*
à dos d'éléphant	*on an elephant*
à mobylette	*by moped*
à moto(cyclette)[1]	*by motorcycle*
à roller[1]	*by roller skates*
à vélo[1]	*by bicycle*
Also:	
à pied	*on foot*
Je vais à l'école **à** pied.	*I walk (= go on foot) to school.*

---

1. Note that although correct usage requires '**à**' with these means of transportation, '**en**' [which is normally reserved for vehicles *inside* which one travels (see p.87)] is often used by native French speakers today.
Il roule/circule **en** Harley Davidson.
Il vient au bureau **en** vélo/**en** roller.

10. **à** denotes *possession*

- with **être à** *(to belong to)* [Here **à** precedes both the noun and the (stressed) pronoun.]

Ces vélos sont **à** mes frères.	*These bikes belong to my brothers.*
L'avenir est **à** eux.	*The future belongs to them.*
A qui est cette montre? -	*Whose watch is this? -*
La montre est **à** moi.	*The watch belongs to me.*

- with **appartenir à** *(to belong to)* [Here **à** precedes the noun only.]

La voiture appartient **à** ma sœur.	*The car belongs to my sister.*
But:	
La voiture lui appartient.	*The car belongs to her.*

- after a *possessive adjective + noun* before a stressed pronoun for emphasis or clarification of ownership

C'est sa maison **à** elle/**à** lui.	*That is **her/his** house.*
C'est mon argent **à** moi.	*That is **my** money.*
Also in:	
C'est un(e) ami(e) **à** moi.	*He (she) is a friend of mine.*
un cousin **à** lui	*a cousin of his*

11. **à** + *definite article* is used after **jouer** when this verb is followed by the name of a *sport* or *game*

- *sports*

jouer **au** badminton	*to play badminton*
jouer **au** ballon	*to play ball*
jouer **au** baseball	*to play baseball*
jouer **au** basketball	*to play basketball*
jouer **au** football	*to play soccer*
jouer **au** football américain	*to play football*
jouer **au** golf	*to play golf*
jouer **au** hockey (sur glace)	*to play (ice) hockey*
jouer **au** ping-pong	*to play table tennis*
jouer **au** rugby	*to play rugby*
jouer **au** tennis	*to play tennis*
jouer **aux** boules	*to play lawn bowling*
jouer **aux** quilles	*to play skittles*

- *games* (here the definite article is not always used after **à**)

jouer **au** baby-foot	*to play fussball*
jouer **au** billard	*to play pool, to play billiards*
jouer **au** bridge	*to play bridge*
jouer **à** cache-cache	*to play hide-and-seek*
jouer **à** chat (perché)	*to play (off ground) tag*
jouer **au** chat et **à la** souris	*to play cat and mouse*
jouer **aux** cartes	*to play cards*
jouer **à** colin-maillard	*to play blind man's buff*
jouer **aux** dames (chinoises)	*to play (Chinese) checkers*
jouer **aux** échecs	*to play chess*
jouer **aux** gendarmes et **aux** voleurs	*to play cops and robbers*
jouer **au** loto	*to play lotto*
jouer **à la** marelle	*to play hopscotch*
jouer **au** monopoly	*to play monopoly*
jouer **au** poker	*to play poker*
jouer **à** pile ou face	*to play heads or tails*
jouer **à la** poupée	*to play dolls*
jouer **à** quitte ou double	*to play double or nothing*
jouer **à la** roulette (russe)	*to play (Russian) roulette*
jouer **à** des jeux vidéo	*to play video games*
jouer **à** des jeux d'argent	*to gamble*
A quoi joues -tu?	*What (sport or game) do you play?*
Ils ont joué/tiré/décidé **à** pile ou face.	*They tossed for it, they decided it on the flip of a coin.*

12. à introduces the *distance* of a locality

Versailles est **à** 20 kilomètres de Paris.	*Versailles is 20 kilometers from Paris.*
C'est loin d'ici? - C'est **à** dix minutes à pied.	*Is it far from here?- It's ten minutes from here on foot.*
Béziers est **à** deux heures de Montpellier.	*Béziers is two hours from Montpellier.*
à deux pas de...	*just a stone's throw from..., near*
C'est **à** deux pas d'ici.	*It's just a stone's throw from here.*
Elle habite **à** deux pas de chez moi.	*She lives right near my house.*
A deux pas de la Conciergerie se trouve la Sainte Chapelle.	*Right near the Conciergerie is the Sainte Chapelle.*

La banque est **à** deux/quelques rues d'ici.	*The bank is two/a few blocks from here.*
New York est **à** 45 minutes d'avion.	*New York is 45 minutes away by plane.*

13. à precedes the *price* or *value* of an item

une robe **à** 500 euros	*a five hundred euro dress*
Les chaussures sont **à** 200 euros.	*The shoes cost 200 euros.*
un billet (d'avion) **à** 100 euros[1]	*a 100 euro (plane) ticket*
Je voudrais deux timbres **à** 46 centimes.	*I would like two stamps at 46 cents.*

14. à (+ l'heure) expresses English *per, an* (+ hour) with *speed*

Le TGV[2] roule à 300 kilomètres **à** l'heure.	*The TGV drives at (a speed of) 300 kilometers* ***an*** *hour.*

15. à is used after certain verbs and expressions when these are followed by an *infinitive*

[For a detailed list of these verbs and expressions see p. 212-215, 219-222]

Je n'arrive pas **à** ouvrir la porte.	*I can't (manage to) open the door.*
N'hésitez pas **à** me contacter.	*Don't hesitate to contact me.*
Il est prêt **à** partir.	*He is ready to leave.*
Elle a tendance **à** travailler trop.	*She tends to work too much.*
J'aurai du mal **à** la convaincre.	*I'll have a hard time convincing her.*

16. à is used in the following *exclamations*, *wishes* and *commands*

A bas...!	*Down with...!*
A bas l'examen!	*Down with the exam!*
A genoux!	*Down on your knees!*
A la bonne heure!	*Well done! Good! Marvellous!*
A table!	*Dinner/lunch/breakfast is ready!*
A votre santé!	*Cheers! To your health!*
A la vôtre!	*Cheers! To yours!*

---

1. But: un billet **de** 100 euros = *a 100 euro bill*
2. **TGV** stands for 'le **t**rain à **g**rande **v**itesse', France's high-speed train.

A tes/vos souhaits!	*Bless you!* [When someone sneezes.]
Au feu!	*Fire!*
Au galop!	*Gallop!*
Au secours!	*Help!*
Au suivant!	*The next person please! Who's next?*
Au travail [= **au** boulot (fam.)]!	*(Let's get) to work!*
Au voleur!	*Catch the thief!*
Aux armes!	*To arms! Take your arms!*

17. à indicates the *manner* in which an action is performed

accepter/décider **à l'**unanimité	*to accept/decide unanimously*
accueillir qn **à** bras ouverts	*to welcome sb warmly/with open arms*
acheter/vendre **à** bon marché	*to buy/sell inexpensively*
acheter/vendre **à** moitié prix	*to buy/sell half-price*
acheter qch **à** tempérament/**à** crédit	*to buy sth on credit*
aimer qn **à la** folie	*to love someone madly*
boire **à** petites gorgées	*to sip*
chasser qn **à** coups de bâtons	*to throw sb out with the stick*
cueilli **à la** main	*handpicked*
cuit **à la** vapeur[1]	*steamed*
écrire **au** crayon/**à l'**encre	*to write in pencil/in ink*
élire qn **au** suffrage universel	*to vote for sb by universal suffrage*
s'enfuir **à** toutes jambes	*to run away as fast as one can*
faire qch **à l'**excès	*to do sth excessively*
fait **à la** main	*handmade, made by hand*
fait **à la** machine	*machine made*
faire qch **à la** perfection	*to do sth perfectly/to perfection*
faire qch **au** nez et **à la** barbe de qn	*to do sth right in front of sb*
Ils ont fait de la contrebande **au** nez et **à la** barbe des douaniers.	*They smuggled (items) under the very nose of the customs officials.*
fermer la porte **à** clé	*to lock the door*
fermer la porte **à** double tour	*to lock the door (turning the key twice)*

---

1. lit.: *cooked with steam*

lire **à** haute voix	*to read out loud*
marcher **à l'**électricité/**au** gaz	*to run on electricity/on gas*
Dans cette cuisine, tout marche **à l'**électricité.	*In this kitchen, everything runs on electricity.*
marcher **à** pas de géant	*to walk with giant strides*
marcher **à** pas de loup	*to walk stealthily*
marcher **à** quatre pattes	*to walk on all fours, to crawl*
parler **à** haute voix/**à** voix basse	*to speak in a loud/low voice*
partir **au** pas de course	*to rush off*
pleurer **à** chaudes larmes	*to cry bitterly, to cry one's eyes out*
pleuvoir **à** verse/**à** sceaux	*to pour, to rain cats and dogs*
nourrir **au** sein	*to breastfeed*
reconnaître qn **à** sa voix	*to recognize sb by his/her voice*
regarder qch **à la** loupe/**au** microscope	*look at sth with a magnifying glass/with a microscope*
rire **aux** éclats	*to roar with laughter*
rouler **à** vive allure/**à** grande vitesse	*to drive at high speed*
rouler **au** pas	*to drive very slowly*
rouler **à** tombeau ouvert[1]	*to drive like a madman*
sauter **à la** corde	*to jump rope*
suivre les instructions **à la** lettre	*to follow instructions to the letter*
taper **à la** machine	*to type*
tirer **à l'**arc	*to shoot with a bow and arrow*
tirer **à** balles réelles	*to shoot with real bullets*
tirer **au** revolver sur qn	*to shoot sb with a gun*
travailler **au** pair	*to work in exchange for room and board*
travailler **à** temps partiel (= à mi-temps)/**à** plein temps	*to work part-time/full-time*
traverser le fleuve **à la** nage	*to swim across the river*
traverser l'océan **à la** rame	*to row across the ocean*
vivre **au** jour le jour	*to live from one day to the next, to live from hand to mouth*
vouloir qch **à** tout prix	*to want sth at any cost/at all costs*

---

1. lit.: *to drive with an open tomb*

18. **à la (à l')** + *feminine adjective of nationality* or *proper noun* expresses 'in the manner of', 'in the style of'

s'habiller/manger **à la** française	*to dress/eat in the French manner*
des jardins **à la** française	*French-style gardens*
un repas **à l'**italienne	*an Italian-style meal*
du homard **à l'**armoricaine	*lobster Britanny-style*
filer **à l'**anglaise[1]	*to leave without notice*
être assis **à la** turque[2]	*to be sitting cross-legged*
des poèmes **à la** Victor Hugo	*poems in the style of Victor Hugo*

19. **à** (+ definite article) expresses *rate* (English: *by*)

acheter/vendre qch **à la** douzaine	*to buy/sell sth by the dozen*
à la livre	*by the pound*
au kilo	*by the kilogram*
au litre	*by the liter*
au mètre	*by the meter*

20. **à** is used after *c'est* before a *noun* or *disjunctive pronoun* in the expression *être **à** qn de* + inf. (see p. 237)

C'est **à** moi (toi, lui...) de jouer.	*It's my (your, his...) turn to play.*
C'est **à** Jean de faire le premier pas.	*It's up to John to take the first step.*

21. **à** combines two *identical nouns*, *adverbs* or *adjectives* in the following fixed expressions (English: *by*)

côte **à** côte	*side by side*
coude **à** coude	*shoulder to shoulder, side by side*
goutte **à** goutte	*drop by drop*
pas **à** pas	*step by step*
petit **à** petit	*little by little*
peu **à** peu	*little by little*
tour **à** tour	*in turn, by turns, alternately*
un **à** un	*one by one*
Also:	
être face **à** face	*to be face-to-face, facing each other*
être terre **à** terre	*to be down to earth* [person]
le tête-**à**-tête	*the tête-à-tête, the private meeting*

---

1. lit.: *to leave in the English manner*
2. lit.: *to sit in the Turkish manner*

22. With some French verbs, **à** is the equivalent of English *from*

acheter qch **à** qn	*to buy sth **from** sb*
arracher qch **à** qn	*to snatch sth **from** sb*
cacher qch **à** qn	*to hide sth **from** sb*
commander qch **à** qn	*to order sth **from** sb*
emprunter qch **à** qn	*to borrow sth **from** sb*
enlever qch **à** qn	*to take sth away **from** sb*
louer qch **à** qn	*to rent sth **from** sb*
ôter qch **à** qn	*to take sth (abstract) away **from** sb*
prendre qch **à** qn	*to take sth **from** sb*
retirer qch **à** qn	*to take sth away **from** sb*
saisir qch **à** qn	*to seize sth **from** sb*
voler qch **à** qn	*to steal sth **from** sb*

23. **à** is part of numerous *adverbial* or *prepositional phrases* and *expressions*

à mon avis (= **à** mon sens)	*in my opinion*
à bon escient	*judiciously, with discrimination*
à mauvais escient	*wrongly*
à bout portant Il a tiré un coup de feu **à** bout portant.	*point-blank* *He shot point-blank.*
à but non-lucratif	*non-profit (with no profit)*
à une condition	*on one condition*
à ma connaissance	*to my knowledge*
à ma (sa...leur) consternation	*to my (his...their) dismay*
à contre-cœur	*reluctantly*
à dessein	*deliberately*
à destination de Les passagers **à** destination de Paris sont priés de se rendre à la porte 14.	*with the destination of, to* *The passengers to Paris are asked to go to gate 14.*
à fond	*thoroughly*
à peu de/**à** grands frais	*at little/at great expense*
à ma (ta, votre...) guise	*just as I (you...) wish or please*
à huis clos	*behind closed doors*
à mon (ton, son...) insu	*without my (your, his, her...) knowledge*
à jamais	*forever*

à jeun	*sober, with an empty stomach*
Soyez **à** jeun!	*Don't eat or drink anything!*
à jour	*up to date*
à merveille	*marvellously, wonderfully*
à mesure que	*as*
à mesure que le temps passait	*as time went by*
à mi-chemin entre...	*halfway between...*
à moitié	*half*
Le verre est **à** moitié vide/plein.	*The glass is half empty/full.*
faire qch **à** moitié	*to do sth halfway*
à nouveau	*again*
à part entière	*full(y), in its own right*
Ce sont des partenaires **à** part entière.	*They are full-fledged partners.*
à peine	*hardly*
à perte de vue	*as far as the eye can see*
à peu près	*about, approximately*
à ta/votre place	*in your place, if I were you*
à plus forte raison	*all the more so*
à plusieurs reprises	*repeatedly, on several occasions*
à maintes reprises	*again and again, many times*
à point[1]	*medium* [meats]
Je voudrais mon bifteck **à** point.	*I would like my steak medium.*
(pas) **à** ce point	*(not) to that extent*
à tel point que...	*to such extent that...*
à ce point de vue	*in this respect*
à tous points de vue	*in every respect*
à (la) portée de la main	*within reach, within arms reach*
à première vue	*at first sight*
à présent	*at present, now*
à priori	*at first sight, initially*
à propos	*by the way, at the right time*
Vous arrivez **à** propos.	*You arrive at the right time.*
à ce propos	*in this connection*
à tout propos	*continually, on every occasion*
mal **à** propos	*at the wrong time*
à proprement parler	*strictly speaking*
à rebours	*backward(s)*

---

1. *well done* [meats] = bien cuit *rare* [meats] = saignant *very rare* [meats] = bleu

à regret	*with regret, regretfully*
à mes (tes, ses...) risques et périls	*at my (your, his...) own risk*
à mon (grand) soulagement	*to my (big) relief*
à succès C'est un film **à** succès.	*successful* [actor, play, film] *It's a successful movie.*
à suivre	*to be continued*
à ma (grande) surprise	*to my (big) surprise*
à temps[1]	*in time*
à court terme **à** long terme	*short-term* *long-term*
à titre de [+ noun]	*as, in the capacity of* [+ a + noun]
à titre d'exemple	*as an example, for instance*
à titre de précaution	*as a precaution*
à titre d'emprunt	*as a loan*
Also:	
à titre de comparaison	*by comparison*
à titre d'essai	*on a trial basis*
à titre [+ adj.] (or: **à** + adj. + titre)	*in a* [+ adj.] *way*
à titre confidentiel	*confidentially, in a confidential way*
à titre exceptionnel	*exceptionally, in an exceptional way*
à titre préventif	*preventively*
à titre privé	*in a private capacity*
à juste titre	*rightfully, rightly so*
au même titre que	*in the same way as*
à [+ number (or: quelques) + noun + près]	*with/by only* [+ number (or: a few) + noun]
à quelques exceptions près	*with only a few exceptions*
(échapper) **à** quelques secondes près	*(to escape) by only a few seconds*
à une différence près	*with only one difference*
à une heure près	*by only one hour*
Also:	
à cela près	*except for that*
à cette exception près	*with this exception, apart from this*
à tort	*wrongly, wrongfully*
être accusé **à** tort	*to be wrongly accused*
à tort ou **à** raison	*rightly or wrongly*
(parler) **à** tort et **à** travers	*(to speak) thoughtlessly, at random*

---

1. Do not confuse ***à*** *temps* = ***in*** *time* and ***à l'****heure* = ***on*** *time*

à tour de rôle	*in turn, taking turns*
à tous les coups	*every time*
à toute heure	*at any time*
à toute vitesse	*at full/top speed*
à vol d'oiseau	*in a straight line* [distance], *as the crow flies*
à volonté	*at will, as much as you wish*
à vrai dire	*really, to tell the truth, frankly*
à vue d'oeil	*before your very eyes*
à mes yeux	*in my opinion*
à la bonne franquette	*informal, simple* [meal]
C'est **à la** bonne franquette.	*It's an informal (= simple) meal.*
à la demande de	*at the request of*
à la demande de tous	*at everyone's request*
à la dérobée	*furtively, stealthily*
à la différence de	*unlike, contrary to*
A la différence de son père, il adore le sport.	*Unlike his father, he adores sports.*
à la seule différence que...	*with the only difference that...*
à la (or: **dans** la) fleur de l'âge	*in the prime of life*
à la fois (= **en** même temps)[1]	*at the same time*
à la hâte	*hastily, in a rush*
à la ligne	*new paragraph* [instructions in a dictation]
à la limite de	*on the verge of*
à la longue	*in the long run*
à la même heure[1]	*at the same (clock) time*
à la mode	*fashionable, in fashion*
à la mode de	*in the style of*
à la place (de)	*instead (of)*

---

1. Do not confuse the following expressions which all mean '*at the same time*'.

- **à la fois** = '*at the same time*' *(= simultaneously)*
  Il fait deux choses **à la fois**. *He does two things **at the same time**.*
- **à la même heure** = '*at the same (clock) time*'
  Je vous retrouve demain **à la même heure** au même endroit.
  *I meet you tomorrow **at the same time** at the same place.*
- **à la même époque** = '*at the same time (period)*'
  l'année dernière **à la même époque** *last year **at the same time***

à la queue leu leu	*in single file, one after the other*
à la recherche de	*in search of*
à la réflexion	*on second thoughts, after thinking*
à la retraite	*retired*
à la rigueur	*if need be, as a last resort*
à la suite de	*following*
à l'abri de	*sheltered/protected from*
se mettre **à** l'abri	*to take shelter*
à l'accoutumée	*as usual*
à l'aide de	*with the help of*
à l'avance (= d'avance)	*ahead of time, in advance*
Prévenez-moi de votre arrivée deux jours **à l'**avance.	*Inform me of your arrival two days ahead of time.*
à l'aveuglette	*blindly, at random*
à l'égard de	*about, concerning, with regard to*
à cet égard	*in this respect*
à tous (les) égards	*in all respects*
à bien des égards	*in many repects*
à l'envers	*the wrong way, back to front, inside out, upside down*
Il porte la casquette **à l'**envers.	*He wears the cap back to front.*
C'est le monde **à l'**envers.	*The world is turned upside down.*
La photo est **à l'**envers dans le projecteur.	*The picture is upside down in the projector.*
à l'exception de	*with the exception of, except for*
à l'exemple de	*following sb's footsteps, like*
(arriver, être) **à l'**heure	*(to arrive, to be) on time*
à l'heure actuelle	*at the present time*
à l'improviste	*unexpectedly, without warning*
à l'inverse de (= contrairement **à**)	*contrary to*
à l'issue de	*at the end of*
à l'occasion de	*on the occasion of*
à l'œil (fam.)	*for free*
à l'opposé de	*in contrast to, contrary to*
à l'origine	*originally*
au besoin	*if need be*
au bout du compte	*ultimately, in the end*

au cas où	*in case*
Au cas où tu aurais besoin de moi.	*In case you needed me.*
au contraire	*on the contrary*
au détriment de	*to the detriment of*
au dire de qn	*according to sb*
Au dire de ses amis, il est gentil.	*According to his friends, he is nice.*
au fait	*by the way*
au fond	*basically*
Au fond, ce n'est pas un homme méchant.	*Basically, he is not a mean man.*
au fur et **à** mesure	*as one goes along*
Je rangerai les livres **au** fur et **à** mesure.	*I will put the books away as I go along.*
au fur et **à** mesure de	*as and when*
au fur et **à** mesure des besoins	*as and when the need arises*
au fur et **à** mesure que	*as, progressively, proportionally*
au fur et **à** mesure que le temps passe	*as time passes*
au hasard	*at random*
au juste	*exactly*
Que voulez-vous **au** juste?	*What exactly do you want?*
Je ne sais pas **au** juste.	*I don't know exactly.*
au large de	*off the coast of*
au loin	*in the distance*
au même endroit	*at the same place*
au moins	*at least* [quantity]
au moyen de	*by means of, using*
au nom de	*on behalf of*
au péril de	*at the risk of*
au péril de sa vie	*at the risk of his life*
au pire	*at the (very) worst*
au plus	*at the most*
tout **au** plus	*at the very most*
au plus tard/tôt	*at the latest/earliest*
au plus vite (= le plus vite possible)	*as quickly as possible*
au poil (fam.)	*terrific*
au (du) point de vue [+ adj. or noun]	*from the/a* [+ adj.] *point of view*
au point de vue religieux	*from a religious standpoint*
au point de vue argent	*from the financial point of view*
au point de vue efficacité	*as far as efficiency is concerned*
au premier abord	*at first sight*

au premier chef	*primarily, first and foremost*
au ralenti	*slow-motion*
au risque de	*at the risk of*
au sein de	*within*
au sein d'une famille	*within a family*
au sens figuré	*in a figurative sense*
au sens propre	*in a literal sense*
au vu et **au** su de qn	*to sb's know, with sb's knowledge*
au vu et **au** su de tout le monde	*openly, with everyone's knowledge*
aux environs de (= **aux** alentours de)	*around, approximately*
aux frais de qn	*at sb's expense*
aller **à la** pêche	*to go fishing*
aller **à la** rencontre de qn	*to go and meet sb*
appeler **à** l'aide	*to call for help*
boire **à la** bouteille	*to drink out of the bottle*
couler **à** flot(s)	*to flow freely*
La bière coulait **à** flots.	*The beer was flowing freely.*
dîner **à la** fortune du pot	*to have a potluck dinner*
être **à** bout/**à** bout de forces	*to be exhausted*
Ils sont **à** bout de forces.	*They can't take it any more.*
être **à** bout de nerfs	*to be at the end of one's rope*
être **à** bout de patience	*to be at the end of one's patience*
être **à** bout de souffle	*to be out of breath*
être **à** court de qch	*to be short of sth, to run out of sth*
Je suis **à** court d'idées/d'argent.	*I am running out of ideas/money.*
être **à** couvert de	*to be sheltered from*
être **à** égalité	*to be tied* [sports]
être **à l'**affût de	*to be on the lookout for*
être/se sentir **à l'**aise	*to be/feel comfortable*
être/se sentir mal **à l'**aise	*to be/feel ill at ease/uncomfortable*
Je me sens toujours mal **à l'**aise dans sa compagnie.	*I always feel uncomfortable in his company.*
être **au** chaud	*to be in the warmth*
être **au** courant (de)	*to be informed/to know (about)*
être **au** chômage	*to be unemployed*
être mauvais/bon **au** goût	*to taste bad/good*
être **au** gré de qn	*to be to sb's liking*
à son gré	*to his/her liking*

être **au** régime	*to be on a diet*
(ne pas) être **à la** hauteur	*(not) to be up to it*
Je ne suis pas **à la** hauteur.	*I am not up to (= not qualified for) it.*
être **à la** page	*to be up to date*
être **à la** portée de qn	*to be within sb's reach*
être **à** (**la**) portée de la main	*to be within reach, to be at hand*
être **à la** recherche de qch	*to be looking for sth*
écouter **aux** portes	*to eavesdrop*
être **aux** aguets	*to be on the lookout*
être **aux** anges	*to be in the seventh heaven*
être **aux** mains de qn	*to be in sb's hands*
Paris était **aux** mains des Anglais.	*Paris was in the hands of the British.*
être **aux** petits soins avec qn	*to pamper sb*
être **aux** prises avec	*to battle with*
frapper **à** la porte	*to knock on the door*
manger **à** sa faim	*to eat one's fill*
Avez-vous mangé **à** votre faim?	*Did you eat enough?*
mener qch **à** bien	*to complete sth successfully*
mettre **à** jour	*to update, to bring up to date*
mettre qn **à** la porte	*to throw/kick sb out*
mettre **à l'**épreuve	*to put to a test*
se mettre **à l'**œuvre	*to get down to work*
mettre qn **au** courant	*to inform sb*
mettre **au** monde	*to give birth to*
mettre **au** point	*to perfect*
perdre **au** change	*to lose on the exchange (= the deal)*
se plier **à** qch	*to submit/yield to sth*
prendre qch **à** cœur	*to take sth to heart*
prendre qn **au** dépourvu	*to catch someone off-guard*
prendre qch **à la** légère	*to take sth lightly*
prendre qch/qn **au** sérieux	*to take sth/sb seriously*
prendre son courage **à** deux mains	*to take one's courage in both hands*
repartir **à** zéro	*to start from scratch*
revenir **au** même	*to amount to the same thing*
Ça revient **au** même.	*That comes up to the same.*
rire **au** nez de qn	*to laugh in someone's face*
sauter **au** cou de qn	*to throw one's arms around someone's neck, to hug sb*
Elle m'a sauté **au** cou.	*She threw her arms around me.*

tenir qn **au** courant	*to keep sb informed/updated/posted*
se tenir **au** courant	*to keep abreast of current events*
tirer **à la** courte paille/**au** sort	*to draw straws/lots*
tomber **à l'**eau	*to fall through* [projects]
vendre/acheter qch **au** détail	*to sell/buy sth retail*
venir **au** monde	*to be born*
C'était avant que je vienne **au** monde.	*That was before I was born.*

24. **à** is used before an infinitive[1] in a series of *fixed expressions*

à louer	*for rent*
à vendre	*for sale*
à savoir	*namely, that is to say*
à suivre	*to be continued*
dans les semaines/années **à** venir	*in the coming weeks/years*

25. **à** + *article* or *possessive adjective* + *noun*[2] frequently replaces the conjunction *quand* + subordinate clause

A mon arrivée à Paris (= *quand* je suis arrivé à Paris), j'ai tout de suite pris un taxi.	*When I arrived in Paris, I took a taxi immediately.*
Elle était fatiguée **à l'**arrivée.	*She was tired when she arrived.*
A son départ, il neigeait.	*It was snowing when he left.*
A mon retour, j'irai faire des courses.	*When I come back, I'll go shopping.*
Au retour d'une fête, il a eu un accident.	*He had an accident when he came back from a party.*
Elle vient chercher/prendre ses enfants **à** la sortie de l'école.	*She picks up her children when school is out.*
Au réveil/**à** son réveil, il allume la radio.	*When he wakes up, he turns on the radio.*
à la mort de mon père	*when my father died*
à la rentrée	*when the school year starts/started*
à notre entrée	*when we enter(ed)*

1. For the use of **à** between a conjugated verb and an infinitive see p. 212-215.
2. Note that these nouns are derived from verbs.

26. **à** introduces the complement after the following *adjectives*

(être) apte **à** qch	*(to be) capable* ***of****/qualified* ***for*** *sth*
(être) disposé **à** qch	*(to be) ready* ***for*** *sth*
(être) favorable **à** qch	*(to be) in favor* ***of*** *sth*
(être) prêt **à** qch	*(to be) ready* ***for*** *sth*
(être) utile **à** qch	*(to be) useful* ***for*** *sth*

Proverbs, sayings, and idioms

A chacun son goût.	*Each to his own taste. There's no accounting for taste.*
A la guerre comme **à** la guerre.	*In times of hardship, you have to make the best of things.*
Revenons **à** nos moutons.	*Let's get back to our subject.*
apporter de l'eau **au** moulin de qn	*to fuel sb's arguments*
avoir plus d'une corde **à** son arc	*to have more than one string to one's bow*
ne pas avoir froid **aux** yeux	*to fear nothing, to be fearless*
courir deux lièvres **à** la fois	*to have too many irons in the fire*
être **au** bon endroit **au** bon moment	*to be in the right place at the right time*
geler **à** pierre fendre	*to freeze hard*
joindre l'utile **à** l'agréable	*to combine the useful with pleasure*
Le temps est **à** la pluie.	*It looks like rain.*
à travail égal, salaire égal	*equal pay for equal work*
Ça saute **aux** yeux.	*That is evident.*
à la lumière du jour/d'une bougie	*by day/candle light*
à la Saint-Glinglin	*when hell freezes over*
C'est **à** double tranchant. (fig.)	*It's a two-sided sword. (fig.)*
C'est gentil **à** vous.	*That's nice of you.*
à ce qu'on dit	*according to what they say*
attention **à**	*watch out for, beware of*
avoir droit **à**	*to be entitled to*
comparé **à**	*in comparison with*
Il y a une raison **à** cela.	*There's a reason for that.*

B. The preposition **de**

1. **de** introduces the *object* [*noun* or *(stressed) pronoun*] after certain verbs and expressions[1]

Il abuse **de l'**alcool et **du**[2] tabac.	*He overuses alcohol and tobacco.*
Avez-vous peur **de** la violence?	*Are you afraid of violence?*
Tout le monde a besoin **d'**amis.[3]	*Everyone needs friends.*
Ça dépend **du** temps qu'il fera.	*It depends on the weather.*
Il manque **d'**assurance.[3]	*He lacks self-confidence.*
Je ne peux pas me passer **de** café.[3]	*I cannot do without coffee.*
Qu'est-ce que tu penses **d'**eux?	*What do you think of them?*
Te souviens-tu **de** cette tempête?	*Do you remember this storm?*

Mistakes to avoid

Incorrect	*Correct*	*English meaning*
Il a besoin ~~de l'~~argent.	Il a besoin **d'**argent.[3]	*He needs money.*
Il manque ~~du~~ tact.	Il manque **de** tact.[3]	*He lacks tact.*

2. **de** + *definite article* is used after **jouer** when this verb is followed by the name of a *musical instrument*[4]

jouer **du**[2] clavecin	*to play the harpsichord*
jouer **du** hautbois	*to play the oboe*
jouer **du** piano	*to play the piano*
jouer **du** saxophone	*to play the saxophone*
jouer **du** trombone	*to play the trombone*
jouer **du** violon	*to play the violin*
jouer **du** violoncelle	*to play the cello*
jouer **du** xylophone	*to play the xylophone*
jouer **de la** batterie	*to play drums*
jouer **de la** clarinette	*to play the clarinet*

---

1. For a detailed list of these verbs and expressions, see p. 80-82, 181-182, 184-187.
2. The preposition **de** contracts with the masculine singular and plural definite articles: de + le = **du**, de + les = **des**.
3. Note that *avoir besoin **de** (to need)*, *manquer **de** (to lack)*, and *se passer **de** (to do without)* are *not* followed by the definite article unless something specific is referred to.
4. For the use of **à** after 'jouer' before a game or sport, see p. 33-34.

jouer **de la** cornemuse	*to play the backpipe*
jouer **de la** flûte	*to play the flute*
jouer **de la** flûte douce	*to play the recorder*
jouer **de la** guitare	*to play the guitar*
jouer **de la** harpe	*to play the harp*
jouer **de la** mandoline	*to play the mandoline*
jouer **de la** trompette	*to play the trumpet*
jouer **de la** vielle	*to play the hurdy-gurdy*
jouer **de l'**accordéon	*to play the accordion*
jouer **de l'**harmonica	*to play the harmonica*
jouer **de l'**harmonium	*to play the harmonium*
jouer **de l'**orgue	*to play the organ*

3. **de** introduces the *noun* or *(stressed) pronoun* after numerous adjectives, corresponding to English 'of', 'about', 'with' and 'for'

être/tomber amoureux **de** qn	*to be/fall in love* ***with*** *sb*
Est-il amoureux **de** Chantal?	*Is he in love* ***with*** *Chantal?*
être avare **de** qch	*to be sparing/stingy* ***with***
Il est très avare **de** son temps.	*He is very stingy* ***with*** *his time.*
être capable **de** qch	*to be capable of sth*
Elle est capable **d'**une grande affection.	*She is capable of a great affection.*
être conscient **de** qch	*to be aware of sth*
Elle est consciente **de** sa faiblesse.	*She is aware of her weakness.*
être content **de** qn/qch	*to be pleased* ***with*** *sb/sth*
Je suis très content **de** toi.	*I am very pleased* ***with*** *you.*
être convaincu **de** qch	*to be convinced of sth*
Il est convaincu **de** sa culpabilité.	*He is convinced of his guilt.*
être déçu **de** (or: **par**) qch	*to be disappointed* ***by/about*** *sth*
Etes-vous déçu **de** son attitude?	*Are you disappointed* ***by*** *his attitude?*
être dégoûté **de** qch	*to be disgusted* ***with*** *sth*
Elle est dégoûtée **de** son métier.	*She is disgusted* ***with*** *her job.*
être désolé **de** (or: **pour**) qch	*to be sorry* ***about*** *sth*
Je suis désolé **de** ces changements.	*I am sorry* ***about*** *these changes.*
être enchanté **de** qch	*to be delighted* ***with*** *sth*
Ils étaient enchantés **de** leur séjour en Autriche.	*They were delighted* ***with*** *their stay in Austria.*
être fâché **de** qch	*to be angry* ***about*** *sth*
Je suis fâché **de** votre conduite.	*I am angry* ***about*** *your behavior.*

être familier **de** qch	*to be familiar* ***with*** *sth*
Il est familier **de** la littérature française.	*He is familiar* ***with*** *French literature.*
être fatigué **de** qch	*to be tired of sth*
Je suis fatigué **de** la grève.	*I am tired of the strike.*
être fier **de** qn/qch	*to be proud of sb/sth*
Elle est fière **de** son succès.	*She is proud of her success.*
être fou **de** qch	*to be crazy* ***about*** *sth*
Elle est folle **de** la France et **de** ses produits.	*She is crazy* ***about*** *France and its products.*
être heureux **de** qch	*to be happy* ***about*** *sth*
Ils sont heureux **de** leur réussite.	*They are happy* ***about*** *their success.*
être incertain **de** qch	*not to be sure* ***about*** *sth*
Je suis incertain **de** mes sentiments.	*I am not sure* ***about*** *my feelings.*
être indigné **de** qch	*to be outraged* ***by*** *sth*
Nous sommes indignés **de** la situation.	*We are outraged* ***by*** *the situation.*
être inquiet **de** qch	*to be worried* ***about*** *sth*
Elle est inquiète **de** son retard.	*She is worried* ***about*** *him being late.*
être passionné **de** (or: **pour**) qch	*to have a passion* ***for*** *sth*
Il est passionné **d'**opéra.	*He has a passion* ***for*** *opera.*
être ravi **de** qch	*to be delighted* ***about*** *sth*
Je suis ravi **de** votre visite.	*I am delighted* ***about*** *your visit.*
être reconnaissant (à qn) **de** qch	*to be thankful (to sb)* ***for*** *sth*
Elle est reconnaissante **de** son aide.	*She is thankful* ***for*** *his/her help.*
Je vous suis reconnaissant **de** votre soutien.	*I am thankful to you* ***for*** *your support.*
être responsable **de** qch	*to be responsible* ***for*** *sth*
Vous êtes responsable **de** vos actions.	*You are responsible* ***for*** *your actions.*
être satisfait **de** qn/qch	*to be satisfied* ***with*** *sb/sth*
Il est satisfait **du** résultat.	*He is satisfied* ***with*** *the result.*
être sûr **de** qn/qch	*to be sure of/****about*** *sb/sth*
Es-tu sûr **de** son honnêteté?	*Are you sure of his honesty?*
Nous sommes sûrs **de** nous.	*We are sure of ourselves.*
être triste **de** qch	*to be sad* ***about*** *sth*
Il est triste **de** la mort de sa tante.	*He is sad* ***about*** *the death of his aunt.*

Mistakes to avoid

Incorrect	*Correct*	*English meaning*
Il est content ~~avec~~ sa vie.	Il est content **de** sa vie.	*He is happy* ***with*** *his life.*
Elle est amoureuse ~~avec~~ lui.	Elle est amoureuse **de** lui.	*She is in love* ***with*** *him.*

4. de introduces the ***place of origin*** (English: *from, out of*)

- **de** (without article) is used with names of *cities*[1], *islands* and *countries* that are *not* preceded by an article, i.e. with places which use 'à' to express 'in' and 'to'

Il vient **de** Strasbourg.	*He comes from Strasbourg.*
Ils sont partis **de** Tahiti.	*They left (from) Tahiti.*
Caroline est **de** Monaco.	*Caroline is from Monaco.*

- **de** (without article) is used with *continents, feminine countries, feminine French provinces, feminine American states* and *feminine Canadian provinces,* i.e. with places which use 'en' to express 'in' and 'to'

L'avion arrive **d'**Europe.	*The plane arrives from Europe.*
Nous venons **de** France.	*We come from France.*
Ils sont partis **d'**Italie.	*They left (from) Italy.*
Elle vient **de** Floride.	*She comes from Florida.*
Il est **de** Colombie Britannique.	*He is from British Columbia.*
Il reviendra **de** Provence en hiver.	*He will come back from Provence in winter.*

- **de** (without article) is used with *masculine countries, masculine French provinces, masculine American States* and *masculine Canadian provinces* starting with a vowel

d'Israël, **d'**Iran, **d'**Anjou	*from Israel, from Iran, from Anjou*
d'Andorre, **d'**Oregon	*from Andorra, from Oregon*
l'avion **d'**Alberta[2]	*the plane from Alberta*

---

1. But if the article is part of the city name, *du, de la* and *des* are used (see p. 282).

Ils viennent **du** Havre.	*They come from Le Havre.*
Elle arrive **de la** Haye.	*She arrives from The Hague.*
Il revient **des** Baux-de-Provence.	*He returns from Les Baux-de-Provence.*

2. Note that to indicate the place of departure of a plane or train, **de** can be reinforced by 'en provenance'.
L'avion **en provenance de** Paris / **de** Suisse / **du** Canada va arriver dans une heure.
The plane from Paris / Switzerland / Canada is going to arrive in one hour.

- **de** + definite article is used with *masculine countries, masculine American States, masculine Canadian provinces, masculine French provinces* starting with a consonant, as well as with *plural countries* and some *islands*

Elle est partie **du** Mexique.	*She left (from) Mexico.*
D'où êtes-vous? - Je suis originaire **des** Etats-Unis.	*Where are you from? -* *I am from the United States.*
J'ai reçu une lettre **des** USA.	*I received a letter from the U.S.*
Elle vient **des** Pays-Bas.	*She comes from the Netherlands.*
Il est **du** Colorado.	*He is from Colorado.*
Es-tu **du** Québec?	*Are you from Québec?*
Elle est **du** Périgord.	*She is from Périgord.*
Ils arrivent **des** Antilles.	*They arrive from the West Indies.*
Also:	
le vent **du** nord/**du** sud	*the north/south wind*
But:	
le vent **d'**est/**d'**ouest	*the east/west wind*

- **de** + definite article (or other determiner) is used to indicate the place of origin with localities other than geographic expressions

Il sort **de** la maison.	*He goes out of the house.*
Je sors un mouchoir **de** mon sac.	*I take a handkerchief out of my bag.*
Son porte-monnaie est tombé **de** sa poche.	*Her wallet fell out of her pocket.*

5. **de** gives the *point of departure* or *starting time*, often in conjunction with **à** (English: *from...to, from...till*)

Quelle est la distance **de** Paris à Chartres?	*How far is it from Paris to Chartres?*
Ils sont allés **de** la Tour Eiffel à la Place de la Concorde.	*They went from the Eiffel Tower to Concord Square.*
de la tête aux pieds	*from head to toe*
Comptez **de** un à dix.	*Count from one to ten.*
du matin au soir	*from morning till night*
du début (jusqu') à la fin	*from beginning to end*

de février à juin	*from February to June*
du jour au lendemain	*from one day to the next, overnight*
Le français ne s'apprend pas **du** jour au lendemain.	*French cannot be learned overnight.*
Je travaille **de** huit heures à midi.	*I work from eight o'clock till noon.*
En France, la scolarité est obligatoire **de** six à seize ans.	*In France, schooling is mandatory from six to sixteen years.*
Le magasin est ouvert **du** lundi au vendredi.	*The store is open from Monday till Friday.*

Also in:

d'un instant à l'autre	*any moment now*
Il doit arriver **d'**un instant à l'autre.	*He must arrive any moment now.*
d'une minute à l'autre	*any minute now, at any minute*
d'ici trois mois/quinze jours	*three months/two weeks from now*
d'ici quelques années	*a few years from now*
d'ici vingt ans	*twenty years from now*
d'ici juillet	*by July*
d'ici la fin de l'année	*by the end of the year*
d'ici la semaine prochaine	*by next week*
d'ici ce soir	*by this evening*
d'ici peu	*before long*
d'ici là	*in the meantime, by then*
Il y a dix ans **de** cela.	*It's been ten years since then.*
(**d'**) aujourd'hui en huit	*a week from today*
de naissance	*from/by birth*
être sourd **de** naissance	*to be deaf from birth*
C'est **de** naissance chez lui.	*He was born like that.*
Il est Français **de** naissance.	*He is French by birth.*

6. **de** is used before nouns to express *possession* (English uses a noun + apostrophe + *s* or a plural noun + apostrophe)

la chambre **de** Marie	*Mary's room*
C'est le père **de** ma mère.	*He is my mother's father.*
Voilà la voiture **du** professeur.	*Here is the teacher's car.*
J'ai trouvé le sac **de** la femme.	*I found the woman's purse.*
Ce sont les cahiers **des** étudiants.	*These are the students' notebooks.*
la maison **de** mes amis	*my friends' house*

7. de indicates the ***cause*** (English: *with, from*)

- between a verb and a noun

étouffer **de** rage	*to choke with anger*
s'évanouir/trembler **de** peur	*to faint/tremble with fear*
hurler **de** douleur	*to scream with pain*
mourir **d'**ennui[1]	*to be bored to death*
mourir **d'**envie de + inf.	*to be dying to + inf.*
Je meurs **d'**envie de parler.	*I am dying to speak.*
mourir **de** froid	*to freeze to death*
mourir **de** soif	*to be dying with thirst*
mourir **de** mort naturelle	*to die from natural death*
mourir **de** vieillesse	*to die from old age*
Je meurs **de** curiosité.	*I am dying with curiosity.*
Je meurs **d'**impatience.	*I am dying with impatience.*
Je meurs **de** faim.	*I am starving.*
Je meurs **de** honte.	*I am dying with shame.*
Je meurs **de** sommeil.	*I am dead-tired.*
J'étais mort **de** peur.[2]	*I was frightened to death.*
Il est mort **d'**un cancer/**du** Sida.	*He died from cancer/from Aids.*
On est mort **de** rire.	*We were dying with laughter.*
pâlir **d'**envie/**de** jalousie[3]	*to turn green with envy*
pleurer/sauter **de** joie	*to cry/jump with joy*
rougir **de** honte	*to blush with shame*
tomber **de** fatigue	*to drop with tiredness*

- between an adjective and a noun

être malade **de** chagrin	*to be sick with chagrin*
être pâle/rouge **de** colère	*to be white/purple with anger*
Nous étions fous **de** bonheur.[4]	*We were extremely happy.*
Il est ivre/fou **de** joie.[5]	*He is thrilled.*
Elle était folle **d'**inquiétude.	*She was worried sick.*
Tu es muet **d'**admiration.	*You are speechless with admiration.*

Also in the expression

être hors de soi **de** qch	*to be beside oneself with sth*
Il était hors de lui **de** fureur.	*He was beside himself with rage.*

---

1. lit.: *to die with boredom*
2. lit.: *I was dying with fear.*
3. lit.: *to turn pale with envy*
4. lit.: *We were crazy with happiness.*
5. lit.: *He is drunk/crazy with joy.*

8. **de** is used after **quelqu'un**, **quelque chose**, **rien**, **personne** and **quoi** when an adjective follows

quelqu'un **d'**expérimenté	*someone experienced*
quelque chose **d'**intéressant	*something interesting*
rien **de** grave	*nothing serious*
personne **de** compétent	*nobody competent*
Quoi **de** neuf?	*What's new?*
Quoi **d'**autre?	*What else?*

9. **de** is used after a *superlative* (English: *in*, *of*)

Paris est la plus belle ville **du** monde.	*Paris is the most beautiful city* ***in*** *the world.*
Marie est la plus intelligente **de** tous les étudiants.	*Mary is the most intelligent one* ***of*** *all the students.*

10. **de** (instead of *que*) is used to express 'than' after **plus** and **moins** when a *number* follows

Plus **de** trois millions de Français gagnent leur vie dans l'industrie viticole.	*More than three million Frenchmen make their living in the wine industry.*
Moins **de** trois mois se sont écoulés.	*Less than three months went by.*
Ce film est interdit aux moins **de** dix-huit ans.	*Noone under eighteen is admitted to this movie.*
Also: plus **de** la moitié des étudiants	*more than half of the students*

11. **de** introduces the *infinitive* after certain verbs, adjectives and expressions[1]

J'ai oublié **de** mettre la table.	*I forgot to lay the table.*
Elle est fière **d'**avoir gagné le prix.	*She is proud to have won the prize.*
Je n'ai pas le temps **de** le[2] faire.	*I don't have the time to do it.*
C'est à vous **de** juger.	*It's up to you to judge.*

---

1. For a detailed list of these expressions see p. 223-227; p. 232-242; p. 267-268.
2. There is *no* contraction between 'de' and 'le' when 'le' is a personal pronoun.

12. de is used before a noun after certain past participles[1] (often expressing 'with' and indicating a content or lack thereof)

accablé **de**	*overwhelmed* ***with***
Il est accablé **de** douleur.	*He is overwhelmed with pain.*
bondé **de**	*packed* ***with****, crammed* ***with***
Le métro est bondé **de** touristes.	*The subway is packed with tourists.*
bordé **de**	*bordered* ***with***
La Loire est bordée **de** châteaux.	*The Loire is bordered with castles.*
bourré **de**	*stuffed* ***with***
Ses poches étaient bourrées **de** pièces d'or.	*His pockets were stuffed with gold pieces.*
chargé **de**	*laden* ***with****, loaded* ***with***
C'est une ville chargée **d'**histoire.	*It's a city laden with history.*
couvert **de**	*covered* ***with***
Le toit est couvert **de** neige.	*The roof is covered with snow.*
débordé **de**	*overloaded/overwhelmed* ***with***
Je suis débordé **de** travail.	*I am overloaded with work.*
décoré **de**	*decorated* ***with***
L'arbre de Noël est décoré **de** boules et **de** guirlandes.	*The Christmas tree is decorated with ornaments and garlands.*
dénué **de**	*devoid of, lacking in*
Elle n'est pas dénuée **d'**imagination.	*She is not lacking imagination.*
dépouillé **de**	*bare of, devoid of*
Les arbres sont dépouillés **de** feuilles.	*The trees are devoid of leaves.*
dépourvu **de**	*deprived of, devoid of, lacking in*
Nous étions dépourvus **de** vivres.	*We were deprived of food.*
doté **de**	*equipped/endowed* ***with***
Il était doté **d'**un fantastique sens de l'humour.	*He was endowed with a fantastic sense of humor.*
entouré **de**	*surrounded* ***with****/by*
Le champ est entouré **d'**arbres.	*The field is surrounded by trees.*

---

1. Note that the verbs from which these past participles stem also use **de** before their complement to express 'with':
couvrir **de** (*to cover with*), décorer **de** (*to decorate with*), doter **de** (*to equip with*), entourer **de** (*to surround with*), farcir **de** (*to stuff with*), garnir **de** (*to garnish with*), munir **de** (*to provide with*), orner **de** (*to adorn with*), remplir **de** (*to fill with*), etc. See p. 184-187.

farci **de**	*stuffed* ***with***
la dinde est farcie **de** marrons.	*The turkey is stuffed with chestnuts.*
garni **de**	*garnished/decorated* ***with***
La viande est garnie **de** fruits.	*The meat is garnished with fruit.*
inondé **de**	*flooded* ***with***
La chambre est inondée **de** lumière.	*The room is flooded with light.*
inondé **de** sang/**de** sueur	*bathed in blood/sweat*
muni **de**	*equipped* ***with***
Cet appareil photo est muni **d'**un flash.	*This camera is equipped with a flash.*
orné **de**	*adorned* ***with***
Sa chambre était ornée **de** fleurs.	*Her room was adorned with flowers.*
paré **de**	*adorned* ***with****, decorated* ***with***
La table est parée **d'**oeillets.	*The table is adorned with carnations.*
privé **de**	*deprived of*
une région privée **d'**eau potable	*a region deprived of drinking water*
Il sera privé **de** dessert.[1]	*He will go without dessert.*
Ils sont privés **d'**électricité.	*They are without (electric) power.*
rempli **de**	*filled* ***with***
La dictée est remplie **de** chausse-trapes.	*The dictation is filled with pitfalls.*
submergé **de**	*inundated* ***with****, swamped* ***with***
Je suis submergé **de** travail/boulot.	*I am inundated with work.*
taché **de**	*stained* ***with***
La chemise était tachée de sang.	*The shirt was stained with blood.*
truffé **de** (fam.)	*peppered/larded/filled* ***with***
Son discours était truffé **de** citations.	*His speech was filled with quotations.*

Also after the following adjectives

libre **de**	*free of/from*
être libre **de** soucis	*to be free of worries*
être libre **de** préjugés	*to be free from prejudice*
être libre **de** ses actes[2]	*to do as one wishes*
être libre **de** ses choix	*to choose freely*
plein **de**	*full of/filled* ***with***
un panier plein **de** confiseries	*a basket filled with candy*
Il a les yeux pleins **de** larmes.	*His eyes are full of tears.*
vide **de**	*empty of*
Le train était vide **de** voyageurs.	*The train was empty of passengers.*
une pièce vide **de** meubles	*a room empty of furniture*
Cette expression est vide **de** sens.	*This expression is meaningless.*

---

1. lit.: *He will be deprived of dessert.*

2. lit.: *to be free in one's actions*

13. de (without article) is used between the following *expressions of quantity* and *nouns*

assez **de**	*enough*
assez **de** lait	*enough milk*
autant **de**	*as much, as many*
autant **de** cadeaux	*as many gifts*
beaucoup **de**	*much, a lot of, many*
beaucoup **de** bruit	*a lot of noise*
combien **de**	*how much, how many*
combien **d'**enfants	*how many children*
davantage **de**	*more*
davantage **de** problèmes	*more problems*
énormément **de**	*enormously much/many*
énormément **de** touristes	*enormously many tourists*
moins **de**	*less, fewer*
moins **d'**hommes	*fewer men*
pas mal **de** (fam.)	*quite a few*
Il a fait pas mal **de** fautes.	*He made quite a few mistakes.*
(bon) nombre **de**	*(a good) many*
bon nombre **de** femmes	*a good many women*
(un) peu **de**	*(a) little, few*
peu **de** chance	*little luck*
peu **d'**occasions	*few opportunities*
plein **de** (fam.)	*plenty of*
plein **de** travail	*plenty of work*
plus **de**	*more*
plus **de** difficultés	*more difficulties*
suffisamment **de**	*enough*
suffisamment **de** place	*enough space*
tant **de**	*so much, so many*
tant **d'**imagination	*so much imagination*
un tas/des tas **de** (fam.)	*lots of*
des tas **de** gens	*lots of people*
trop **de**	*too much, too many*
trop **de** monde	*too many people*

Mistakes to avoid

Incorrect	*Correct*	*English meaning*
beaucoup ~~de l'~~argent	beaucoup **d'**argent	*much money*
beaucoup ~~des~~ amis	beaucoup **d'**amis	*many friends*

une assiette **de**	*a plate of*
une assiette **de** charcuterie	*a plate of coldcuts*
un bol **de**	*a bowl of*
un bol **de** café au lait	*a bowl of cafe au lait*
une bouteille **de**	*a bottle of*
une bouteille **de** vin	*a bottle of wine*
une boîte **de**	*a box/can of*
une boîte **de** thon	*a can of tuna*
un bouquet **de**	*a bouquet of*
un bouquet **de** fleurs	*a bouquet of flowers*
une caisse **de**	*a case of*
une caisse **de** champagne	*a case of champagne*
une canette **de**	*a can of*
une canette **de** Coca Cola	*a can of Coke*
une carafe **de**	*a decanter of*
une carafe **d'**eau	*a decanter of water*
une chope **de**	*a mug of*
une chope **de** bière	*a mug of beer*
une corbeille **de**	*a basket of*
une corbeille **de** fruits	*a basket of fruit*
une cuillerée **de**	*a spoonful of*
une cuillerée **de** farine	*a spoonful of flour*
un flacon **de**	*a small bottle of*
un flacon **de** parfum	*a bottle of perfume*
une foule **de**	*a crowd of*
une foule **de** gens	*a crowd of people*
une gorgée **de**	*a sip of*
une gorgée **de** café	*a sip of coffee*
une gousse **de**	*a clove of*
une gousse **d'**ail	*a clove of garlic*
un kilo **de**	*a kilogram of*
un kilo **de** pommes	*a kilogram of apples*
un litre **de**	*a liter of*
un litre **d'**essence	*a liter of gasoline*
un mètre **de**	*a meter of*
un mètre **de** tissu	*a meter of fabric*
une miche **de**	*a loaf of*
une miche **de** pain	*a loaf of bread*

un morceau **de**	*a piece of*
un morceau **de** gâteau	*a piece of cake*
une paire **de**	*a pair of*
une paire **de** chaussures	*a pair of shoes*
un panier **de**	*a basket of*
un panier **de** pain	*a basket of bread*
un paquet **de**	*a package of*
un paquet **de** biscuits	*a package of cookies*
un pichet **de**	*a pitcher of*
un pichet **de** vin	*a pitcher of wine*
une pincée **de**	*a pinch of*
une pincée **de** sel	*a pinch of salt*
un plateau **de**	*a tray of*
un plateau **de** fromage	*a tray of cheese*
une poignée **de**	*a handful of*
une poignée **de** réfugiés	*a handful of refugees*
un pot **de**	*a jar of*
un pot **de** confiture	*a jar of jam*
un sac **de**	*a bag of*
un sac **de** pommes de terre	*a bag of potatoes*
un sachet **de**	*a (small) bag/packet of*
un sachet **de** soupe	*a packet of soup*
un sachet **de** thé/**de** bonbons	*a bag of tea/of candy*
un soupçon **de**	*a hint of*
un soupçon **de** cannelle	*a hint of cinnamon*
une tablette **de**	*a bar of*
une tablette **de** chocolat	*a bar of chocolate*
un tas **de**	*a heap/pile of*
un tas **de** sable	*a pile of sand*
une tasse **de**	*a cup of*
une tasse **de** thé	*a cup of tea*
une tonne **de**	*a ton of*
une tonne **de** vivres	*a ton of food*
une tranche **de**	*a slice of*
une tranche **de** jambon	*a slice of ham*
un tube **de**	*a tube of*
un tube **de** dentifrice	*a tube of toothpaste*
un verre **de**	*a glass of*
un verre **de** jus d'orange	*a glass of orange juice*

14. **de** (+ definite article) is used after the following *expressions of quantity*

bien	*much, many*
Bien **des** gens le connaissent.	*Many people know him.*
encore	*some more*
encore **de la** glace	*some more ice cream*
la plupart	*most*
La plupart **des** élèves sont ici.	*Most of the students are here.*
la plupart **du** temps	*most of the time*
la majorité	*the majority*
la majorité **des** ouvriers	*the majority of the workers*
la moitié	*half*
la moitié **des** participants	*half of the participants*

15. **de** is used between *approximate numbers* and *nouns,* between 'million' and a *noun,* and between 'milliard' and a *noun*

une *douzaine* **d'**œufs	*a dozen eggs*
une *vingtaine* **d'**étudiants	*about twenty students*
des *centaines* **d'**euros	*hundreds of euros*
Elle a une *cinquantaine* **d'**années.	*She is about fifty/in her fifties.*
des *milliers* **de** kilomètres	*thousands of kilometers*
Paris a deux *millions* **d'**habitants.	*Paris has two million inhabitants.*
Notre planète est vieille de quatre *milliards* et demi **d'**années.	*Our planet is four and a half billion years old.*

16. **de** indicates the *material* something is made out of (see also p. 88)

des gants **de** laine	*woolen gloves*
un manteau **de** fourrure	*a fur coat*
un t-shirt **de** coton	*a cotton T-shirt*
une robe **de** soie	*a silk dress*
le rideau **de** fer	*the Iron Curtain*
un sac **de** cuir	*a leather handbag*
un chapeau **de** paille	*a straw hat*
une jambe **de** bois	*a wooden leg*
des bottes **de** caoutchouc	*rubber boots*
une maison **de** pierre	*a stone house*
une boîte **de** carton	*a cardboard box*
une statue **de** marbre	*a marble statue*

Also in a figurative sense:

un coeur **de** granit	*a heart of stone*
une santé **de** fer[1]	*a health of a horse*
une volonté **d'**acier[2]	*an iron will*

17. With literature, works of art and other creations, **de** indicates the *author*, the *artist, and* the *creator* (English: *by)*

J'aime les tableaux **de** Picasso.	*I like the paintings by Picasso.*
Elle adore la poésie **de** Baudelaire.	*She adores the poetry by Baudelaire.*
Nous lisons un roman **de** Balzac.	*We read a novel by Balzac.*
un tailleur **de** Chanel	*a suit by Chanel*
une maison **de** Le Corbusier*	*a house by Le Corbusier*

* Note that *no* contraction takes place between ***à*** or ***de*** and 'le' when 'le' is part of a person's name.

18. de is used to build the *partitive article*

Il achète **du** vin, **de la** bière et **de l'**eau.	*He buys wine, beer and water.*

19. de can precede the agent of a *passive construction* in the passive voice (English: *by*)

Elle est aimée **de** nous tous.	*She is liked by all of us.*

20. de is used *in comparisons before an infinitive* following 'que' after 'aimer mieux' or 'préférer'

J'aime mieux me reposer que **de** voyager.	*I prefer to rest rather than to travel.*
Je préfère rester à la maison plutôt que **de** sortir.	*I prefer to stay at home rather than go out.*

21. de (+ determiner) + (modified) noun indicates the *manner* in which something is done. This construction often replaces an adverb of manner.

Il répondit **d'**un ton fâché.	*He answered angrily.*

---

1. lit.: *a health of iron*
2. lit.: *a will of steel*

Elle m'a regardé **d'**un air furieux.	*She looked at me furiously.*
Il parle **d'**une façon précise.	*He speaks precisely.*
Ils se battaient **de** toutes leurs forces.	*They fought with all their might.*
boire qch **d'**un trait	*to drink sth in one gulp*
citer un texte **de** mémoire	*to quote a text from memory*
connaître qn **de** vue/**de** nom	*to know sb by sight/by name*
écrire **d'**une façon/manière illisible	*to write illegibly*
entrer dans un endroit **de** force	*to enter a place by force*
être opéré **d'**urgence	*to have emergency surgery*
éviter qch **de** justesse	*to barely avoid sth*
manger **de** bon appétit	*to eat heartily/with appetite*
parler **d'**une voix douce	*to speak with a soft voice*
souhaiter qch **de** tout (son) cœur	*to wish sth with all one's heart*
voir qn **de** dos	*to see sb from behind*
voir qch **d'**un bon/mauvais œil	*to look (un) favorably upon sth*

22. de + noun indicates the *means* with which something is done

chercher qn/qch **des** yeux	*to look for sb/sth with the eyes*
cligner **de** l'oeil	*to wink*
écrire **de** la main droite/gauche	*to write with the right/left hand*
faire signe **de** la main à qn	*to signal/wave at sb with the hand*
franchir qch **d'**un bond	*to cross sth with one jump*
indiquer qch **de** la main	*to point at/towards sth*
montrer qn/qch **du** doigt	*to point (the finger) at sb/sth*
tuer **d'**un coup de fusil	*to kill with a gunshot*
faire qch **de** ses (propres) mains	*to do sth with one's (own) hands*
suivre qn **du** regard/**des** yeux	*to follow sb with one's eyes*
voir qch **de** ses propres yeux	*to see sth with one's own eyes*

23. de is part of numerous prepositional phrases giving the location of something or someone (see p. 4-6)

La banque est en face **du** cinéma.	*The bank is across from the cinema.*
L'église est à côté **de** la mairie.	*The church is next to the town hall.*

24. de indicates *age, time, amount* and *measurement (length, width, height,* etc.)

Ce monument a 3000 ans **d'**âge.	*This monument is 3000 years old.*
Elle est âgée **de** soixante ans.	*She is 60 years old.*
une auberge vieille **de** 500 ans	*a 500-year-old hostel*
L'univers est vieux **de** plus de dix milliards d'années.	*The universe is more than ten billion years old.*
L'espérance de vie des Français est actuellement **de** 75 ans pour les hommes et **de** 83 ans pour les femmes.	*The life expectancy of the French is currently 75 years for men and 83 years for women.*
En 2002, le taux de natalité était **de** 1,9 enfant par femme en France.	*In 2002, the birthrate was 1.9 children per woman in France.*
La moyenne d'âge était **de** 30 ans.	*The average age was thirty.*
Vous êtes en retard/en avance **de** trois minutes.	*You are three minutes late/early.*
Le train a dix minutes **d'**avance/**de** retard.	*The train is ten minutes early/late.*
Ma montre avance/retarde **de** dix minutes.	*My watch is ten minutes fast/slow.*
Il y a un décalage horaire **de** neuf heures entre Paris et Seattle.	*The time difference between Paris and Seattle is nine hours.*
Elle est enceinte **de** huit mois.	*She is eight months pregnant.*
En France, la durée de travail hebdomadaire est **de** 35 heures.	*In France, people work 35 hours weekly.*
La température extérieure est **de** vingt degrés.	*The outside temperature is twenty degrees.*
En France, le montant de la TVA[1] est actuellement **de** 19,6 %.	*In France, the VAT amount is presently 19.6 %.*
La pharmacie est distante **de** cinq kilomètres.	*The pharmacy is five kilometers away.*
Le mur a deux mètres **d'**épaisseur.	*The wall is two meters thick.*
une montagne haute **de** 2000 mètres	*a 2000 meter high mountain*
un fleuve large **de** deux kilomètres	*a two kilometer wide river*
Cette rue est longue **de** 1000 mètres.	*This street is 1000 meters long.*

1. la TVA = la **T**axe à la **V**aleur **A**joutée (*the Value Added Tax*)

25. de denotes the difference in *age*, *time*, *measurement* and *amount*

- in expressions such as

Elle a vieilli **de** dix ans.	*She grew ten years older.*
Il est plus âgé que toi **de** six ans.	*He is six years older than you.*
Elle est **de** cinq ans plus jeune que sa sœur.	*She is five years younger than her sister.*
Il est son cadet **de** trois ans.	*He is 3 years younger than he/she.*
J'abrège mes vacances **d'**un jour.	*I am cutting my vacation by a day.*
En octobre, il faut retarder sa montre **d'**une heure.	*In October, one must set back one's watch one hour.*
Elle a grandi **de** cinq centimètres.	*She grew five centimeters taller.*
Il est plus grand que moi **de** trois centimètres.	*He is three centimeters taller than I.*
Le niveau du lac a baissé **de** deux mètres.	*The level of the lake dropped by two meters.*
J'ai grossi/maigri **de** six kilos.	*I put on/lost six kilograms.*
Cette valise est **de** trois kilos plus lourde que l'autre.	*This suicase is three kilograms heavier than the other one.*
Le chômage a baissé/augmenté **de** 2%.	*Unemployment decreased/increased by 2%.*
On a augmenté mon salaire **de** quatre cents euros.	*They raised my salary by four hundred euros.*

- between a *number* (or expression of quantity) + *noun* and **plus, moins** or **trop**

Elle a six ans **de** plus/**de** moins que moi.	*She is six years older/younger than I.*
une fois **de** plus	*one more time*
La Française vit en moyenne huit ans **de** plus que son conjoint.	*The French woman lives on an average eight years longer than her husband.*
On lui donnerait 10 ans **de** moins.	*She looks ten years younger.*
En France, les femmes gagnent en moyenne 30% **de** moins que les hommes.	*In France, women earn on an average 30% less than men.*
Il y a plusieurs verres **de** trop.	*There are several glasses too many.*

26. de gives a *quality*

C'est un homme **de** talent.	*He is a talented man.*
une personne **de** bonne volonté	*a person of good will*
un produit **de** qualité	*a quality product*

27. de indicates a *duration*

un voyage **de** dix jours	*a ten-day trip*
Il y a environ une heure **de** route.	*It's about a one-hour drive.*

28. de is between *two nouns in apposition*

la ville **de** Paris	*the city of Paris*
l'île **de** Ré	*Ré Island*
le mois **de** juillet	*the month of July*

29. de follows the adjective *drôle* when it precedes the noun

un drôle **de** type	*a strange guy*
Il a un drôle **d'**air.	*He has a strange look.*
C'est une drôle **d'**idée.	*That's a strange idea.*

30. de precedes the adjective *libre* when it follows the verb *avoir* + *time period* or *space*

Si tu as un moment **de** libre.	*If you have a free moment.*
J'ai le reste de la matinée **de** libre.	*I have the rest of the morning free.*
Beaucoup de Français ont deux heures **de** libre pour le déjeuner.	*Many French have two hours off for lunch.*
Il n'y a plus une seule place **de** libre dans le parking.	*There isn't a single free place left in the parking lot.*

31. de indicates the *bodypart* where someone is operated on or where there is an *infirmity*

Il a été opéré **du** nez/**du** cœur.	*He had nose/heart surgery.*
Elle a été amputée **d'**un bras.	*One of her arms was amputated.*
Elle est aveugle **de** l'oeil gauche et sourde **de** l'oreille droite.	*She is blind in the left eye and deaf in the right ear.*
Il est paralysé **des** deux jambes.	*He is paralyzed in both legs.*
saigner **du** nez	*to have a nosebleed*
être dur **d'**oreille	*to be hard of hearing*

32. **de** is used after *être* when prices are indicated

Le prix de la chambre est **de** 200 euros par nuit.	*The price of the room is 200 euros per night.*

33. After an indication of clock time, **de** + article (+ *matin*, *après-midi* or *soir*) expresses **A.M.** and **P.M.**

à deux heures **du** matin	*at two A.M.*
Il est trois heures **de** l'après-midi.	*It is three P.M.*
vers huit heures **du** soir	*at about eight P.M.*

34. **de** combines two *nouns* which have become a unit

un accident **de** voiture	*a car accident*
une agence **de** voyage	*a travel agency*
un agent **de** change	*a broker*
un animal **de** compagnie	*a pet*
un animateur **de** télévision	*a talk-show host*
un arbre **de** Noël	*a Christmas tree*
l'argent **de** poche	*the pocket money, the allowance*
l'Armée **de** Terre	*the army, the ground forces*
l'arrêt **d'**autobus	*the bus stop*
l'article **de** fond	*the feature article, the cover story*
un asile **d'**aliénés	*a lunatic asylum*
une auberge **de** jeunesse	*a youth hostel*
les bijoux **de** fantaisie	*the fashion jewelry*
un bilan **de** santé	*a medical checkup*
le blanc **d'**oeuf	*the egg white*
un billet **de** banque	*a banknote*
la boîte **de** conserve	*the can*
une boîte **de** nuit	*a nightclub*
un bon **de** réduction	*a coupon*
le bonhomme **de** neige	*the snowman*
une bouche **d'**incendie	*a fire hydrant*
une boucle **d'**oreille	*an earring*
une boule **de** neige	*a snowball*
une bourse **d'**études	*a scholarship, a grant*
les boutons **de** manchettes	*cuff links*
le bulletin **de** naissance	*the birth certificate*
le bureau **de** change	*the foreign exchange office*
la cabine **d'**essayage	*the dressing room*

le cadeau **de** Noël	*the Christmas gift*
le (la) camarade **de** chambre	*the roommate*
le canot **de** sauvetage	*the lifeboat*
le carnet **d'**adresses/**de** chèques	*the address/check book*
une carte **de** crédit	*a credit card*
la carte **d'**embarquement	*the boarding pass*
une carte **d'**identité	*an identification card, an ID*
une carte **de** séjour	*a residence card*
une carte **de** téléphone	*a phone card*
une carte **de** visite	*a calling/business card*
une carte **de** vœux	*a greeting card*
la ceinture **de** sécurité	*the safety belt*
la chair **de** poule	*goosebumps*
la chambre **d'**amis	*the guest room*
la chasse **d'**eau	*the (toilet) flush*
le chauffeur **de** taxi	*the taxi driver*
des chaussures **de** randonnée	*hiking shoes*
le chef **d'**orchestre	*the conductor*
une chemise **de** nuit	*a nightgown*
un chèque **de** voyage	*a traveller's check*
le chiffre **d'**affaires	*the turnover*
le chou **de** Bruxelles	*the Brussels sprouts*
la colonie **de** vacances	*the summer camp*
le commissariat **de** police	*the police station*
le compte **d'**épargne	*the savings account*
le conte **de** fées	*the fairy tale*
le conducteur **d'**autobus	*the bus driver*
le coup **de** feu	*the shot*
un coup **de** fil/**de** téléphone	*a phone call*
le coup **de** foudre	*love at first sight*
un coup **d'**œil	*a glance, a quick look*
un coup **de** soleil	*a sunburn*
une coupure **de** journal	*a newspaper clipping*
le courant **d'**air	*the draft (of cold air)*
une course **de** chevaux	*a horse race*
une course **de** taureaux	*a bullfight*
le court **de** tennis	*the tennis court*

danger **de** mort	*danger of death*
un défilé **de** mode	*a fashion show*
la demoiselle **d'**honneur	*the bridesmaid*
la dent **de** lait	*the baby tooth*
la dent **de** sagesse	*the wisdom tooth*

le dessous **de** verre	*the coaster*
un détecteur **de** fumée	*a smoke detector*
le détournement **d'**avion	*the hijacking*
le distributeur (automatique) **de** billets	*the automatic teller machine (ATM)*
les droits **de** douane	*the customs duties*
la différence **d'**âge	*the age difference*
la diseuse **de** bonne aventure	*the fortune teller*
la disquette **d'**ordinateur	*the computer disk, the floppy disk*
la durée **d'**incubation	*the incubation period*
la durée **de** vie	*the life span*
l'eau **de** javel	*the bleach*
l'effet **de** serre	*the greenhouse effect*
l'émission **de** télévision	*the TV program*
une épingle **de** sûreté	*a safety pin*
l'état **de** grâce	*the grace period*
des états **d'**âme	*moods*
l'examen **de** santé	*the (medical) check-up*
une façon **de** parler	*a manner of speaking*
une faim **de** loup	*a wolf's hunger*
les faits **d'**actualité	*the current events*
une famille **d'**accueil	*a host family*
une faute **de** frappe	*a typing error*
une faute **d'**imprimerie	*a printing mistake*
une faute **d'**inattention/**d'**étourderie	*a careless mistake*
une faute **d'**orthographe	*a spelling mistake*
une femme **d'**affaires	*a businesswoman*
la fête **d'**anniversaire	*the birthday party*
le feu **d'**artifice	*the fireworks*
une feuille **de** papier	*a sheet of paper*
une fièvre **de** cheval	*a very high fever*
la file **d'**attente	*the (waiting) line*
un film **d'**épouvante/**d'**horreur	*a horror movie*
la flaque **d'**eau	*the puddle*
le flocon **de** neige	*the snowflake*
les frais **d'**envoi/**de** port	*the shipping costs*
les frais **d'**inscription/**de** scolarité	*the registration fees, the tuition*
un gant **de** toilette	*a washcloth*
le garçon **d'**honneur	*the best man*
le gardien **de** but	*the goalkeeper*
le gâteau **d'**anniversaire	*the birthday cake*
le gilet **de** sauvetage	*the life jacket*

un grain **de** beauté	*a beauty spot, a mole*
l'heure **de** pointe	*the rush hour*
les heures **d'**ouverture	*the business hours*
l'heure **de** vérité	*the moment of truth*
un homme **d'**affaires	*a businessman*
l'hôtel **de** ville	*the town hall*
l'horloge **de** parquet	*the grandfather clock*
l'image **de** marque	*the image (of a person)*
un institut **de** bronzage	*a tanning booth*
l'issue **de** secours	*the emergency exit*
le jardin **d'**enfants	*the kindergarten*
le jaune **d'**oeuf	*the egg yolk*
un jeu **d'**enfant	*a child's game*
les jeux **de** hasard/**d'**argent	*gambling*
la joie **de** vivre	*the love of life, the joy of living*
les jumelles **de** théâtre	*opera glasses*
le jus **de** fruits	*the fruit juice*
la lame **de** rasoir	*the razor blade*
la lampe **de** poche	*the flashlight*
le lavage **de** cerveau	*the brainwashing*
une leçon **de** conduite	*a driving lesson*
une lettre **de** licenciement	*a pink slip*
la liberté **d'**expression	*the freedom of speech*
la limitation **de** vitesse	*the speed limit*
un livre **de** cuisine	*a cookbook*
le livre **de** poche	*the paperback book*
la longueur **d'**onde	*the wavelength*
la lune **de** miel	*the honeymoon*
le magasin **d'**alimentation	*a food store*
le magasin **de** chaussures	*the shoe store*
le magasin **de** produits diététiques	*the health food store*
le magasin **d'**usine	*the outlet store*
le maillot **de** bain	*the bathing suit*
la maison **d'**édition	*the publisher*
une maison **de** retraite	*a nursing home*
le maître **d'**hôtel	*the head waiter*
la maîtresse **de** maison	*the lady of the house*
le mal **de** mer	*the seasickness*
un mal **de** tête	*a headache*
la manière **de** vivre	*the way of life*

le marchand **de** sable	*the sandman*
un match **de** football	*a soccer game*
la messe **de** minuit	*the midnight mass*
une mine **d'**or	*a gold mine*
le mode **d'**emploi	*the instructions for use*
le mode **de** vie	*the way of life, the lifestyle*
le mont-**de**-piété	*the pawn shop*
le nid **de** poule	*the pothole (in street)*
le niveau **de** vie	*the standard of living*
le nom **de** jeune fille	*the maiden name*
le nom **de** plume	*the pen name*
la note **de** téléphone	*the phone bill*
les objets **de** valeur	*the valuables*
le pain **d'**épices	*the ginger bread*
une panne **d'**électricité	*a blackout, a power outage*
le papier **d'**aluminium	*the aluminum foil*
un parc **d'**attraction	*a theme park, an amusement park*
une patience **d'**ange	*an angelic patience*
les pays **d'**outre-mer	*the overseas countries*
la peine **de** mort	*the death penalty*
le permis **de** conduire	*the driver's licence*
une pièce **d'**identité	*a piece of ID*
des pièces **de** rechange	*spare parts*
une pièce **de** théâtre	*a play (theatre)*
un pilote **de** course	*a race car driver*
la piste **d'**atterrissage	*the landing field*
le point **de** congélation	*the freezing point*
le point **d'**ébullition	*the boiling point*
un poisson **d'**avril	*an April fool's joke*
une pomme **d'**amour	*a candy apple*
la pomme **de** terre	*the potato*
un pot **de** vin	*a bribe*
le pouvoir **d'**achat	*the purchasing power*
la prime **de** licenciement	*severance pay*
la prise **de** courant	*the electrical outlet, the plug*
les produits **de** beauté	*the cosmetics*
le professeur **de** français[1]	*the French teacher*

1. Do not confuse:

le professeur **de** français	*the French teacher* (who teaches French)
le professeur français	*the French teacher* (who is French)

la purée **de** pommes de terre — *mashed potatoes*

le rayon **de** soleil — *the sunbeam*
une reconnaissance **de** dette — *an IOU*
un remède **de** cheval — *a drastic remedy*
la robe **de** chambre — *the robe*
une robe **de** mariée — *a wedding dress*
une robe **de** soirée — *an evening gown*
des ronds **de** serviettes — *napkin holders*

le sac **de** couchage — *the sleeping bag*
le sac **de** voyage — *the travel bag*
le salaire **de** départ — *the starting salary*
la salle **d'**attente — *the waiting room*
la salle **de** séjour — *the living room*
le salon **de** coiffure — *the beauty parlor*
un secret **de** Polichinelle — *an open secret*
la serviette **de** toilette — *the towel*
le seuil **de** pauvreté — *the poverty level*
la situation **de** famille — *the marital status*
le ski **de** fond — *the cross-country skiing*
la sortie **de** secours — *the emergency exit*
la station **de** métro — *the subway station*
la station **de** radio — *the radio station*
la station **de** ski — *the ski resort*
le Syndicat **d'**Initiative — *the chamber of commerce*

la table **de** nuit — *the nightstand, the bedside table*
le tableau **d'**affichage — *the bulletin board*
le tableau **de** bord — *the dashboard*
les taches **de** rousseur — *the freckles*
la taie **d'**oreiller — *the pillowcase*
le talon **d'**Achille — *the Achilles heel*
le tapis **d'**Orient — *the Oriental rug*
le taux **de** change — *the exchange rate*
la tempête **de** neige — *the snowstorm*
le terrain **de** football — *the football field*
le terrain **de** golf — *the golf course*
le ticket **de** caisse — *the cash register receipt*
le trafiquant **de** drogue — *the drug dealer*
un traitement **de** faveur — *a preferential treatment*
le traitement **de** texte — *the word processing*
une transfusion **de** sang — *a blood transfusion*
le tremblement **de** terre — *the earthquake*

un trou **d'**air	*an air pocket*
un trou **de** mémoire	*a (memory) blank*
le tuyau **d'**arrosage	*the (garden) hose*
la vague **de** chaleur/**de** froid	*the heat/cold wave*
les verres/lentilles **de** contact	*the contact lenses*
les vêtements **d'**hiver	*the winter clothes*
le violon **d'**Ingres	*the hobby*
une voiture **d'**occasion	*a secondhand car*
une voiture **de** sport/**de** location	*a sports/rental car*
le voyage **de** noces	*the honeymoon (trip)*

de is followed by the definite article in the following nouns

l'Armée **de l'**Air	*the Air Force*
la carte **des** vins	*the wine list*
le code **de la** route	*the highway code*
les conducteurs **du** dimanche	*the Sunday drivers, the bad drivers*
le contrôle **des** naissances	*the birthcontrol*
le coucher **du** soleil	*the sunset*
le cours **du** soir	*the evening class*
le coût **de la** vie	*the cost of living*
les droits **de l'**homme	*human rights*
l'eau **du** robinet	*tap water*
un emploi **du** temps	*a schedule*
la fête **des** Mères/**des** Pères	*Mother's/Father's Day*
le fossé **des** générations	*the generation gap*
le garde **du** corps	*the bodyguard*
la grève **de la** faim	*the hunger strike*
l'hôtesse **de l'**air	*the stewardess*
le journal **du** dimanche	*the Sunday paper*
le langage (or: la langue) **des** signes	*the sign language*
le lever **du** soleil	*the sunrise*
le mal **de l'**air/**du** pays	*the air-/homesickness*
les pirates **de l'**air	*the hijackers*
le plat **du** jour	*the special of the day* [restaurant]
le rayon **de la** boucherie	*the meat department* [in a store]
la remise **des** diplômes	*the graduation (ceremony)*
le rhume **des** foins	*the hay fever*
la salle **des** urgences	*the emergency room*
le sens **de l'**humour	*the sense of humor*
le sens **de l'**orientation	*the sense of orientation*
la zone **des** bagages	*the baggage claim*

35. de indicates a *timespan* in expressions such as

de jour	*by day(light)*
de nuit	*by night*
de jour et **de**[1] nuit	*by day and night*
de mon temps	*in my time*
du temps de	*at the time of*
du temps de Napoléon	*at the time of Napoleon*
du vivant de	*during the lifetime of*
de son/leur vivant	*during his/her/their lifetime*
de nos jours	*nowadays*
Also:	
jamais **de** la vie	*not on your life*

36. de is part of a series of expressions containing de...en

d'année en année	*from year to year*
de fil en aiguille	*one thing leading to another*
de fond en comble	*from top to bottom, thoroughly*
de jour en jour	*from day to day*
(marcher) **de** long en large	*(to go) up and down, to and fro*
de moins en moins	*less and less*
de mieux en mieux	*better and better*
de plus en plus	*more and more*
de temps en temps	*from time to time*
de ville en ville	*from city to city*

37. de is part of numerous verbal expressions

aller **de** pair (avec qch)	*to go hand in hand (with sth)*
Ça va **de** pair.	*That goes hand in hand.*
Les deux vont **de** pair.	*Both go hand in hand.*
changer **de** train/**d'**avion[2]	*to change trains/planes*
changer **d'**avis	*to change one's mind*
J'ai changé **d'**avis.	*I changed my mind.*

---

1. Note that in French, contrary to English, the prepositions are repeated.
2. Note that in French, contrary to English, 'train' and 'avion' are singular.

être **de** bonne foi	*to be honest, to act in good faith*
être **de** mauvaise foi	*to be dishonest*
être **de** bonne/**de** mauvaise humeur	*to be in a good/bad mood*
être **de** garde/**de** service	*to be on call/on duty* [doctor, nurse]
être **de** l'avis de qn	*to be of someone's opinion*
Je suis **de** votre avis.	*I agree with you.*
être **de** passage	*to be passing through*
être **de** retour	*to be back*
Je serai **de** retour à minuit.	*I will be back at midnight.*
être **de** trop	*to be unwanted, to be in the way*
être **de** valeur	*to be valuable*
faire **de** son mieux	*to do one's best*
jouer **de** l'argent	*to gamble*
jouer **de** plusieurs instruments	*to play several instruments*
mettre qch **de** côté	*to put/set sth aside*
mettre qn **de** bonne/**de** mauvaise humeur	*to put sb in a good/bad mood*
payer **de** sa poche	*to pay out of one's own pocket*
perdre qn **de** vue	*to lose sight of sb*
prendre qch **d'**assaut	*to storm sth*
savoir/apprendre qch **de** source sûre	*to know/learn sth from a reliable source*
tirer qn **d'**affaire	*to get sb out of trouble*
se tirer **d'**affaire	*to manage, to get out of difficulties*

38. de is part of many prepositional, adverbial and other expressions

d'abord	*at first*
d'accord!	*agreed! ok!*
d'ailleurs	*besides, moreover, incidentally*
d'autant plus (que)	*all the more (since)*
d'avance	*in advance, beforehand*
Il faut payer **d'**avance.	*One must pay in advance.*
Je vous remercie **d'**avance.	*I thank you in advance.*
D'avance merci!	*Thanks in advance!*
d'un certain âge	*elderly*
une dame **d'**un certain âge	*an elderly lady*

de l'autre côté de	*on the other side of*
de ce côté	*on this side*
d'un côté...**de** l'autre	*on (the) one hand...on the other*
D'un côté il est gentil, **de** l'autre il est très fier.	*On the one hand he is very nice, on the other he is very proud.*
de crainte/**de** peur de (+ inf. or noun)	*for fear of*
de droite[1]	*right-wing, on the right*
un parti **de** droite	*a right-wing party*
le trottoir **de** droite	*the sidewalk on the right*
de courte durée	*short-lived*
d'emblée (= **du** premier coup)	*from the outset, there and then*
de cette façon/manière	*this way*
de la même façon/manière	*in the same way*
Dieu aime tous les êtres **de** la même manière.	*God likes all beings in the same manner.*
d'une façon ou **d'**une autre	*in one way or another, somehow*
d'une façon/manière (+ adj.)	*in a (+ adj.) way*
(se comporter) **d'**une façon étrange	*(to behave) in a strange way*
d'une manière différente	*in a different way*
de gauche[1]	*left-wing, on the left*
un parti **de** gauche	*a left-wing party*
la porte **de** gauche	*the door on the left*
de grâce	*for pity's sake*
de bonne/mauvaise grâce	*willingly/grudgingly*
de bon gré	*willingly, gladly*
de mauvais gré	*reluctantly*
de bonne heure	*early*
d'habitude	*usually, ordinarily*
de l'heure	*per hour (pay)*
Il est payé 100 euros **de** l'heure.	*He is paid 100 euros per hour.*
de justesse	*just barely, narrowly*
Ils ont échappé **de** justesse.	*They narrowly escaped.*
de loin	*by far, from a distance, from afar*
Je préfère **de** loin le beurre français.	*I prefer the French butter by far.*
Il vient **de** loin.	*He comes from far away.*
On est presbyte quand on voit mal **de** loin.	*One is near-sighted when one sees badly in the distance.*

1. following a noun

de longue date	*long-standing*
de même	*likewise, the same*
Bon appétit! - A vous **de** même.	*Enjoy your meal! - You also.*
de nouveau	*again*
d'occasion	*secondhand*
d'ordinaire	*usually*
de l'ordre **de** [+ number]	*in the height of* [+ number]
La dépense est **de** l'ordre **de** dix euros.	*The expenditure is in the height of ten euros.*
d'où	*hence*
d'où son nom	*hence his name*
de la part de qn	*on behalf of sb*
Remerciez votre ami **de** ma part.	*Thank your friend on my behalf.*
Salue tes parents **de** ma part.	*Greet your parents from me.*
de part et **d'**autre	*on either side, on both sides*
d'une part...**d'**autre part	*on (the) one hand...on the other hand*
de parti pris	*deliberately*
de plein fouet	*full-force*
de plus belle	*more than ever, even more*
de premier ordre	*topnotch, first-rate*
de (or: **en**) plus	*furthermore, moreover, besides*
de préférence	*preferably*
de près	*closely, from close up*
à y regarder **de** plus près	*looking at it more closely*
Je l'ai vu **de** près.	*I saw him closely.*
On est myope quand on voit mal **de** près.	*One is farsighted when one sees badly up close.*
de son propre chef	*on one's own*
de quelle couleur est...	*what color is...*
de quoi (+ inf.)	*enough to, the means to*
Il a **de** quoi manger.	*He has enough to eat.*
de rigueur	*(socially) required, mandatory*
Le smoking/la prudence est **de** rigueur.	*The tuxedo/caution is required.*
de la sorte	*(in) this way*
de suite	*in a row*
trois jours **de** suite	*three days in a row*
de surcroît	*moreover, what is more*

de toujours	*very old*
un ami **de** toujours	*a very old friend*
de toute apparence	*seemingly*
de toute évidence	*seemingly*
de toute façon (= en tout cas)	*in any case, at any rate, anyhow*
de toute urgence	*urgently*
de travers	*the wrong way*
avaler **de** travers	*to go down the wrong way* [food]
Tout va **de** travers aujourd'hui.	*Everything goes wrong today.*
de vive voix	*orally*
du côté de	*in the neighborhood /on the side of*
du côté de l'église	*near the church*
un oncle **du** côté de mon père	*an uncle on my father's side* [family]
du coup	*as a result*
du fond du cœur	*from the bottom of one's heart*
Je vous remercie **du** fond du cœur.	*I thank you from the bottom of my heart.*
du moins	*at least*
du reste	*besides, furthermore*

39. **de** precedes the complement after the following nouns

l'amour **de**	*the love **for***
Il a perdu l'amour **de** son métier.	*He lost the love for his job.*
merci **de**	*thanks **for***
Merci **de** (or: **pour**) votre aide.	*Thanks for your help.*
la raison **de**	*the reason **for***
Il sait la raison **de** cette réaction.	*He knows the reason for this reaction.*
trêve **de**	*enough of*
Trêve **de** plaisanterie!	*Joking aside!*

40. **de** + *noun* frequently replaces a conjunction + subordinate clause

Il n'est pas sûr **de** la date de son départ.	*He is not sure when he will leave.*

41. **de** is also used after the word 'espèce' to reinforce an insult

espèce **d'**idiot/**d'**imbécile/**de** lâche!	*you idiot/fool/coward!*

42. de introduces the (first or second) object [*noun* or *(stressed) pronoun*] after the following verbs and expressions[1]

abriter qn/qch ***de*** qch Il faut abriter ce tableau **du** soleil.	*to shelter/protect sb/sth from sth* *We must protect this painting from the sun.*
s'absenter *de* qch Il s'est absenté **de** son bureau.	*to go away from sth* *He went away from his desk.*
s'abstenir *de* qch Si vous êtes malade, abstenez-vous **de** vin.	*to refrain from sth* *If you are ill, refrain from wine.*
accuser qn ***de*** qch On l'a accusée **de** sorcellerie.	*to accuse sb of sth* *They accused her of witchcraft.*
s'agir *de* qn/qch Il s'agit **de** son avenir.	*to be the question of sb/sth* *It's a question of his future.*
assurer qn ***de*** qch Je puis vous assurer **de** ma reconnaissance.	*to assure sb of sth* *I can assure you of my gratitude.*
attendre qch ***de*** qn Elle fait ce que ses parents attendent **d**'elle.	*to expect sth of sb* *She does what her parents expect of her.*
avertir qn ***de*** qch Je vous avais averti **de** ce danger.	*to warn sb of/about sth* *I had warned you about this danger.*
avoir honte *de* qn/qch Tu devrais avoir honte **de** toi. Il a honte **de** ses actes.	*to be ashamed of sb/sth* *You should be ashamed of yourself.* *He is ashamed of his actions.*
avoir peur *de* qn/qch As-tu peur **de** moi? J'ai peur **de** la nuit.	*to be afraid of sb/sth* *Are you afraid of me?* *I am afraid of the night.*
bénéficier *de* qch Nous avons bénéficié **des** soldes.	*to profit from* *We profited from the sales.*
se charger *de* qch Je me charge **de** cette affaire.	*to take care of sth, to see to sth* *I take care of this business.*

---

1. Note that this section only lists verbs and expressions where 'de' corresponds to 'of' or 'from' in English. For more French verbs and expressions requiring 'de' before their complement, see p. 181-182 (no preposition in English), and p. 184-187 (a different preposition in English).

convaincre qn ***de*** qch	*to convince sb of sth*
L'avocat a convaincu le tribunal **de** l'innocence de l'accusé.	*The lawyer convinced the court of the innocence of the accused.*
dater ***de***	*to date from, to date back to*
Cet édifice date **du** 19e siècle.	*This building dates from the 19th century.*
se débarrasser ***de*** qn/qch	*to get rid of sb/sth*
Je voudrais bien me débarrasser **de** lui.	*I would like to get rid of him.*
décourager qn ***de*** qch	*to deter sb from sth*
Il m'a découragé **de** ce voyage.	*He deterred me from this trip.*
dépouiller qn ***de*** qch	*to deprive/rob sb of sth*
Les révolutionnaires ont dépouillé les prêtres **de** leurs biens.	*The revolutionaries robbed the priests of their belongings.*
descendre ***de*** qch	*to get out of (a means of transportation)*
Elle est descendue **du** train/**du** taxi/ **de l'**avion/**de la** voiture.	*She got off the train/out of the taxi/ off the plane/out of the car.*
dissuader qn ***de*** qch	*to dissuade sb from sth*
J'ai essayé de la dissuader **de** cette idée.	*I tried to dissuade her from this idea.*
s'écarter ***de*** qch	*to move away from sth*
Ecarte-toi **de** ce cheval.	*Move away from this horse.*
s'échapper ***de*** qch	*to escape from sth*
On ne s'échappe pas **de** cette prison.	*One doesn't escape from this prison.*
s'éloigner ***de*** qn/qch	*to move away from sb/sth*
Eloigne-toi **de** lui!	*Move away from him!*
médire ***de*** qn	*to speak ill of sb*
Il ne faut pas médire **de** son voisin.	*One must not speak ill of one's neighbor.*
se méfier ***de*** qn/qch	*to be wary of sb/sth*
Méfiez-vous **des** pickpockets.	*Be wary of pickpockets.*
se moquer ***de*** qn/qch	*to make fun of sb/sth*
Ils se moquent **du** professeur.	*They make fun of the teacher.*
s'occuper ***de*** qch/qn	*to take care of sth/sb*
On s'occupe **de** vous?	*Are you being taken care of?* [store]
partir ***de***	*to leave (from)*
L'avion part **de** Roissy.	*The plane leaves (from) Roissy.*

penser ***de***[1]	*to think of* [= to have an opinion of sb/sth]
Je vais te dire ce que je pense **de** cette situation.	*I am going to tell you what I think of this situation.*
prendre soin ***de*** qn/qch	*to take care of sb/sth*
Elle prend soin **de** moi/**de** la maison.	*She takes care of me/of the house.*
profiter ***de*** qch	*to take advantage of sth*
Je profite **de** l'occasion.	*I take advantage of the opportunity.*
protéger qn ***de*** qch	*to protect sb from sth*
Ce chapeau va vous protéger **du** soleil.	*This hat will protect you from the sun.*
priver qn ***de*** qch	*to deprive sb of sth*
On l'a privé **de** ses droits.	*They deprived him of his rights.*
rêver ***de*** qch	*to dream of sth*
Je rêve **d'**un voyage en Inde.	*I am dreaming of a trip to India.*
Il rêve **de** fruits succulents.	*He is dreaming of delicious fruit.*
se sortir ***de*** qch	*to get out of sth* [a predicament]
Il s'est sorti **d'**une épreuve.	*He got out of an ordeal.*
souffrir ***de*** qch	*to suffer from sth*
Elle souffrait **de** sa méchanceté.	*She suffered from his meanness.*

Proverbs, sayings, and idioms

La parole est **d'**argent, le silence est **d'**or.	*Speech is silver but silence is golden.*
Faute **de** grives, on mange des merles.[2]	*Beggars can't be choosers.*
Des goûts et **des** couleurs on ne discute pas.	*Tastes differ. There is no accounting for taste.*
Un **de** perdu, dix **de** retrouvés.	*There's plenty more fish in the sea.*
Croix **de** bois, croix **de** fer, si je mens, je vais en enfer.[3]	*Cross my heart and hope to die.*
tomber **de** Charybde en Scylla	*to fall from the frying pan into the fire*
Je ne suis pas né(é) **d'**hier.	*I wasn't born yesterday.*
C'est **de** la part **de** qui?	*Who is calling?* [telephone]

1. For the difference between *penser à* and *penser de*, see p. 194.
2. lit.: *For lack of thrushes, one eats blackbirds.*
3. lit.: *Cross of wood, cross of iron, if I lie I go to hell.*

Donne-moi **de** tes nouvelles.	*Let hear from you. Keep in touch.*
Je n'ai pas fermé l'oeil **de** la nuit. (= Je n'ai pas dormi **de** la nuit.)	*I didn't sleep a wink last night.*
et ainsi **de** suite	*and so on and so forth*
de vous à moi	*between the two of us*
de gré ou **de** force[1] Il le fera **de** gré ou **de** force.	*whether sb likes it or not* *He'll do it whether he likes it or not.*
de guerre lasse	*from sheer weariness*
de longue haleine un travail **de** longue haleine	*lengthy* *a lengthy operation*
il n'y a pas **de** quoi	*you are welcome*
de rien	*you are welcome*
Pardon! - Il n'y a pas **de** mal!	*Excuse me! - There is no harm done.*
Il y va **de** sa vie.	*His life is at stake.*
comme **d'**habitude	*as usual*
fin **de** citation	*unquote*
tout **de** suite	*right away*
du tac au tac répondre **du** tac au tac	*tit for tat* *to snap back*
pour **de** bon Il quittera la France pour **de** bon.	*for good* *He will leave France for good.*
coûter les yeux **de** la tête[2]	*to cost an arm and a leg*
être sain **de** corps et **d'**esprit	*to be sound in body and mind*
parler **de** la pluie et **du** beau temps	*to make small talk*
parler **de** tout et **de** rien	*to speak about anything*
passer **de** bouche à oreille	*to be passed on by word of mouth*
regarder qn **de** travers	*to give sb a dirty look*
se lever **du** pied gauche[3]	*to get up on the wrong side of the bed*
tomber **des** nues[4]	*to be flabbergasted*
vivre **d'**amour et **d'**eau fraîche[5]	*to live on love alone*
voir qch **du** bon côté	*to look on the bright side of sth*
voler **de** ses propres ailes[6]	*to stand on one's own feet*

---

1. lit.: *out of one's own free will or by force*
2. lit.: *to cost the eyes of the head*
3. lit.: *to get up with the left foot*
4. lit.: *to fall from the clouds*
5. lit.: *to live on love and fresh water*
6. lit.: *to fly with one's own wings*

Translation difficulties

- English 'from' (followed by a place) is *not* translated with **de** but with other prepositions after verbs such as *prendre, boire, aller chercher, récupérer, manger.*

*She took the calendar **from** the desk.*	Elle a pris le calendrier **sur** le bureau.
*Go and get my keys **from** my room.*	Va chercher mes clés **dans** ma chambre.
*Can I get back my suitcase **from** under your seat?*	Est-ce que je peux récupérer ma valise **sous** votre siège?
*to eat **from / out of** a plate*	manger **dans** une assiette
*to drink **from / out of** a glass*	boire **dans** un verre

- English 'from' (when followed by a noun usually referring to a person) is translated with **à** after the verbs *acheter, arracher, cacher, commander, emprunter, enlever, louer, ôter, prendre, retirer, saisir, voler.*[1]

*I bought this watch **from** a jeweller in Paris.*	J'ai *acheté* cette montre **à** un bijoutier de Paris.
*He snatched the bag **from** the lady.*	Il a *arraché* le sac **à** la dame.
*We hid the truth **from** our parents.*	Nous avons *caché* la vérité **à** nos parents.
*He borrowed money **from** his friends.*	Il a *emprunté* de l'argent **à** ses amis.
*You can borrow this book **from** the university library.*	Vous pouvez *emprunter* ce livre **à** la bibliothèque de l'université.
*They rented a room **from** the old lady.*	Ils ont *loué* une chambre **à** la vieille dame.
*I took the hope away **from** my father.*	J'ai *ôté* l'espoir **à** mon père.
*He often takes toys **from** his sister.*	Il *prend* souvent des jouets **à** sa sœur.
*They took away the driver's licence **from** my friend.*	On a *retiré* le permis de conduire **à** mon ami.
*They seized the passports **from** the travellers.*	Ils ont *saisi* les passeports **aux** voyageurs.

---

1. See p. 39 #22

C. The preposition **en**

1. **en** expresses 'in' and 'to'

- before all continents, *feminine* countries, *feminine* French and Canadian provinces, and *feminine* American states[1]

en Australie	*in/to Australia*
en Asie	*in/to Asia*
en Espagne	*in/to Spain*
en Bretagne	*in/to Britanny*
en Bourgogne	*in/to Burgundy*
en Californie	*in/to California*
en Floride	*in/to Florida*
en Colombie Britannique	*in/to British Columbia*
en Nouvelle-Ecosse	*in/to Nova Scotia*

Nous allons voyager **en** Amérique.[2]	*We are going to travel **in** America.*
Ils vont **en** Europe.	*They go/travel **to** Europe.*
Il habite **en** France.	*He lives **in** France.*
J'ai passé un mois **en** Normandie.	*I spent a month **in** Normandy.*

except:

When these continents, countries, French or Canadian provinces, and American states are modified, **dans** [+ def. article] replaces **en** (see p. 121)

dans l'Europe du vingtième siècle	*in twentieth-century Europe*
dans toute la France	*in all of France*

- before all *masculine* countries, *masculine* French regions, *masculine* American states and *masculine* Canadian provinces which start with a vowel

en Israël	*in/to Israel*
en Anjou	*in/to Anjou*
en Alaska	*in/to Alaska*
en Alberta	*in/to Alberta*

---

1. American states and Canadian provinces are generally feminine when their French form ends in '**e**' (see p. 300 and p. 302).
2. Note that the verb **voyager** followed by a preposition + a place name expresses 'to travel ***in***' a place. To translate *'to travel **to**'*, one uses ***aller***.
   Nous **allons** *en* France. We *travel **to*** France.

- before some big *islands*

en Corse	*in/to Corsica*
en Sicile	*in/to Sicily*
en Sardaigne	*in/to Sardinia*

2. **en** followed by a noun or adjective indicates a *location* also in the following expressions

en banlieue[1]	*in/to a suburb, in/to the suburbs*
en bas	*downstairs*
en haut	*upstairs*
en bas/**en** haut de la page	*on the bottom/top of the page*
en boîte	*in a can, in/to a nightclub*
des légumes **en** boîte	*canned vegetables*
aller/sortir **en** boîte	*to go/go out to a nightclub*
en classe[1]	*in/to class*
en conserve	*in a can*
des petits pois **en** conserve	*canned peas*
en coulisse	*behind the scenes, backstage*
en enfer	*in/to hell*
en face	*across the way*
en famille	*(with)in the family*
en scène	*on the stage*
en ligne	*on-line (via computer)*
en ce lieu	*in this place*
en lieu sûr	*in a safe place*
en mer	*at sea*
en montagne (= **dans** les montagnes)	*in/to the mountains*
en plein air	*outdoors, in the open air*
le cinéma **en** plein air	*the drive-in cinema*
en première page	*on the first page*
en prison[1]	*in/to prison*
en province	*in/to the province(s)*
en salle de réanimation	*in intensive care*
en terminale	*in the last grade of high school*
en ville[1]	*in/to town*

---

1. But 'dans' is generally used when the place is modified

dans une banlieue chic	*in an elegant suburb*
dans la banlieue de Paris	*in the suburbs of Paris*
dans la classe de français	*in the French class*
dans une prison éloignée	*in a remote prison*
dans la ville où je suis né(e)	*in the town where I was born*

3. en expresses 'by' with *means of transportation* inside which one travels

en auto	*by car*
en autobus	*by bus*
en autocar	*by (intercity) bus*
en avion[1]	*by plane*
en barque/**en** canoë	*by (rowing) boat/by canoe*
en bateau[1]	*by ship, by boat*
en carrosse	*by (horse-drawn) coach*
en chemin de fer	*by railroad*
en hélicoptère (or: **par** hélicoptère)	*by helicopter*
en métro (or: **par** le métro)	*by subway*
en taxi	*by taxi*
en train (or: **par** le train)	*by train*
en tramway	*by streetcar, by light-rail*
en voiture	*by car*
Also:	
en auto-stop	*by hitchhiking*
en traineau	*by sleigh*

But:

- **dans** is used instead of **en** when a specific vehicle is referred to
  Compare:
  Ils sont venus **en** voiture. — *They came by car.*
  Ils sont venus **dans** la nouvelle voiture de Paul. — *They came in Paul's new car.*
- **à** is generally used with means of transportation *on* (rather than *inside)* which one travels (see p. 32)

4. en expresses 'in' before *months, years* and *seasons*

en avril[2] (or: **au** mois d'avril)	*in April*
en 1980	*in 1980*
en l'an 1999	*in the year 1999*
en quelle année	*in what year*
en quelle saison?	*in what season?*
en hiver	*in (the) winter*
en plein hiver	*in the midst of winter*

---

1. But ***par*** is used before *avion* and *bateau* when *things* are being transported.
   envoyer une lettre **par** avion/**par** bateau — *to send a letter by air/by sea*
2. With names of months, French uses **en**, even when they are modified.
   en mars dernier/prochain — *last/next March*

en été	*in (the) summer*
en automne	*in the fall*

But:

au printemps	*in (the) spring*
au dix-septième siècle	*in the 17th century*
dans les années trente	*in the thirties*

5. en indicates a certain *time point* or *period* in expressions such as

en ce moment	*right now, at this time*
en ce temps-là	*in those days*
en temps normal	*in normal times*
en temps de paix/guerre	*in times of peace/war*
en semaine	*on a weekday, during the week*
En semaine, je me lève à huit heures.	*On weekdays, I get up at 8 o'clock.*
en début de semaine	*at the beginning of the week*
en fin de semaine	*at the end of the week*
en début d'après-midi	*in the early afternoon*
en fin d'après-midi	*in the late afternoon*
en fin de matinée	*late in the morning*
en fin de journée	*at the end of the day*
en plein jour	*in broad daylight*
en pleine nuit	*in the dead of night*
mardi **en** huit	*a week from Tuesday*

Also in:

(être) **en** première/deuxième année[1]	*(to be) a freshman/sophomore*
(être) **en** troisième/quatrième année[2]	*(to be) a junior/senior*

6. en denotes the *material an object is made of*[3]

en acier (inoxydable)	*out of (stainless) steel*
en argent	*out of silver*
une montre **en** argent	*a watch (made) out of silver*

---

1. lit.: *in the first/second year*
2. lit.: *in the third/fourth year*
3. Answering the question: **En** quoi est...? *What is...made of?*
Note that **de** can also be used to indicate the material something is made of (see p. 62).
In some instances, **en** and **de** before a material are interchangeable, **en** however emphasizes the material more than **de**.
un sac **de** cuir = *a leather bag* un sac **en** cuir = *a bag made of leather*

en bois	*out of wood*
un chèque **en** bois (fam.)	*a rubber check*
en brique	*out of brick*
en caoutchouc	*out of rubber*
en carton	*out of cardboard*
des assiettes/des verres **en** carton	*paper plates/cups*
en chocolat	*out of chocolate*
des œufs **en** chocolat	*chocolate eggs*
en cire	*out of wax*
en coton	*out of cotton*
en cristal	*out of crystal*
en cuir	*out of leather*
en cuir verni	*out of patent leather*
en cuivre	*out of copper*
en daim	*out of suede*
en dentelle	*out of lace*
en étain	*out of pewter*
en étoffe	*out of fabric*
en fer	*out of iron*
en fer forgé	*out of wrought iron*
en fibre de verre	*out of fiberglass*
en ivoire	*out of ivory*
en laine	*out of wool*
en laiton	*out of brass*
en marbre	*out of marble*
en métal	*out of metal*
en or	*out of gold*
en osier	*out of wicker*
une corbeille **en** osier	*a wicker basket*
en pierre	*out of stone*
en papier	*out of paper*
en peluche	*out of plush*
un ours **en** peluche	*a teddy bear*
en plastique	*out of plastic*
en platine	*out of platinum*
en plomb	*out of lead*
en porcelaine	*out of china*
en soie	*out of silk*
en tissu	*out of fabric*
en tissu éponge	*out of terry cloth*
en velours	*out of velvet*
en velours côtelé	*out of corduroy*
en verre	*out of glass*

7. en is used before the present participle to form the *gerund*

en voyageant	*by travelling*

8. en + *unit of time* expresses 'in' (meaning 'within'), indicating the period of time needed to complete an action

J'ai lu le livre **en** cinq heures.	*I read the book* ***in*** *(= within) five hours.*
Il a fini le travail **en** un temps record.	*He finished the work* ***in*** *record time.*
La Tour Eiffel a été achevé **en** deux ans.	*The Eiffel Tower was completed* ***in*** *two years.*

But:
dans + *unit of time* expresses 'in', indicating the period of time at the *end* of which an action will take place (see p. 124)

Je reviendrai **dans** quelques jours.	*I'll come back* ***in*** *(= after) a few days.*

9. en indicates a *physical* or *mental state*

(être) **en** bonne/**en** mauvaise santé	*(to be) healthy/ill*
(être) **en** liesse	*(to be) jubilant*
(être) **en** forme	*(to be) in good shape*
(être) **en** paix	*(to be) in peace*
(être/se mettre) **en** colère (contre qn)	*(to be/get) angry (with sb)*

10. en expresses 'in' with *languages* and *academic subjects*

Comment dit-on 'lit' **en** anglais?	*How does one say 'lit' in English?*
En quelle langue pensez-vous?	*In which language do you think?*
Je suis bon/mauvais **en** chimie.	*I am good/bad in chemistry.*
Elle est calée (fam.) **en** physique.	*She is brilliant in physics.*
Il est fort/faible/nul **en** informatique.	*He is strong/weak/hopeless in computer science.*

Also:

un étudiant **en** droit	*a law student*
un étudiant **en** langues	*a language student*
un étudiant **en** médecine	*a student of medicine*

But:

dans un excellent français	*in excellent French*
dans le français courant	*in common French*

11. **en** indicates the *manner* in which something is done in expressions such as

chanter **en** canon	*to sing in a round*
faire qch **en** vitesse	*to do something quickly*
se garer **en** double file	*to double park*
payer/régler **en** espèces/**en** liquide	*to pay cash*
payer/régler **en** euros	*to pay in euros*
prendre/attraper qn **en** flagrant délit	*to catch sb red-handed*
téléphoner **en** PCV	*to call collect*
vivre **en** union libre	*to live together* (without being married)
en file indienne	*in single file*
en tête-à-tête	*intimately*

12. **en** combines two nouns, the second noun indicating a *particularity* of the first one

le compte **en** banque	*the bank account*
un escalier **en** colimaçon	*a spiral staircase*
le metteur **en** scène	*the stage director*
la mise **en** scène	*the stage setting*
des oeufs **en** gelée	*eggs in aspic*
du pâté **en** croûte	*pâté baked inside dough*
des patins **en** ligne	*roller blades*
les pays **en** voie de développement	*the developing countries*
le rédacteur/la rédactrice **en** chef	*the editor in chief*
une route **en** lacets	*a twisting road*
un téléviseur **en** couleur	*a color television*
les transports **en** commun	*public transportation*
un tueur **en** série	*a serial killer*
des virages **en** épingle à cheveux	*hairpin curves*
des yeux **en** amande	*almond-shaped eyes*

13. **en** translates 'in' before *colors* and with *clothing*

un film **en** noir et blanc	*a black and white movie*
Auriez-vous ce chemisier **en** rouge?	*Would you have this blouse in red?*
une porte peinte **en** bleu	*a door painted in blue*
être **en** tenue décontractée	*to be in/wear casual clothes*
être **en** bras de chemise	*to be in one's shirtsleeves*
les dames **en** robes longues	*the ladies in the long dresses*
le monsieur **en** costume gris	*the man in the grey suit*

14. en is used before the object after the following verbs, verbal expressions, and adjectives

avoir confiance **en** qn/qch	*to trust/have confidence in sb/sth*
J'ai confiance **en** lui.	*I trust him.*
Je n'ai pas confiance **en** moi.	*I am not self-confident.*
s'y connaître **en** qch	*to know much about sth*
Il s'y connaît **en** musique.	*He knows much about music.*
consister **en** qch	*to consist of sth*
L'examen consiste **en** cinq épreuves.	*The exam consists of five tests.*
croire **en** qn/qch	*to (firmly) believe in sb/sth*
Elle croit **en** Dieu.	*She believes in God.*
Je crois **en** l'avenir.	*I believe in the future.*
se déguiser **en** qn/qch	*to disguise oneself as sb/sth*
Je me suis déguisée **en** princesse.	*I disguised myself as a princess.*
être divisé **en** qch	*to be divided into sth*
La France est divisée **en** 22 régions.	*France is divided into 22 regions.*
être expert **en** qch	*to be an expert in sth*
Elle est très experte **en** psychologie.	*She is a great expert in psychology.*
s'habiller **en** qn/qch	*to dress up as sb/sth*
Les enfants s'habillaient **en** prêtres.	*The children dressed up as priests.*
se perfectionner **en** qch	*to become perfect in sth*
Il veut se perfectionner **en** français.	*He wants to become perfect in French.*
se spécialiser **en** qch	*to major in sth*
Elle se spécialise **en** mathématiques.	*She majors in mathematics.*
traiter qn **en** qn	*to treat sb like sb*
Nous l'avons traité **en** ennemi.	*We treated him like an enemy.*

15. en is used to express a *transformation* (English: *into*)

casser/briser qch **en**	*to break sth into*
Il a cassé le vase **en** mille morceaux.	*He broke the vase into 1000 pieces.*
changer qch **en**	*to change sth into*
Ils ont changé leurs francs **en** euros.	*They changed their francs into euros.*
se changer **en**	*to change into*
La neige s'est changée **en** pluie.	*The snow changed into rain.*
convertir qch **en**	*to convert sth into*
On peut convertir du sucre **en** alcool.	*One can convert sugar into alcohol.*
traduire qch **en**	*to translate sth into*
Je dois traduire ce texte **en** français.	*I must translate this text into French.*

transformer qch/qn **en**	*to turn/convert sth/sb into*
Il a transformé l'eau **en** vin.	*He turned water into wine.*
se transformer **en**	*to turn into*
En hiver, les routes se transforment **en** patinoire.	*In winter, the roads turn into an ice rink.*

16. **en** is used in the following *commands*

En avant!	*Forward! Let's get going!*
En route!	*Let's go!*
En vitesse!	*Make it snappy!*
En voiture!	*All aboard!*

17. **en** can express 'as', 'for' in the following contexts

En cadeau, je demandais toujours des livres.	*For a gift, I always asked for books.*
En entrée, j'ai mangé des escargots, et **en** dessert, j'ai pris une glace.	*I ate snails as entrée, and I had ice cream for dessert.*
Je te parle **en** ami.	*I speak to you as a friend.*
Il voyage **en** touriste.	*He travels as a tourist.*

18. **en** is also part of the following expressions

avoir/prendre qch/qn **en** horreur	*to loathe/begin to loathe sth/sb*
J'ai la couleur orange **en** horreur.	*I loathe the color orange.*
avoir qch **en** tête/vue	*to have sth in mind*
avoir qch **en** commun (avec qn)	*to have sth in common (with sb)*
Ils n'ont pas beaucoup **en** commun.	*They don't have much in common.*
couper **en** dés	*to dice, to cut in cubes*
demander qn **en** mariage	*to propose to sb*
éclater **en** sanglots	*to burst into tears*
écrire **en** majuscules	*to write in capital letters*
écrire **en** toutes lettres	*to write out*
entrer **en** collision avec	*to collide with*
entrer **en** vigueur/**en** application	*to come into effect*
envoyer qch **en** exprès	*to send sth special delivery*

envoyer qch **en** recommandé	*to send sth by certified mail*
être **en** augmentation	*to be on the rise*
être/arriver **en** avance[1]	*to be/arrive early (= ahead of time)*
être **en** baisse La criminalité est **en** baisse.	*to be dropping, to be falling* *The crime rate is falling.*
être/mettre **en** berne	*to be/put at half-mast* [flag]
être **en** bon/**en** mauvais état	*to be in a good/bad condition*
être **en** bons/**en** mauvais termes avec	*to be on good/bad terms with*
être **en** cavale	*to be on the run*
être **en** cause	*to be concerned, to be in question*
être **en** compétition	*to compete*
être **en** congé (sabbatique)	*to be on (sabbatical) leave*
être **en** consultation	*to be with a patient*
être **en** contradiction avec qn	*to contradict sb*
être **en** crise	*to be in a crisis*
être **en** deuil (de qn)	*to be in mourning (for sb)*
être **en** difficulté	*to be in difficulties, to be in trouble*
être **en** diminution	*to be decreasing, to be falling*
être **en** échec scolaire	*to be failing* (*school*)
être **en** (état d') alerte	*to be on (the) alert*
être **en** faillite	*to be bankrupt*
être **en** feu	*to be on fire, to be burning*
être **en** fleurs	*to bloom, to be in blossom*
être **en** fuite	*to be on the run, to be at large*
être/se mettre **en** grève	*to be/go on strike*

---

1. Do not confuse the expression **en avance** (*early)* with the adverb **tôt** (*early*)
   - **tôt** means *early* in a general sense

     Il est très **tôt**. — *It is very early.*
     Je me lève **tôt**. — *I get up early.*
   - **en avance** expresses *ahead of (a certain) time*, *ahead of schedule*

     Ils sont **en avance**. — *They are early (= ahead of time).*
     J'arrive toujours **en avance**. — *I always arrive early (= ahead of time).*
     Elle est partie **en avance**. — *She left early (= ahead of time).*

   Do not confuse **en avance** with **d'avance** (= à l'avance) which means '*in advance*', '*beforehand*'.

être **en** guerre	*to be at war*
être **en** hausse	*to be going up (in price or amount)*
être **en** infraction (avec la loi)	*to break the law*
être **en** instance de divorce	*to be engaged in divorce proceedings*
être **en** jeu	*to be at stake*
Sa réputation est **en** jeu.	*His reputation is at stake.*
être **en** manque	*to suffer from withdrawal symptoms*
être **en** mesure de + inf.	*to be in a position to, to be able to*
être **en** nage	*to be bathed in perspiration*
être **en** panne	*to be out of order, to be broken*
être **en** panne sèche	*to be out of gasoline*
être **en** promotion	*to be on special*
être **en** question	*to be in question*
être/se mettre **en** quête de qch	*to be/go looking for sth*
être **en** réclame	*to be on special*
être **en** recul	*to be falling, to be on the decline*
être **en** règle	*to be in order* [papers, etc.]
être **en** rendez-vous	*to be at an appointment*
être **en** réparation	*to be under repair*
être **en** retard[1]	*to be late (= not on time)*
être **en** retard dans son travail	*to be behind in one's work*
être **en** retraite	*to be retired*
être **en** réunion	*to be in a meeting*
être/se croire/se sentir **en** sécurité	*to be/believe to be/feel safe*
être **en** séjour chez qn	*to be staying with sb*
être **en** service	*to be in operation/open/running*
être **en** solde	*to be on sale*

---

1. Do not confuse the expression **en retard** (*late*) with the adverb **tard** *(late)*
   - **tard** means *late* in a general sense

     Il est trop **tard**. — *It is too late.*
     Je suis rentré très **tard**. — *I went home very late.*
   - **en retard** expresses *not on time*

     Le professeur est **en retard**. — *The teacher is late (= not on time).*
     Nous sommes arrivés **en retard**. — *We arrived late (= not on time).*
     Il paie toujours ses factures **en retard**. — *He always pays his bills late.*

être **en** tête Son nom est **en** tête de la liste.	*to be at the head of/in the lead* *His name is at the top of the list.*
être **en** train de + inf. Je suis **en** train d'écrire une lettre.	*to be in the process of (doing)* *I am in the process of writing a letter.*
être **en** transit	*to be in transit/on a stopover*
être/partir **en** vacances	*to be/leave/go on (a) vacation*
être **en** vie (= être vivant)	*to be alive*
être **en** vente[1]	*to be for sale, to be sold in a store*
être **en** vente libre Ce médicament est **en** vente libre.	*to be freely available* *This medication is available over the counter.*
être/rester **en** vigueur	*to be/stay in effect*
être **en** visite chez qn/à un endroit Il est/vient **en** visite à Bordeaux.	*to pay sb/a place a visit* *He pays Bordeaux a visit.*
être **en** vogue	*to be in fashion, to be fashionable*
être **en** voie de disparition	*to be nearing extinction*
être/partir **en** voyage (d'affaires)	*to be/leave on a (business) trip, to be/go out of town*
fondre **en** larmes	*to burst into tears*
garder qch **en** mémoire/**en** souvenir	*to keep sth in mind/in one's memory*
laisser qch **en** gage	*to leave sth as security*
laisser qn **en** paix	*to leave sb alone (= in peace)*
maintenir **en** vie	*to keep alive*
mettre **en** application	*to implement*
mettre **en** conserve/**en** boîte	*to can*
mettre qch **en** danger/**en** péril	*to endanger/jeopardize sth*
mettre qn **en** difficulté	*to put sb in a difficult position*
mettre qn **en** garde (contre)	*to put sb on his guard (against)*
mettre qch **en** lumière	*to highlight sth*
mettre qch **en** marche	*to start/start up/switch on sth*

---

1. Do not confuse **à vendre** (*for sale*) and **en vente** (*for sale*)

Cette maison est **à** vendre.	*This house is for sale. (= to be sold)*
Cet article est **en** vente chez votre pharmacien.	*This article is for sale (= available) at your pharmacist.*

mettre qch **en** œuvre	*to implement sth, to put into effect*
mettre qch **en** ordre	*to put sth in order*
mettre qch **en** pratique	*to put sth into practice, to carry out*
se mettre **en** route	*to set out, to start out on one's way*
mettre qch **en** vente	*to put sth up for sale*
monter **en** flèche	*to soar, to rise like an arrow*
Les prix montent **en** flèche.	*Prices climb rapidly.*
monter **en** haut de	*to climb up*
Il est monté **en** haut de la Tour Eiffel.	*He climbed up the Eiffel Tower.*
partir **en** fumée	*to go up in smoke*
passer qch **en** contrebande	*to smuggle sth*
passer qch **en** revue	*to review sth*
poursuivre qn **en** justice	*to sue sb (in a court of law)*
prendre qn **en** affection	*to become fond of sb*
prendre qn/qch **en** charge	*to take care of sb/sth*
prendre qch **en** compte	*to take sth into account*
prendre qch **en** considération	*to take sth into consideration*
prendre qch **en** main	*to take sth in hand*
prendre/retenir qn **en** otage	*to take/hold sb hostage*
prendre qn **en** photo	*to take a picture of sb*
regarder qch **en** face	*to face sth*
(re)mettre qch **en** question/**en** cause	*to call sth into question*
rester **en** contact avec qn	*to keep in touch with sb*
rester **en** route	*to remain behind*
sauter **en** parachute	*to make a parachute jump*
stationner **en** infraction	*to be parked illegally*
Votre voiture stationne **en** infraction.	*Your car is illegally parked.*
tenir qn **en** échec	*to hold sb in check*
tenir qn **en** haleine	*to hold sb in suspense*
tenir **en** laisse	*to keep on a leash*
tenir/avoir qch **en** réserve	*to keep/have sth in stock*
tomber **en** bas de l'escalier	*to fall down the stairs*
tomber **en** désuétude	*to become obsolete*
tomber **en** panne	*to break down*

tourner **en** rond	*to go round in circles/get nowhere*
vendre/acheter **en** gros	*to sell/buy wholesale*
venir **en** aide à qn	*to come to the help of sb*
venir **en** tête	*to come first*
en apparence	*seemingly*
en attendant	*in the meantime, meanwhile*
en arrière	*backwards, behind*
Ne reste pas **en** arrière!	*Don't stay behind!*
Je suis **en** arrière.	*I lag behind.*
regarder **en** arrière	*to look back, to look behind*
aller/marcher **en** arrière	*to go/walk backward(s)*
se pencher **en** arrière	*to lean backward(s)*
faire un pas **en** arrière	*to take a step backward(s)*
en aucun cas/**en** aucune manière	*in no way*
en avant	*forward*
C'est un pas **en** avant.	*That's a step forward.*
en bordure de	*alongside, by, along the edge of*
une maison **en** bordure de mer	*a house by the ocean*
en bordure de la forêt	*on the edge of the forest*
en bas âge	*at a young age*
en cachette	*secretly, on the sly*
en caractères gras	*in bold type*
en caractères d'imprimerie	*in print*
en cas de	*in case of, in the event of*
en cas de besoin	*if need be*
en cas de doute	*in case of doubt*
en cas d'urgence	*in (the case of) an emergency*
en cas d'incendie/de verglas	*in the event of a fire/of black ice*
en catimini	*secretly*
en ce moment[1]	*now, at this time*
en ce qui concerne	*as for, concerning*
en ce qui me concerne	*as far as I am concerned*
en chemin (= **en** route)	*on/along the way*
en civil	*in plain clothes (= not in uniform)*
un policier **en** civil	*a plain-clothes policeman*

---

1. But: **à** ce moment-là *at that time*

en compagnie de	*in the company of*
en comparaison de	*compared with, in comparison with*
en conclusion	*in conclusion*
en (toute) connaissance de cause	*with (full) knowledge of the facts*
en conséquence	*consequently, as a result*
agir **en** conséquence	*to act accordingly*
en cours	*under way*
en danger	*in danger*
en d'autres termes	*in other words*
en définitive	*when all is said and done*
en dehors de	*outside, apart from*
traverser **en** dehors des clous	*to cross the street outside the pedestrian crossing*
en dépit de	*in spite of*
(faire qch) **en** dernier	*(to do sth) last*
en désespoir de cause	*out of despair, as a last resort*
en direct	*live* [TV/radio broadcast]
un entretien **en** direct	*a live interview*
en désordre	*in a mess, messy* [room, etc.]
en douceur	*gently, softly*
en échange de	*in exchange for*
en effet	*as a matter of fact, indeed*
en entier	*entirely, in its entirety*
J'ai lu le livre **en** entier.	*I read the book in its entirety.*
en fait	*actually, as a matter of fact*
en file indienne	*in single file*
en fin de compte	*when all is said and done, ultimately*
en fonction de	*according to*
en général	*usually, generally, as a rule*
en grande partie	*to a big extent*
en gros	*roughly*
Voilà **en** gros ce qui s'est passé.	*Here is roughly what happened.*
en gros et au détail	*wholesale and retail*
en guise de	*instead of, as, by way of*

en hommage à qn	*in tribute to sb*
en italique(s)	*in italics*
en marge de	*outside*
en matière de	*as far as...is concerned*
En matière d'art, je préfère...	*As far as art is concerned, I prefer...*
en même temps (= à la fois)[1]	*at the same time (= simultaneously)*
en mémoire de qn	*in memory of sb*
en moyenne	*on an average*
en mon (ton, son...) nom	*in my (your, his, her...) name*
en outre	*besides, moreover, furthermore*
en particulier	*particularly, in particular*
en partie	*partially*
en permanence	*permanently, constantly, non-stop*
en personne	*personally*
en perspective	*in prospect*
Il a des soucis **en** perspective.	*Worries are in store for him.*
en plus	*besides, moreover, in addition*
Les boissons sont **en** plus.	*The beverages are extra.*
en plus de	*in addition to*
en pratique	*in practice*
(faire qch) **en** premier	*(to do sth) first*
Tu passes **en** premier. Servez-moi **en** premier! Ils sont arrivés **en** premier.	*You go first.* *Serve me first!* *They arrived first.*
en premier lieu	*first of all*
en principe	*usually, as a rule, theoretically*
en priorité	*first and foremost*
en privé	*in private*
en proportion de	*in proportion to*
en provenance de	*(coming) from*
J'attends le train **en** provenance d'Allemagne.	*I am waiting for the train (coming) from Germany.*
en public	*in public*

1. Do not confuse '*en même temps*' with '*à la même heure*' (see footnote p. 42).

en quantité	*in large amounts*
en quelque sorte	*in some way, in a way, as it were*
en raison de (= à cause de) **en** raison du mauvais temps	*because of, on account of* *because of the bad weather*
en réalité	*in reality*
en règle générale (= en général)	*as a rule, generally*
en remerciement de	*as thanks for*
en réponse à	*in answer to*
en représailles à	*in retaliation for*
en retour de	*in return for*
en revanche	*on the other hand*
en rien	*in no way*
en route	*on the way*
en secret	*secretly*
en sens inverse	*in the opposite direction*
en silence	*silently*
en somme	*all in all, in short*
en souvenir	*as a souvenir, as a keepsake*
en souvenir de **en** souvenir de la tragédie	*in memory (remembrance) of* *in memory of the tragedy*
en (tant que) [+ noun] **en** tant que professeur	*as a* [+ noun], *being a* [+ noun] *as a teacher*
en théorie	*in theory*
en tout	*in all*
en tout cas/**en** tout état de cause	*in any case*
en toute occasion	*on all occasions*
en toute franchise	*in all honesty*
en un clin d'œil	*in the twinkling of an eye*
en un mot	*in short, to cut a long story short*
en un rien de temps	*in no time*
en un tour de main/un tournemain	*in a split second*
en vain	*in vain*
en vérité	*in truth, truly, actually*
en vue	*in sight*

Proverbs, sayings, and idioms

Chaque chose **en** son temps.	*Everything in its time.*
Heureux au jeu, malheureux **en** amour.	*Lucky in games, unlucky in love.*
Il faut laver son linge sale **en** famille.	*One must not wash one's dirty linen in public.*
En avril, ne te découvre pas d'un fil, **en** mai, fais ce qu'il te plaît.	*In April, do not remove one stitch, in May, do as you please.*
arriver comme mars **en** carême[1]	*to come as sure as night follows day*
avoir le vent **en** poupe	*to have the wind in one's sails, to be successful*
voir tout **en** rose	*to look at the bright side of things*
voir tout **en** noir	*to look at the dark side of things*
en chair et **en** os	*in the flesh*

Note:

en is generally *not* followed by the definite article *except* in the following expressions

en l'absence de	*in the absence of*
en l'air	*in the air*
des mots (paroles) **en l'**air	*idle talk*
des menaces **en l'**air	*empty threats*
les mains **en l'**air!	*hands up!*
tirer **en l'**air	*to shoot in the air*
en l'an	*in the year*
en l'an 2000	*in the year 2000*
en l'espace de	*in the (time) space of*
en l'espace d'une seconde	*(with) in one second*
en l'honneur de	*in honor of*
en l'occurence	*in this case, as it turns out*
en la matière	*on the subject*
Je ne suis pas expert(e) **en la** matière.	*I am not an expert on the subject.*

1. lit.: to arrive like March in Lent
(Lent = period of 46 days between Mardi Gras and Easter)

D. The preposition **par**

1. **par** expresses 'through', 'via', and 'out of' with a place

Je ne suis jamais passé **par** ici.	*I never passed through here.*
Nous revenons **par** Paris.	We *come back via Paris.*
Je vais aller à Sète **par** Nice.	*I am going to go to Sète via Nice.*
Il n'est pas entré/sorti **par** la porte mais **par** la fenêtre.	*He didn't come in/go out through the door but through the window.*
Le cambrioleur a sauté **par** la fenêtre.	*The burglar jumped out of the window.*
Il a quitté le palais **par** une porte secrète.	*He left the palace through a secret door.*
regarder **par** la fenêtre	*to look out of the window*
se pencher **par** la fenêtre	*to lean out of the window*
jeter qch **par** la fenêtre	*to throw sth out of the window*
regarder **par** le trou de la serrure	*to look through the keyhole*

2. **par** indicates the *means or manner* by which something is done or obtained (English: *with, by*)

Il voulait atteindre son but **par** des flatteries.	*He wanted to reach his goal with flatteries.*
Il a appris la nouvelle **par** la radio/ **par** un ami.	*He learned the news by the radio/ from a friend.*
payer/régler **par** chèque[1]	*to pay by check*
payer **par** carte de crédit[1]	*to pay by credit card*
payer **par** mandat	*to pay with a money order*
acheter/vendre qch **par** correspondance	*to buy/sell sth by mail order*
savoir/apprendre qch **par** cœur	*to know/learn sth by heart*
savoir qch **par** expérience	*to know sth by/from experience*
obtenir qch **par** la force	*to obtain sth by force*
mourir **par** injection mortelle	*to die by lethal injection*

---

1. But:

payer **en** espèces	*to pay cash*
payer **avec** des chèques de voyage	*to pay with traveler's checks*

3. **par** indicates some *means of transportation* and *communication*

monter/descendre **par** l'ascenseur[1]	*to go up/down by elevator*
monter/descendre **par** l'escalier	*to go up/down by (way of) the stairs*
venir/arriver/voyager **par** le train[2]	*to come/arrive/travel by train*
par le métro[3]	*by subway*
par la route	*by the road (= by car or truck)*
par mer et **par** terre	*by land and sea*
envoyer une lettre **par** avion	*to send a letter airmail*
envoyer un colis **par** bateau	*to send a package by sea*
envoyer une lettre **par** la poste	*to send a letter through the mail*
par le même courrier	*with the same mail*
par courrier électronique[4]	*by e-mail*
par courrier ordinaire	*by surface mail*
(répondre) **par** retour du courrier	*(to answer) by return mail*
par télécopieur/**par** fax	*by fax*
(envoyer un message) **par** internet	*(to send a message) via internet*
(joindre/contacter qn) **par** téléphone	*(to reach/contact sb) by phone*

4. **par** expresses the *cause* before abstract nouns (English: *out of*)

par amitié pour qn	*out of friendship for sb*
par amour du métier	*out of love for the job*
par crainte de [+ inf. or noun] **par** crainte de sous-estimer la neige	*out of/for fear of* *for fear of underestimating the snow*
par curiosité	*out of curiosity*
par désespoir	*out of despair*
par égard pour qn/qch	*out of consideration for sb/sth*
par ennui	*out of boredom*
par étourderie	*out of absent-mindedness*
par faiblesse	*out of weakness*
par gentillesse	*out of kindness*
par goût de l'aventure	*out of love for adventure*

---

1. also: **en** ascenseur
2. also: **en** train
3. also: **en** métro
4. also: **par** e-mail, **par** courriel

par ignorance	*out of ignorance*
par instinct	*out of instinct*
(agir) **par** intérêt	*(to act) out of self-interest*
par jalousie	*out of jealousy*
par lâcheté	*out of cowardice*
par lassitude	*out of weariness*
par manque de temps	*owing to lack of time*
par méchanceté	*out of wickedness, out of spite*
par nécessité	*out of need*
par peur de [+ inf. or noun] **par** peur de l'inconnu	*out of fear of* *out of fear of the unknown*
par pitié	*out of pity*
par plaisir	*out of pleasure, for the fun of it*
par politesse	*out of politeness*
par précaution/**par** prudence	*as a precaution*
par solidarité	*out of solidarity*
par vanité	*out of vanity*

5. **par** indicates the acting *agent* in a *passive action* (English: *by*)

La Tour Eiffel a été construite **par** Gustave Eiffel.	*The Eiffel Tower was built* ***by*** *Gustave Eiffel.*
Le piéton a été percuté/renversé **par** un camion.	*The pedestrian was hit/run over* ***by*** *a truck.*
La tapisserie de la Reine Mathilde représente la conquête de l'Angleterre **par** les Normands.	*The tapestry of Queen Mathilda represents the conquest of England* ***by*** *the Normans.*
Henri IV fut tué **par** Ravaillac.	*Henry IV was killed* ***by*** *Ravaillac.*
La Marseillaise[1] a été écrite **par** Rouget de Lisle en 1792.	*The Marseillaise was written* ***by*** *Rouget de Lisle in 1792.*
Parlé **par** 160 millions de personnes, le français est une langue internationale par excellence.	*Spoken* ***by*** *160 million people, French is an international language par excellence.*
Elle est suivie **par** un médecin.	*She is being treated* ***by*** *a doctor.*
Le voyage a été gâché **par** la météo.	*The trip was ruined* ***by*** *the weather.*

1. *La Marseillaise* is the name of the French national anthem.

Il s'est fait écraser **par** une voiture.	*He was run over **by** a car.*
Elle a été frappée **par** la foudre.	*She was hit **by** lightning.*
La forêt a été endommagée **par** la tempête.	*The forest was damaged **by** the storm.*
Je suis tenté **par** cette offre.	*I am tempted **by** this offer.*
être aveuglé **par** le soleil	*to be blinded **by** the sun*
être fasciné **par** qch	*to be fascinated **by** sth*
être frappé **par** qch	*to be struck **by** sth*
être vexé **par** qn	*to be upset/offended **by** sb*

6. **par** followed by an expression of time indicates the *frequency* with which something occurs, or an *amount per unit of time* (English *a, per*)

Je me brosse les dents trois fois **par** jour.	*I brush my teeth three times **a** day.*
Nous allons au cinéma deux fois **par** mois.	*We go to the movies twice **a** month.*
En France, on travaille 35 heures **par** semaine et 270 jours **par** an.	*In France, people work 35 hours **per** week and 270 days **a** year.*
Elle tape 300 mots **par** minute.	*She types 300 words **per** minute.*
La chambre coûte 200 euros **par** nuit.	*The room costs 200 euros **per** night.*

7. **par** is used before the infinitive after the verbs **commencer** (with the meaning 'to start out doing sth'), and **finir** (with the meaning 'to end up doing sth', 'to finally do sth')

Il a *commencé **par*** pleurer et *fini **par*** rire.	*He started out crying and ended up laughing.*
Elle a *fini **par*** changer d'avis.	*She finally changed her mind.*

8. **par** followed by an expression of weather or temperature expresses 'in' and 'on'

par beau temps	*in good weather*
par mauvais temps	*in bad weather*
par temps chaud	*in warm weather, when it is warm*
par temps clair	*on a clear day*

par temps ensoleillé	*in sunny weather*
par temps d'orage	*in stormy weather*
par temps de pluie	*in rainy weather*
par temps de brouillard	*in fog, when it's foggy*
par tous les temps	*in any weather*
par n'importe quel temps	*in any weather*
par un temps pareil	*in weather like this*
par ce temps-là	*in this kind of weather*
par ce froid	*in this cold*
par cette chaleur	*in this heat*
Also:	
par moins 10 degrés	*when it's minus 10 degrees*
par une belle nuit d'été	*on a beautiful summer('s) night*
par une journée pareille	*on a day like this*

9. **par** is part of the following nouns

le contrôle **par** radar	*the radar control*
la télévision **par** câble	*cable television*
la vente **par** correspondance	*the mail-order sale*
un cours **par** correspondance	*a correspondence course*

10. **par** is used in the following expressions

appeler les choses **par** leur nom	*to call things by their name*
appeler qn **par** son prénom	*to call sb by his/her first name*
commencer **par** le commencement	*to start at the beginning*
passer **par** la tête de qn	*to pass through sb's head*
répondre **par** oui ou **par** non	*to answer with yes or no*
tenir/prendre qn **par** la main	*to hold/take sb by the hand*
Elle est suédoise **par** son père et française **par** sa mère.	*She is Swedish by her father and French by her mother.*
Qu'est-ce que vous entendez **par** là? (= Qu'est-ce que vous voulez dire **par** là?)	*What do you mean by that?*
année **par** année	*year by year*

11. par is used in the following *exclamations* and *directions*

par exemple!	*Well! What do you know!*
par ici	*this way, it's in this direction*
par là	*that way, it's in that direction*

12. par is part of the following adverbial and other expressions

par accident	*accidentally, by accident*
par ailleurs	*otherwise, moreover, furthermore*
par bonheur	*luckily, by good fortune*
par chance	*luckily*
par conséquent	*consequently, as a result*
par contre	*on the other hand*
par écrit	*in writing*
par enchantement	*by magic, magically*
par endroits	*in some places, here and there*
par erreur	*by mistake*
par excellence	*par excellence, unequalled*
par exemple	*for example, for instance*
par habitude	*by habit*
par hasard	*by any chance*
par inadvertance	*unintentionally*
par intervalles	*every now and then, intermittently*
par la suite	*subsequently*
On ne sait pas ce qui va se passer **par** la suite.	*One doesn't know what is going to happen subsequently.*
par le menu	*minutely, in great detail*
Je vais vous raconter l'histoire **par** le menu.	*I am going to tell you the story in great detail.*
par malchance	*unluckily, as ill luck would have it*
par malheur	*unfortunately*
par mégarde	*by mistake, inadvertently*
par mesure de précaution	*as a precautionary measure*
par mesure de sécurité	*as a safety precaution*
par milliers	*by the thousands*

par miracle	*miraculously*
par moments	*at times*
par opposition à	*in contrast to*
par ordre alphabétique	*in alphabetical order*
par ordre chronologique	*in chronological order*
par ouï-dire	*by hearsay*
par (or: **dans**) le passé	*in the past*
par rapport à	*in relation to, with regard to*
par surprise	*by surprise*
par tous les moyens	*by every possible means*

13. par indicates a *location* in the expression

par terre	*on the ground, on the floor*
Ils sont assis **par** terre.	*They are sitting on the floor.*
tomber **par** terre	*to fall to the ground*
jeter qch **par** terre	*to throw sth on the ground*

14. par introduces the complement in the following expressions

être déçu **par** qn	*to be disappointed by/about/with sb*
Il est déçu **par** ses enfants.	*He is dispappointed with his children.*
se distinguer de qn/qch **par** qch	*to differ from sb/sth by sth*
Il se distingue de ses amis **par** son accent.	*He differs from his friends by his accent.*
s'illustrer **par** qch	*to win fame through sth*
Il s'est illustré **par** son courage.	*He won fame through his courage.*
être intéressé **par** qn/qch	*to be interested in sb/sth*
Il n'est pas intéressé **par** la politique.	*He is not interested in politics.*
à en juger **par** qch	*judging from/by sth*
à en juger **par** sa réponse...	*judging from his answer...*
ne jurer que **par** qn/qch	*to swear by sb/sth*
Il ne jure que **par** elle.	*He swears by her.*
être préoccupé **par** qch	*to be concerned about sth*
Je suis préoccupé **par** les problèmes de l'entreprise.	*I am concerned about the problems of the business.*
se terminer **par** qch	*to end in/with sth*
Le mot 'corps' se termine **par** 's'.	*The word 'corps' ends in 's'.*

Sayings and idioms

brûler la chandelle **par** les deux bouts	*to burn the candle at both ends*
mener qn **par** le bout du nez	*to lead sb by the nose*
prendre le taureau **par** les cornes	*to take the bull by the horns*
être toujours **par** monts et **par** vaux	*to be always on the move*
jeter l'argent **par** les fenêtres	*to waste money*
manger les pissenlits **par** la racine	*to push up daisies*
ne pas y aller **par** quatre chemins Il n'y va pas **par** quatre chemins.	*not to beat about the bush* *He is direct.*
(marcher) un **par** un/deux **par** deux	*(to walk) one by one/two by two*
par les temps qui courent	*the times we live in, these days*
C'est tiré **par** les cheveux.	*That's far-fetched.*
Nous sommes ici **par** la volonté du peuple et nous n'en sortirons que **par** la force des baïonnettes. (Mirabeau)	*We are here by the will of the people and we will leave only by the force of bayonets.*

Translation difficulties

English 'per' is translated with

1. par

- when 'per' is followed by a unit of time indicating the *frequency* with which sth occurs or an *amount per unit of time* (see p. 106 # 6)

In the flooded areas, the water rises three centimeters **per** hour.	Dans les régions inondées, l'eau monte trois centimètres **par** heure.

But:

***per** hour* referring to *speed* and *pay* is translated in the following manner:

– *speed* **per** hour = **à l'heure** (see p. 35)

– *earnings* **per** hour = **de l'heure**

*My brother earns seven dollars **per hour.***	Mon frère gagne sept dollars **de l'heure**.

- when 'per' indicates *distribution*

There were six students ***per*** *apartment.*	Il y avait six étudiants **par** appartement.
The French consume 22 kilos of cheese ***per*** *year* ***per*** *person.*	Les Français consomment 22 kilos de fromage **par** an **par** personne.

2. **the definite article** (le, la, les) when 'per' is followed by a *weight, measurement* or *quantity*

In France, gasoline costs 1.08 euro ***per*** *liter.*	En France, l'essence coûte 1,08 euro **le** litre.
Truffles cost between 500 and 1000 euros ***per*** *kilo.*	La truffe vaut entre 500 et 1000 euros **le** kilo.
Nougat costs 2 euros ***per*** *100 grammes.*	Le nougat est à 2 euros **les** cent grammes.
Pizza costs 2.50 euros ***per*** *piece.*	La pizza coûte 2,50 euros **la** part.

E. The preposition **pour**

1. **pour** indicates the *purpose* or an *aim*

- followed by an infinitive (English: *in order to*[1])

J'ai fait ça **pour** vous aider.	*I did that (in order) to help you.*
Ils ont pris un taxi **pour** ne pas manquer le train.	*They took a taxi in order not to miss the train.*
Il a dit ça **pour** rire.	*He said that for fun.*
Combien de temps faut-il **pour** aller à Lyon?	*How long does it take to go to Lyon?*
Il faut travailler **pour** vivre et non pas vivre **pour** travailler.	*One must work in order to live and not live in order to work.*
Il faut du courage **pour** faire ça.	*One must have courage to do that.*
Il faut le voir **pour** le croire.	*One must see it to believe it.*
Il travaille à l'usine **pour** gagner sa vie.	*He works at the factory in order to make a living.*

1. Note that when English 'to' before an infinitive can be replaced by 'in order to', it must be translated with ***pour***.

- followed by a noun (English: *for*)

des vêtements **pour** hommes	*clothes for men*
le wagon **pour** fumeurs	*the car for smokers*
c'est **pour** votre bien	*it's for your own good*
un livre **pour** enfants	*a book for children*
voilà les devoirs **pour** lundi	*here is the homework for Monday*
des pastilles **pour** la toux	*cough drops*
une chambre **pour** une personne	*a single room*
une chambre **pour** deux personnes	*a double room*

2. **pour** indicates the *destination*

- when used with the name of a *place*

C'est bien le train **pour** Paris?	*Is this the train to Paris?*
Elle part **pour** Nice demain.	*She is leaving for Nice tomorrow.*
Il a pris un billet de seconde **pour** Marseille.	*He bought a second-class ticket for Marseille.*

- when used with a *person*

J'ai une surprise **pour** toi.	*I have a surprise for you.*
Il a un cadeau **pour** vous.	*He has a gift for you.*
Est-ce qu'il y a du courrier **pour** moi?	*Is there any mail for me?*

3. **pour** expresses 'for' in the sense of 'in place of'

Je répondrai **pour** toi.	*I will answer for you.*
Il est ici **pour** sa mère.	*He is here for his mother.*

4. **pour** indicates the *cause* [followed by a noun or the past infinitive] (English: *for*)

Elle a épousé le vieil homme **pour** son argent.	*She married the old man for his money.*
La route est fermée **pour** travaux.	*The road is closed for repair.*
Il est admiré **pour** son courage.	*He is admired for his courage.*

Il a été puni **pour** son insolence.	*He was punished for his insolence.*
Je l'aime **pour** sa franchise.	*I like him for his frankness.*
Elle a été arrêtée **pour** avoir brûlé un feu rouge.	*She was stopped for having run a red light.*
J'ai eu une contravention **pour** excès de vitesse.	*I got a ticket for speeding.*
Il est mort **pour** avoir trop fumé.	*He died for having smoked too much.*

5. **pour** indicates a *viewpoint*

C'est bien fait **pour** toi (lui...eux).	*That serves you (him...them) right.*
Tant pis/mieux **pour** elle.	*So much the worse/better for her.*
Heureusement **pour** nous.	*Luckily for us.*
C'est trop cher **pour** moi.	*That is too expensive for me.*
Ce garçon est grand **pour** son âge.	*This boy is tall for his age.*
Il fait froid **pour** la saison.	*It's cold for the season.*
C'est dommage **pour** vous.	*It's too bad for you.*

6. **pour** indicates the *total value*

Des timbres **pour** cinq euros s.v.p.	*Five euros-worth of stamps please.*
J'ai mis **pour** vingt euros d'essence.	*I put in twenty euros-worth of gas.*

7. **pour** followed by an expression of time expresses 'for' indicating the anticipated duration of an action in the future (in relation to the time of speaking), especially after the verbs *aller, partir, sortir,* and *venir* (see also p. 119)

Il est parti **pour** quinze jours.	*He left for two weeks.*
Je suis obligé de sortir **pour** deux heures.	*I have to go out for two hours.*
Elle est ici **pour** quatre semaines.	*She is here for four weeks.*
Also in:	
Tu pars **pour** combien de temps?	*How long will you be gone?*

8. **pour** indicates a *proportion* in the expression ***pour cent***

dix **pour** cent	*ten per cent*

9. pour can mean 'for the sake of'

Il a tout abandonné **pour** son indépendance.	*He gave up everything for his independence.*

10. pour after *ce+être* and followed by an expression of time or by 'quand' indicates that an action will take place at some time in the future

Ça sera **pour** une autre fois.	*We'll do it another time.*
Le bébé, c'est **pour** quand?	*When is the baby due?*
C'est **pour** aujourd'hui ou **pour** demain?	*Will it happen today or tomorrow?*

11. pour introduces the infinitive after certain expressions in verb + verb constructions (see p. 243-245)

12. pour is used in questions asking for directions

Pardon, Monsieur, **pour** aller à la gare du Nord s.v.p.?	*Excuse me, Sir, how do I get to the Gare du Nord please?*
Comment fait-on **pour** aller à la rue Barge?	*How does one get to Barge Street?*

13. pour is part of the following expressions

pour ainsi dire	*so to speak*
pour autant	*for all that*
pour cause de [+ noun]	*because of, on account of, due to*
pour cause de blessure/maladie/grève	*because of injury/illness/a strike*
pour ce qui est de [+ determiner + noun]	*with respect to, as far as...is/are concerned*
pour ce qui est de mon salaire	*as far as my salary is concerned*
pour ce qui est de l'étiquetage/des films	*with respect to the labelling/movies*
pour cette raison	*for that reason*
pour comble de malheur	*to make things worse*
pour commencer	*to begin with*
pour de bon	*for good, forever*
pour de vrai	*for real*
pour finir	*as a conclusion*

pour l'instant/**pour** le moment	*for the moment, for the time being*
pour longtemps	*for a long time*
pour ma part	*for my part*
pour la plupart	*for the most part*
pour quelle raison?	*for what reason?*
pour rien	*for nothing, in vain*
attendre **pour** rien	*to wait in vain*
travailler **pour** rien	*to work for next to nothing*
C'était **pour** rien.	*It was free (of charge).*
pour rien au monde	*not for anything in the world*
pour une fois	*for once*
pour toujours	*forever*
pour terminer	*in conclusion*

14. **pour** introduces the object after the following verbs and expressions

avoir peur **pour** qch/qn	*to fear for sth/sb*
Il a peur **pour** sa couronne.	*He fears for his crown.*
avoir une aversion **pour** qch/qn	*to have an aversion to sth/sb*
avoir une préférence **pour** qn/qch	*to have a preference for sb/sth*
n'avoir d'yeux que **pour** qn	*to have eyes only for sb*
craindre **pour** qch	*to fear for sth*
Ils craignent **pour** leur emploi.	*They fear for their jobs.*
se disputer **pour** qch	*to argue over sth*
être aux petits soins **pour** qn	*to wait on sb hand and foot*
être bon **pour** qn	*to be good to sb*
en être quitte **pour** (la peur)	*to get off with (a fright)*
être désolé **pour** (or: **de**) qch	*to be sorry for/about sth*
Je suis désolé **pour** ce qui s'est passé.	*I am sorry for what happened.*
Je suis désolé **pour** cet oubli.	*I am sorry about this oversight.*
être doué **pour** qch	*to be gifted for sth*
Vous êtes très doué **pour** les langues.	*You are very talented for languages.*
être inquiet **pour** qn/qch	*to be worried about sb/sth*
Ils sont inquiets **pour** l'avenir.	*They worry about the future.*

s'en faire **pour** qn Ne t'en fais pas **pour** moi.	*to worry about sb* *Don't worry about me.*
féliciter qn **pour** (or: **de**) qch Je te félicite **pour** ton succès.	*to congratulate sb on sth* *I congratulate you on your success.*
s'inquiéter **pour** qn Ne vous inquiétez pas **pour** moi.	*to worry about sb* *Don't worry about me.*
louer qn **pour** (or: **de**) qch	*to praise sb for sth*
lutter/se battre **pour** qch	*to fight for sth*
opter **pour** qn/qch	*to opt for sb/sth*
partir **pour** [+ nom de lieu] Je pars **pour** Lyon.	*to leave for* [+ place name] *I am leaving for Lyon.*
passer **pour** [+ adj.]	*to be considered* [+ adj.]
passer **pour** [+ nom] Elle pourrait passer **pour** sa fille.	*to be taken for* [+ noun] *She could be taken for her daughter.*
se passionner **pour** qch	*to have a passion for sth*
pencher **pour** qch	*to be in favor of sth*
se porter garant **pour** qn	*to vouch for sb*
prendre qn/qch **pour** (= tenir qn **pour**) **Pour** qui me prenez-vous?[1] Je l'ai pris **pour** son père. Vous me prenez **pour** un imbécile. Je l'ai pris **pour** plus intelligent qu'il ne l'est. Je vous ai pris **pour** quelqu'un d'autre. Don Quijote prend les moulins **pour** des géants agitant leurs bras.	*to take sb/sth for* *Who do you think I am?* *I took him for his father.* *You take me for an idiot.* *I took him for more intelligent than he is.* *I took you for someone else.* *Don Quixote takes the windmills for giants (who are) moving their arms.*
prendre qn **pour** époux/épouse Monsieur Jean Dutronc, voulez-vous prendre **pour** épouse Mademoiselle Céline Carpentier?	*to take sb to be one's husband/wife* *Mr. John Dutronc, do you want to take Miss Céline Carpentier to be your wife?*
se prendre **pour** qn Elle se prend **pour** une vedette.	*to consider oneself to be sb* *She considers herself to be a movie star.*

1. lit.: *For whom do you take me?*

se prononcer **pour** qch	*to declare oneself in favor of sth*
punir qn **pour** (or: **de**) qch	*to punish sb for sth*
récompenser qn **pour** qch	*to reward sb for sth*
remercier qn **pour** (or: **de**) qch	*to thank sb for sth*
Je vous remercie **pour** votre carte.	*I thank you for your postcard.*
voter **pour** qn/qch	*to vote for sb/sth*
sans égard **pour** qn	*without regard/consideration for sb*
merci **pour**	*thanks for*
Merci **pour** votre appel.	*Thanks for your call.*
Merci **pour** le cadeau.	*Thanks for the gift.*
Merci **pour** tout.	*Thanks for everything.*
félicitations **pour**	*congratulations* ***on***

Proverbs, sayings, and idioms

Chacun **pour** soi et Dieu **pour** tous.	*Everyone for himself and God for us all.*
Il faut de tout **pour** faire un monde.	*It takes all sorts to make a world.*
Oeil **pour** œil, dent **pour** dent.	*An eye for an eye and a tooth for a tooth.*
C'est trop beau **pour** être vrai.	*It's too good to be true.*
C'est meilleur **pour** la santé.	*It's healthier.*
pour le meilleur et **pour** le pire	*for better or worse*
pour l'amour de Dieu	*for heaven's/God's sake*
beaucoup de bruit **pour** rien	*much ado about nothing*
pour une raison ou **pour** une autre	*for one reason or another*
pour comble de malheur	*to make things worse*
la raison **pour**[1] laquelle...	*the reason why...*
Et **pour** cause!	*And for a very good reason!*
pour un oui ou **pour** un non	*for the slightest thing, over trifles*
pour en savoir plus, appelez le...	*for further information, call...*
garder une poire **pour** la soif[2]	*to save sth for a rainy day*
C'était **pour** rire.	*It was meant as a joke.*

1. But: la raison **de** son absence (*the reason* ***for*** *his absence*)
2. lit.: *to keep a pear for the thirst*

tenir qn **pour** responsable (de qch)	*to hold sb responsible (for sth)*
travailler **pour** des prunes	*to work for nothing*
une fois **pour** toutes	*once and for all*
avoir **pour** conséquence	*to result in*
Ces mesures avaient **pour** conséquence le licenciement de beaucoup d'ouvriers.	*These measures resulted in the laying off of many workers.*
juste **pour** savoir	*just wondering!*
C'est **pour** offrir?	*Are you giving it as a gift?*
C'est **pour** cela que...	*That is why...*
en avoir **pour** [un certain temps]	*to take* [+ time expression]
J'en ai **pour** une minute.	*It will only take me a minute.*
J'en ai encore **pour** deux heures.	*It will take me another two hours.*
Je n'en ai pas **pour** longtemps.	*I won't be long. It will not take me a long time.*
y être **pour** qch	*to be to blame, to have sth to do with it, to be responsible for it*
Si elle pleure, tu y es bien **pour** quelque chose.	*If she cries, you certainly have something to do with it.*
n'y être **pour** rien	*to have nothing to do with it*
Je n'y suis **pour** rien.	*I am not to blame.*
Il n'y est **pour** rien à vos problèmes.	*He has nothing to do with your problems.*
y être **pour** peu dans une affaire	*to count for little in a matter*
y être **pour** beaucoup	*to be largely responsible*
Il y est **pour** beaucoup.	*He is largely responsible. A lot of credit should go to him.*

Translation difficulties

English **for** + *time period* has the following equivalents in French

1. for + *time period* referring to an action or situation which started in the *past* and continues in the *present* is translated with **depuis**

*I have studied (have been studying) French **for** five years.* (And I still do.)	J'étudie[1] le français **depuis** cinq ans.

---

1. Note that unlike in English, the verb is in the *present tense* in a sentence with *depuis* when the action started in the past and continues in the present (see p. 164).

2. **for** + *time period* referring to an action or situation which was completed in the *past* is translated with **pendant**[1] (which can be omitted if the time period follows the verb immediately)

*He studied in Paris **for** five years.* (But he no longer does.)	Il a étudié à Paris **pendant** 5 ans. (or: Il a étudié cinq ans à Paris.)
*Last year, we travelled **for** one month.*	L'année dernière nous avons voyagé (**pendant**) un mois.

3. **for** + *time period* referring to the intended duration of an action or situation (usually in the *future*) is translated with **pour**. 'Pour' + *time period* indicates a period that is not yet completed at the moment when the speaker refers to it, and frequently follows the verbs *aller, venir, sortir* and *partir.*[2]

*They go to Europe **for** a month.*	Ils vont en Europe **pour** un mois.
*She came **for** a few days.*	Elle est venue **pour** quelques jours.
*They are leaving for Africa **for** two years.*	Ils partent pour l'Afrique **pour** deux ans.
*I committed myself **for** six years.*	Je me suis engagé **pour** six ans.
Also:	
*The French president is elected **for** five years by universal and direct suffrage.*	Le président français est élu **pour** cinq ans au suffrage universel direct.
How much longer?[3]	**Pour** combien de temps encore?

Mistakes to avoid

Incorrect	*Correct*	*English meaning*
J'ai vécu à l'étranger ~~pour~~ deux ans.	J'ai vécu à l'étranger **pendant** deux ans.	*I lived abroad **for** two years.* (But I no longer do.)

---

1. Note that **pendant** also means 'during' (see p. 165).
2. See also p. 113.
3. *(For) how long* is translated by
   - '*depuis* combien de temps' when the past action continues in the present (p. 163)
   - '*pendant* combien de temps' when the action was completed in the past (p. 165)
   - '*pour* combien de temps' when the action will take place in the future (see above)

F. The preposition **dans**

1. **dans** expresses 'in', often meaning 'inside'

dans l'annuaire	*in the phone book*
dans l'armoire	*in the closet*
dans l'ascenseur	*in the elevator*
dans l'avenue[1] (or: **sur** l'avenue)	*in the avenue*
dans la boîte	*in the box*
dans la boutique	*in the store*
dans le centre ville	*in the town center, downtown*
dans ma chambre	*in my room*
dans le ciel[2]	*in the sky*
dans les coulisses	*in the wings, backstage*
dans la cour	*in the courtyard*
dans le courrier	*in the mail*
dans l'eau	*in the water*
dans l'espace	*in outer space*
dans les environs	*in the vicinity, in the neighborhood*
Il y a 100 centimes **dans** un euro.	*There are 100 cents in one euro.*
dans un fauteuil[3]	*in an armchair*
dans la file (d'attente)	*in line*
dans l'hexagone[4]	*in France*
dans la guerre	*in the war*
dans le jardin	*in the yard/garden*
(lire qch) **dans** un journal	*(to read sth) in a newspaper*
dans un lieu (= **dans** un endroit)	*in a place*
Il est interdit de fumer **dans** (tous) les lieux publics.	*It is forbidden to smoke in (all) public places.*
dans un livre	*in a book*
dans la main[5]	*in(side) the hand*
dans la maison	*in the house*
dans la marge	*in the margin*

---

1. But: **sur** la route = *on the road* **sur** le boulevard = *on the boulevard*
2. But: **au** ciel = *in/to heaven*
3. But: **sur** une chaise = *in a chair*
4. lit.: *in the hexagone.* Note that the French often refer to their country with the term **hexagone** because of its shape (a six-sided geometrical figure).
5. Do not confuse '**à** la main' and '**dans** la main'

Il a un bouquet de fleurs **à** la main.	*He has a bouquet of flowers* ***in*** *his hand.*
Il cache une pièce de monnaie **dans** la main.	*He is hiding a coin* ***in****(side) his hand.*

dans le monde entier	*in the whole world*
dans les montagnes	*in the mountains*
dans la neige	*in the snow*
dans le noir/l'obscurité	*in the dark*
dans mon pays	*in my country*
dans la poche	*in the pocket*
dans le portefeuille	*in the wallet*
dans une revue/un magazine	*in a magazine*
dans la rue[1]	*in the street*
dans le tiroir	*in the drawer*
dans la valise	*in the suitcase*
dans la voiture	*in the car*

2. dans + definite article expresses 'in' or 'to'

- with a *modified continent* or *country* (replacing *en* and *au*)

Nous avons voyagé **dans** toute l'Afrique.	*We travelled in all of Africa.*
dans l'Europe moderne	*in modern Europe*
dans l'Italie du Nord	*in Northern Italy*
dans l'Allemagne d'après-guerre	*in post-war Germany*
dans la France entière	*in all of France*
dans le Japon du 16e siècle	*in 16th-century Japan*

But:

When the modifying expression is an integral part of the place name, the 'normal' preposition is used before the modified continent or country

en Amérique du Nord	*in North America*
en Amérique latine	*in Latin America*
en Asie du Sud-Est	*in South East Asia*

---

1. But a different preposition is used with '*rue*' in the following expressions:

jeter/mettre qn **à** la rue	*to throw sb out **into** the street*
être **à** la rue	*to be out **on** the street (= to have no home)*
les personnes **à** la rue	*the people **on** the street (= the homeless)*
l'homme **de** la rue	*the man **in** the street (= the average citizen)*

Note also:
When the *street name* is mentioned, there is usually *no* preposition and *no* article.

Ils habitent Rue de Rennes.	*They live on Rennes Street.*
Le restaurant Maxim's se trouve Rue Royale.	*The restaurant Maxim's is located on Royal Street.*

en Asie centrale	*in central Asia*
en Afrique/Asie de l'Est	*in East Africa/Asia*
en Afrique du Nord	*in North Africa*

- with *cities* when they are *modified* (**dans** *with* article), when 'inside the city' is stressed (**dans** *without* article), and before the expression 'la/une ville de'

dans le Paris du 17e siècle	*in 17th-century Paris*
J'aime marcher **dans** Paris.	*I like to walk in(side) Paris.*
dans la Rome antique	*in ancient Rome*
dans la ville de Lyon	*in the city of Lyon*
dans une ville de Russie	*in a city of Russia*

Also:

dans la capitale allemande	*in the German capital*

But:

One uses **à** to express 'in' or 'to' with a city name when the city is not modified or when simply a location is to be stated.

Ils habitent (**à**)[1] Marseille.	*They live* **in** *Marseille.*
Ils vont **à** Bordeaux.	*They go* **to** *Bordeaux.*

- with other *modified locations*

dans la classe de français[2]	*in French class*
dans la banlieue parisienne[3]	*in the suburbs of Paris*
(en vente) **dans** toutes les bonnes drogueries[4]	*(for sale) in all good drugstores*
dans une école privée[5]	*in/to a private school*

- with most *French departments*[6]

dans l'Allier

dans les Bouches-du-Rhône

dans le Finistère

---

1. Note that with the verb 'habiter', **à** can be omitted before a city name.
2. But: **en** classe = *in class*
3. But: **en** banlieue = *in the suburb(s)*
4. But: **à** la droguerie = *in/to the drugstore*
5. But: **à** l'école = *in/at/to school*
6. See geographical names p. 299-300

- with masculine *French provinces and regions* beginning with a consonant

dans le Languedoc	*in/to Languedoc*
dans le Périgord	*in/to Perigord*

But:

en Anjou	*in/to Anjou*

- with *mountains*

dans les Alpes	*in/to the Alps*
dans les Pyrénées	*in/to the Pyrenees*
dans le Jura	*in/to the Jura mountains*

- with most *masculine American states* and *Canadian provinces*

dans le Colorado[1]	*in/to Colorado*
dans le Vermont	*in/to Vermont*
dans le Montana	*in/to Montana*
dans l'Ontario[2]	*in/to Ontario*

- with *cardinal points* denoting the interior of a region

dans l'est	*in/to the east*
dans l'ouest	*in/to the west*
dans le nord	*in/to the north*
dans le sud	*in/to the south*
dans le Midi	*in/to the south of France*

But:

For orientation, **à** is used with cardinal points.

L'Autriche est **au** nord de l'Italie.	*Austria is north of Italy.*

Compare:

Bordeaux est **dans** l'ouest de la France.	*Bordeaux is in the west of France.*
Bordeaux est **à** l'ouest de Paris.	*Bordeaux is west of Paris.*

---

1. Note that it is always correct to say '**dans** l'état de' (to express 'in' or 'to') before *all* American states, no matter whether they are masculine or feminine (see p. 301).

2. Note that it is always correct to say '**dans** la province de' (to express 'in' or 'to') before *all* Canadian provinces, no matter whether they are masculine or feminine (see p. 303).

- with *small islands*

dans l'île d'Elbe	*on the island of/to Elba*

3. dans + *unit of time* expresses 'in' (meaning 'after') indicating the period of time at the end of which an action will take place

Je serai de retour **dans** une heure.	*I will be back* ***in*** *an hour.*[1]
Rappelez-moi **dans** deux semaines.	*Call me back* ***in*** *two weeks.*
Je suis à vous **dans** un instant.	*I am all yours* ***in*** *a moment. (= I will be with you shortly.)*
Il va nous rejoindre **dans** dix minutes.	*He will join us* ***in*** *ten minutes.*
Elle va avoir quarante ans **dans** huit jours.	*She is going to be forty* ***in*** *a week.*

But: .

en + *unit of time* indicates the time needed to complete an action (see p. 90)

Il a écrit le roman **en** trois mois.	*He wrote the novel* ***in*** *(= within) three months.*

4. dans replaces 'en' before a language when this language is modified

dans un allemand parfait	***in*** *perfect German*

5. dans translates 'at', 'to', 'on' (a certain occasion) in the following expressions

aller **dans** des soirées	*to go* ***to*** *parties*
Je l'ai connu **dans** un bal.	*I met him* ***at*** *a dance.*
Il a appris ça **dans** un voyage.	*He learned that* ***on*** *a trip.*
rencontrer qn **dans** un dîner	*to meet sb* ***at*** *a dinner*

6. dans + *les* + number expresses 'approximately', 'around'

Ça va coûter **dans** *les* 500 dollars.	*That is going to cost around $ 500.*
La femme doit avoir **dans** *les* 30 ans.	*The woman must be about 30.*
Il gagne **dans** *les* 9000 euros par an.	*He earns about 9000 euros per year.*

---

1. Or: *an hour from now*

7. '*monter* **dans**' followed by a means of transportation expresses 'to get in', 'to get on'

monter **dans** un avion	*to get on a plane*
monter **dans** l'autobus	*to get on the bus*
monter **dans** le train	*to get on the train*
monter **dans** la voiture	*to get in the car*

But:

dans is *not* used if one does not get *inside* the vehicle

monter **sur** un vélo	*to get on a bike*

8. **dans** is always used after the verb '*entrer*' before the following noun

Je suis entré **dans** la maison.	*I entered the house.*

Also:

entrer **dans** une dépression nerveuse	*to have a nervous breakdown*

But:

à is used after 'entrer' when an institution is entered

Elle veut entrer **au** couvent.	*She wants to enter the convent.*
En quelle année êtes-vous entré **à** l'université?	*In what year did you enter college?*
Les petits Français peuvent entrer **à** l'école maternelle à l'âge de deux ans.	*French children can enter kindergarten at the age of two.*

9. **dans** can mean 'out of', 'from' with verbs such as *boire, manger, découper, copier, prendre,* etc.

Elle mange la soupe **dans** une assiette.	*She eats the soup **out of** a plate.*
J'ai découpé cet article **dans** un journal.	*I cut this article **out of** a newspaper.*
Prends le document **dans** le tiroir.	*Take the document **out of/from** the drawer.*
boire **dans** un verre	*to drink **out of** a glass*
copier qch **dans** un livre	*to copy sth **out of** a book*
vivre **dans** sa valise	*to live **out of** one's suitcase*
retirer de l'argent **dans** le distributeur	*to withdraw money **from** the ATM machine*

10. dans indicates a particular *moment* or *time period* in the following expressions (English: *in, in the course of, during, within*)

dans le passé	*in the past*
dans le présent (or: **au** présent)	*in the present*
dans l'avenir (or: **à l'**avenir)	*in the future*
dans un avenir proche	*in the close future*
dans la prochaine décennie	*in the next decade*
dans les prochains jours/mois	*in the next days/months*
dans les prochaines heures/semaines	*in the next hours/weeks*
dans la semaine	*during the week, within a week*
dans les 24 heures	*within 24 hours*
dans le courant de la semaine/l'année	*in the course of the week/year*
dans la matinée/journée/soirée	*during the morning/day/evening*
tard **dans** la soirée	*late at night*
dans la nuit	*during the night*
dans les jours/mois/années à venir	*in the coming days/months/years*
dans les heures/jours qui viennent	*in the coming hours/days*
dans les années quarante/cinquante	*in the forties/fifties*
dans ma (ta, sa...) jeunesse	*in my (your, his...) youth*
dans mon (ton, son...) enfance	*in my (your, his...) childhood*
dans l'intervalle	*meanwhile, in the meantime*
dans le temps	*in those days, way back*
dans les siècles passés	*in the past centuries*
dans son sommeil	*in his/her sleep*

But:
dans is generally omitted before 'morning', 'afternoon' and 'evening'

le matin	***in*** *the morning*
l'après-midi	***in*** *the afternoon*
le soir	***in*** *the evening*

11. dans is part of the following expressions

dans ce cas	*in this case*
dans certains cas/tous les cas	*in certain cases/every case*
dans l'intérêt de qn/qch	*in the interest of sb/sth*
C'est **dans** votre intérêt.	*It's in your interest.*
dans l'intérêt de la paix	*in the interest of peace*

dans tous les sens	*in all directions*
être **dans** le même bateau	*to be in the same boat*
être **dans** les bonnes/mauvaises grâces de qn	*to be in sb's good/bad graces*
être **dans** ses pensées	*to be in one's thoughts*
être **dans** le rouge	*to be in the red (financially)*
être **dans** une situation difficile	*to be in a difficult situation*
parler **dans** une autre langue	*to speak in another language*
tomber **dans** le piège	*to fall in the trap*
Ce n'est pas **dans** mes moyens.	*It's not within my means.*

12. The following verbs and expressions introduce the complement with **dans** (see also '*entrer*' p. 125)

avoir confiance **dans** qch	*to have confidence in sth*
Je n'ai pas confiance **dans** l'avenir.	*I have no confidence in the future.*
se jeter **dans** qch	*to flow into sth*
La Loire se jette **dans** l'Atlantique.	*The Loire flows into the Atlantic.*
inclure qn **dans** qch	*to include sb in sth*
Nous vous inclurons **dans** nos prières.	*We will include you in our prayers.*
s'illustrer **dans** qch	*to become famous through sth*
Il s'est illustré **dans** le roman.	*He became famous through the novel.*
mettre de l'ordre **dans** qch	*to tidy sth up*
J'ai mis de l'ordre **dans** mes affaires.	*I tidied up my things.*
persévérer **dans** qch	*to persevere in sth*
Persévérez **dans** cette voie.	*Persevere in this path.*
persister **dans** qch	*to persist in sth*
Il persiste **dans** son erreur.	*He persists in his error.*
se plonger **dans** qch	*to bury oneself in sth*
Il se plonge **dans** son travail.	*He buries himself in his work.*
rentrer **dans** qch (fam.)	*to run into sth*
La voiture est rentrée **dans** un arbre.	*The car ran into a tree.*
sombrer **dans** qch	*to sink into sth*
Il est sombré **dans** la dépression.	*He slipped into depression.*
se tromper **dans** qch	*to be mistaken in sth*
Je me suis trompé **dans** mon choix.	*I was mistaken in my choice.*
verser qch **dans** qch	*to pour sth into sth*
Il a versé le café **dans** un bol.	*He poured the coffee in a bowl.*

13. dans indicates a field of expertise after *'être'* and *'travailler'*

être/travailler **dans** le bâtiment	*to be/work in the building trade*
travailler **dans** l'immobilier/l'édition	*to work in real estate/publishing*
être **dans** les affaires/le commerce	*to be in business*
être **dans** l'enseignement	*to be in the field of teaching*
être **dans** l'hôtellerie	*to be in the hotel business*
être **dans** la restauration	*to be in the catering business*

14. dans translates 'on' (giving a location) in the following expressions

dans l'assiette	***on** the plate*
dans l'avion	***on** the plane*
dans le bus	***on** the bus*
dans le dos (de qn)	***on** the back (of sb)*
dans l'escalier	***on** the stairs*
dans l'examen	***on** the test*
(vivre) **dans** une ferme	*(to live) **on** a farm*
dans une île	***on** an island*
(être assis) **dans** les marches	*(to sit) **on** the steps*
dans un ranch	***on** a ranch*
dans le train	***on** the train*

15. dans translates 'behind' in the following expressions

dans les coulisses (fig.)	***behind** the scenes*
faire qch **dans** le dos de qn	*to do sth **behind** sb's back*
Tout le monde parle **dans** ton dos.	*Everyone talks **behind** your back.*
Tout cela se passait **dans** mon dos.	*All that was going on **behind** my back.*

....

Proverbs, sayings, and idioms

C'est une tempête **dans** un verre d'eau.	*It's a storm in a teacup.*
Dans le doute, abstiens-toi!	*When in doubt, do without!*
Ça me fait froid **dans** le dos.	*That gives me the shivers.*

L'affaire est **dans** le sac. (fam.)	*It's in the bag!*
avoir un chat **dans** la gorge	*to have a frog in one's throat*
avoir l'estomac **dans** les talons (fam.)	*to be famished*
avoir des fourmis **dans** les jambes	*to have pins and needles in the legs*
avoir un pied **dans** la tombe	*to be over the hill*
avoir un poil **dans** la main (fam.)	*to be ultra-lazy*
chercher une aiguille **dans** une botte de foin	*to look for a needle in a haystack*
descendre **dans** un hôtel	*to stay at a hotel*
entrer/vivre **dans** la clandestinité	*to go/live underground*
être **dans** le besoin	*to be in need*
être bien/mal **dans** sa peau	*to feel good/bad about oneself*
être **dans** (or: **sur**) la bonne voie	*to be on the right track*
être **dans** de beaux draps (fam.)	*to be in a fine mess*
être **dans** le doute	*to be in doubt*
être **dans** un état sérieux	*to be in serious condition*
être **dans** une impasse	*to have reached (a) deadlock*
être **dans** la lune	*to be absent-minded*
être **dans** les nuages	*to have one's head in the clouds*
être **dans** le pétrin (fam.)	*to be in a mess, to be in trouble*
être **dans** le secret	*to be in on a secret*
être **dans** son tort	*to be in the wrong*
être **dans** le vent	*to be up-to-date, to be 'in'*
ne pas être **dans** son assiette Je ne suis pas **dans** mon assiette.	*to be in bad shape, not to feel well* *I am not myself, I don't feel well.*
être une épine **dans** l'œil de qn	*to be a thorn in sb's eyes*
faire qch la mort **dans** l'âme	*to do sth with a heavy heart*
(marcher) la main **dans** la main	(*to walk*) *hand in hand*
se mettre le doigt **dans** l'œil (fam.)	*to be entirely mistaken*
mettre **dans** le même sac	*to throw in the same pot*
monter **dans** l'échelle sociale	*to climb up the social ladder*
prêcher **dans** le désert	*to talk to deaf ears*
remuer le couteau **dans** la plaie	*to move the dagger in the wound*

rire **dans** sa barbe	*to laugh up one's sleeve*
tomber **dans** l'excès inverse	*to fall into the other extreme*
tomber **dans** l'oubli	*to fall into oblivion*
tomber **dans** les pommes (fam.)	*to faint, to pass out*
tuer **dans** l'oeuf	*to nip in the bud*
vivre **dans** le luxe/**dans** la misère	*to live in luxury/in poverty*
Dans le livre/**dans** le film/**dans** la pièce, il s'agit de...	*The book/the movie/the play is about...*
Dans l'attente de votre réponse, je...	*Looking forward to your answer, I...*
dans des circonstances étranges	*under strange circumstances*
dans ces conditions	*under these conditions*
dans quelles conditions?	*under which conditions?*
dans les plus brefs délais	*as soon as possible*
dans l'ensemble	*on the whole, by and large*
dans l'espoir de [+ inf.]	*with the hope of (doing)*
dans le fond	*basically*
dans la fleur/force de l'âge	*in the prime of life*
dans l'intention de [+ inf.]	*with the intention of (doing)*
dans l'immédiat	*for the time being*
dans la mesure où	*to the extent that, in so far as*
dans quelle mesure?	*to what extent?*
dans une certaine/large/moindre mesure	*to a certain/large/lesser extent*
dans la mesure du possible	*as far as possible*
dans la pratique	*in practice*
dans le sens (inverse) des aiguilles d'une montre	*(counter) clockwise*
dans le sens de la longueur	*lengthwise*
dans un premier temps	*at first, to begin with*
dans un deuxième temps	*second*
dans la théorie	*in theory*
dans la vie	*in life, for a living*
On ne peut pas tout avoir **dans** la vie.	*One cannot have everything in life.*
Qu'est-ce que vous faites **dans** la vie?	*What do you do for a living?*

Translation difficulties

English 'in' is *not* translated with **dans** but with other prepositions in the following instances[1]

in *the photo/picture*	**sur** la photo/l'image
in *the drawing*	**sur** le dessin
in *the tree*	**sur** l'arbre
in *the chair*	**sur** la chaise
in *the country*	**à la** campagne
in *the sun*	**au** soleil
in *the shade*	**à l'**ombre
in *the warmth*[2]	**au** chaud
in *the 20th century*	**au** 20e siècle
in *spring*	**au** printemps
in *the evening*	**au** soir (or: le soir)
in *the morning*	**au** matin (or: le matin)
to be interested ***in***	s'intéresser **à**, être intéressé **par**
in *all weather*	**par** tous les temps
to be ***in*** *a good/bad mood*	être **de** bonne/**de** mauvaise humeur
the man ***in*** *the street*	l'homme **de** la rue
at 3 o'clock ***in*** *the morning*	à trois heures **du** matin
at two o'clock ***in*** *the afternoon*	à deux heures **de l'**après-midi
at 8 o'clock ***in*** *the evening*	à huit heures **du** soir
in *the rain*	**sous** la pluie
in *the shower*	**sous** la douche
in *(a state of) shock*	**sous** le choc
in *1960*	**en** 1960
in *May*	**en** mai
in *summer*	**en** été
in *fall*	**en** automne
in *winter*	**en** hiver
in [+ name of a language]	**en**
in *Spanish*	**en** espagnol

---

1. See also p. 149 #5 and p. 168 #4
2. But: ***in*** *the cold* = **dans** le froid

in [+ time period] (meaning 'within')	**en**
*to do sth **in** (= within) 10 minutes*	faire qch **en** dix minutes
in [+ unmodified feminine country]	**en**
in Italy	**en** Italie
in [+ unmodified masculine country]	**au**
in Denmark	**au** Danemark
in [+ city name]	**à**
in New York	**à** New York

Mistakes to avoid

Incorrect	*Correct*	*English meaning*
J'entre la chambre.	J'entre **dans** la chambre.	*I enter the room.*

G. The preposition **chez**

The preposition **chez** is used

1. with *persons* to express 'at/to the home/house of'

Elle est rentrée **chez** elle[1] à minuit.	*She came home at midnight.*
Ils sont allés **chez** eux.[1]	*They went home.*
Il nous a invités **chez** lui.[1]	*He invited us to his house.*
En France, beaucoup d'étudiants habitent **chez** leurs parents.	*In France, many students live with (= at the home of) their parents.*
Ce soir, nous dînons **chez** Pierre.	*Tonight, we are having dinner at Pierre's.*
Il y a une fête **chez** les Duval.	*There is a party at (the home of) the Duvals.*
Il a passé la nuit **chez** des amis.	*He spent the night with/at the home of friends.*
Je suis resté **chez** moi[1] toute la journée.	*I stayed at home all day.*

---

1. Note that stressed pronouns are used after '*chez*'.

2. with *persons* to express 'at/to the office of', 'at/to the store of', 'at/to the business of'

J'ai rendez-vous **chez** le dentiste.	*I have an appointment at the dentist's.*
Je vais **chez** le médecin.	*I am going to the doctor's (office).*
Elle va/est **chez** le coiffeur.	*She goes to/is at the hairdresser('s).*
chez le boulanger	*to the baker, at the baker's*
chez le boucher	*to the butcher, at the butcher's*
chez le cordonnier	*to the shoemaker, at the shoemaker's*
chez l'épicier	*to the grocer, at the grocer's*
chez le fleuriste	*to the florist, at the florist's*
chez l'opticien	*to the optician, at the optician's*
chez le pharmacien	*to the pharmacist, at the pharmacist's*
chez le poissonnier	*to the fishmonger, at the fishmonger's*
chez le tailleur	*to the tailor, at the tailor's*
chez le marchand de vin	*to the wine merchant, at the wine merchant's*
chez le pâtissier	*to the pastry baker, at the pastry baker's*

Note:

- **chez** can only be followed by a proper name or by a noun or pronoun representing a *person*

Elle achète des croissants **chez** le boulanger.	*She buys croissants at the baker's.*

  With stores, **à** + *article* must be used

à la boulangerie	*to/at the bakery*
à la boucherie	*to/at the butchery*
à l'épicerie	*to/at the grocery*
à la pâtisserie	*to/at the pastry shop*
à la pharmacie	*to/at the pharmacy*
Elle achète des croissants **à la** boulangerie.	*She buys croissants at the bakery.*

- In informal French, **à** is sometimes used instead of **chez**

Je suis allé **au** médecin.	*I went to the doctor.*
Elle est allée **au** coiffeur.	*She went to the hairdresser.*

3. with a *publisher* or a *business* which has the name of the founder or owner

Son roman est paru **chez** Hachette.	*His novel was published by Hachette.*
Ses poèmes ont été publiés **chez** Gallimard.	*His poems were published by Gallimard.*
Mon père travaille **chez** Peugeot.	*My father works for the Peugeot company.*
Elle s'habille (= achète ses vêtements) **chez** Givenchy.	*She buys her clothes at Givenchy's.*
Nous avons dîné **chez** Bocuse.	*We had dinner at Bocuse's (restaurant).*
Mangeons **chez** McDo.	*Let's eat at McDonald's.*

4. with a *group of people* or a *nation* to express 'in/to the country of' or 'among'

Cela se fait **chez** les Européens mais pas **chez** nous.	*That is done in Europe but not in our country.*
Le chômage **chez** les jeunes a baissé.	*Unemployment among young people has decreased.*
Cette maladie se trouve surtout **chez** les personnes âgées.	*This illness is most common among the elderly.*
Chez les catholiques, the mariage civil n'est pas reconnu.	*Among Catholics, the civil wedding is not recognized.*
Le suicide est la deuxième cause de mortalité (après les accidents de la circulation) **chez** les 15 à 24 ans en France.	*Suicide is the number two killer (after traffic accidents) among the 15 to 24 olds in France.*

5. with the name of an *author* to express 'in the work of'

Il y a beaucoup de néologismes **chez** Rabelais.	*There are many neologisms in the work of Rabelais.*
J'ai trouvé cette citation **chez** Molière.	*I found this quote in the work of Molière.*

6. to refer to a *person's character* or *looks*, expressing 'about', 'in' or 'with'

Cela ne me surprend pas **chez** elle.	*That doesn't surprise me **about** her.*
Chez lui, c'est une obsession.	***With** him, that's an obsession.*
C'est rare **chez** un enfant de cet âge.	*That's rare **in** a child of that age.*
Qu'est-ce que tu regardes en premier **chez** une femme?	*What are you looking at first **in** a woman?*
Ce qui est surprenant **chez** toi, c'est ton énergie.	*What is surprising **about** you is your energy.*
Qu'est-ce que vous aimez **chez** ces gens?	*What do you like **about** these people?*

Mistakes to avoid

Incorrect	*Correct*	*English meaning*
Je vais ~~à~~ chez moi.[1]	Je vais **chez** moi.	*I am going home.*

Proverbs, sayings, and idioms

C'est toujours mieux **chez** le voisin que **chez** soi.[2]	*The grass is always greener on the other side.*
On n'est nulle part aussi bien que **chez** soi.	*East or west, home is best.*
Faites comme **chez** vous.	*Make yourself at home.*

---

1. **chez** can be preceded by other prepositions

Il habite **près de chez** moi.	*He lives close to my home.*
La boulangerie est **en face de chez** lui.	*The bakery is across from his house.*
C'est **à côté de chez** toi.	*It's next to your house.*
Elle a été tuée **devant chez** elle.	*She was killed in front of her house.*
Cette robe vient **de chez** Dior.	*This dress comes from Dior's business.*

but **chez** can be preceded by **à** *only* when **à** follows **de**

J'ai pris un taxi ***de*** la gare ***à*** **chez** moi.	*I took a taxi **from** the train station **to** my house.*

2. lit.: *It's always better at the neighbor's than at one's own home.*

H. The preposition **sur**

1. **sur** indicates a location expressing 'on'

sur l'auroroute	*on the expressway*
sur (or: **dans**) l'avenue[1]	*on the avenue*
Elle habite **sur** la Cinquième Avenue.	*She lives on Fifth Avenue.*
sur le boulevard[1]	*on the boulevard*
sur Canal Plus	*on Canal Plus* [TV]
sur la première chaîne	*on channel one* [TV]
sur la une[2]/la deux	*on channel one/two* [TV]
sur le canapé	*on the couch*
sur la carte	*on the map, on the menu*
sur la côte (est/ouest)	*on the (west/east) coast*
sur le côté (droit, gauche)	*on the (right, left) side*
sur la (ma, ta, sa...) droite[3]	*on the (my, your, his, her...) right*
sur l'écran	*on the screen*
sur le petit écran	*on TV*
sur les étals du supermarché	*on the shelves of the supermarket*
sur la/votre gauche[3]	*on the/your left*
sur l'herbe	*on the grass*
sur (l') internet (= **sur** le net)	*on the internet, on the WEB*
sur le mur	*on the wall*
sur le pas de la porte	*on the doorstep*
sur place	*on the premises, on site*
sur la place[1]	*on the square*
sur la plage (or: **à** la plage)	*on the beach*
sur le plancher	*on the floor*
sur le plancher des vaches (fam.)	*on firm ground*
sur la route	*on the road*
sur (la) scène	*on (the) stage*
sur (la) terre	*on earth*

---

1. But:
When avenues, boulevards and squares are accompanied by a *name*, there is usually *no* preposition and *no* article before them.

Les grands couturiers ont leurs boutiques **Avenue** Montaigne.	*The big fashion designers have their stores* ***on*** *Montaigne Avenue.*
Je l'ai croisé **Boulevard** Raspail.	*I ran into him* ***on*** *Raspail Boulevard.*
On s'est donné rendez-vous **Boulevard** Saint-Michel.	*We agreed to meet* ***on*** *St. Michel Boulevard.*
Il y avait une manifestation **Place** de la Bastille.	*There was a demonstration* ***on*** *Bastille Square.*

2. But: **à** la une = ***on*** *the title page* [of a newspaper]
3. Also: **à** droite = ***on*** *the right* **à** gauche = ***on*** *the left*

sur terre et **sur** mer	*on land and sea*
sur le toit	*on the roof*
sur le trottoir	*on the sidewalk*
sur un vol	*on a flight*
Mettez le vase **sur** la table.	*Put the vase on the table.*
mettre une robe **sur** un cintre	*to put a dress on a hanger*
As-tu un stylo **sur** toi?	*Do you have a pen on you?*
Je n'ai pas d'argent **sur** moi.	*I don't have any money on me.*
laisser un message **sur** le répondeur	*to leave a message on the answering machine*

2. **sur** between *numerals* expresses 'out of (every)', 'in' indicating a proportion

Aux USA, un couple **sur** deux divorce.	*In the USA, one out of every two couples divorces.*
Dans un dictionnaire anglais, plus d'un terme **sur** deux est d'origine française.	*In an English dictionary, more than one out of every two terms is of French origin.*
Un Français **sur** six habite à Paris.	*One out of every six Frenchmen lives in Paris.*
Ce magasin est ouvert 24 heures **sur** 24, sept jours **sur** sept.	*This store is open around the clock, seven days a week.*
Aujourd'hui, un enfant **sur** cinq a des parents qui ne sont pas mariés.	*Today, one out of every five children has parents who are not married.*
Le professeur m'a mis 13 **sur** 20 pour ma rédaction.	*The teacher gave me 13 out of 20 for my composition.*
une chance **sur** mille	*one chance in a thousand*
un jour **sur** deux[1]	*every other day*
une semaine **sur** trois	*one week in three*
un week-end **sur** deux	*every other week-end*
un mardi **sur** deux	*every other Tuesday*
Vous avez une chance **sur** deux d'identifier ces deux personnes.	*You have a fifty-fifty chance to identify these two people.*

---

1. Or: tous les deux jours

3. **sur** between two identical nouns indicates *accumulation* and expresses 'after'

faire proposition **sur** proposition	*to make offer after offer*
commettre erreur **sur** erreur	*to make mistake after mistake*
J'ai eu grippe **sur** grippe.	*I had one flu after the other.*
Il a eu deux réussites coup **sur** coup.	*He had two successes one after the other.*

4. **sur** indicates the *subject matter* expressing 'about', 'on'

un article **sur** la révolution	*an article about the revolution*
une étude **sur** le communisme	*a study on/about communism*
un livre **sur** la deuxième guerre mondiale	*a book about the Second World War*

5. in measurements, **sur** combines two *dimensions* expressing 'by'

Le tapis mesure trois mètres **sur** deux.	*The rug measures three meters **by** two.*
Ma chambre a cinq mètres de long **sur** quatre de large.	*My room is five meters long **by** four meters wide.*

6. **sur** introduces the object in the following *verbal expressions*

s'accorder **sur** qch	*to agree about/on sth*
agir **sur** qch	*to act upon/have an effect on sth*
alerter qn **sur** qch	*to alert sb to sth*
s'apitoyer **sur** qn	*to feel sorry for sb*
appuyer **sur** qch	*to press sth*
appuyer **sur** un bouton	*to press a button*
s'appuyer **sur** qch	*to lean/depend/rely on*
Il s'appuya **sur** mon bras.	*He leaned on my arm.*
s'asseoir **sur** qch	*to sit down on sth*
Elle s'est assise **sur** un banc.	*She sat down on a bench.*
s'attarder **sur** qch	*to dwell on sth* [a subject]
attirer l'attention de qn **sur** qch	*to draw sb's attention to sth*
Je voudrais attirer votre attention **sur**...	*I'd like to draw your attention to...*
avoir/se faire une opinion **sur** qch	*to have/form an opinion on sth*

compter **sur** qn/qch	*to count/depend on sb/sth*
Je compte **sur** toi.	*I count on you.*
se concentrer **sur** qch	*to concentrate on sth*
copier **sur** qn	*to copy from sb*
Il copie **sur** son voisin.	*He copies from his neighbor.*
déboucher **sur** qch	*to open onto, to lead to, to result in*
A Paris, un mariage **sur** deux débouche **sur** un divorce.	*In Paris, one out of two marriages ends in a divorce.*
donner **sur**	*to face, to look out on, to overlook*
La fenêtre donne **sur** la mer.	*The window goes out on the ocean.*
économiser **sur** qch	*to save on sth*
s'écraser **sur** qch	*to crash into sth*
écrire qch **sur** qn/qch	*to write sth about sb/sth*
l'emporter **sur** qn	*to beat/defeat sb* [team, candidate]
Il l'a emporté **sur** son adversaire.	*He defeated his opponent.*
l'emporter **sur** qch	*to override/outweigh sth*
En français, le masculin l'emporte toujours **sur** le féminin.	*In French, the masculine always overrides the feminine.*
enchérir **sur** qn/qch	*to bid more than sb/to make a higher bid on sth*
Personne n'a enchéri **sur** moi.	*Nobody bid more than I.*
enquêter **sur** qch	*to carry out an investigation into sth*
épargner **sur** qch	*to save on sth*
être/se mettre d'accord **sur** qch	*to agree about/on sth*
Ils sont d'accord **sur** ce point.	*They agree about that.*
être en avance **sur** qn/qch	*to be ahead of sb/sth*
Cet enfant est en avance **sur** les autres.	*This child is ahead of the others.*
Il est (très) en avance **sur** son temps.	*He is (far) ahead of his time.*
être strict **sur** qch	*to be strict about sth*
Il est strict **sur** la propreté.	*He is strict about cleanliness.*
faire feu **sur** qn	*to fire at sb*
faire le point **sur** qch	*to give an up-to-the minute report on*
faire pression **sur** qn	*to put pressure on sb*
focaliser **sur** qch	*to focus on sth*
foncer **sur** qn/qch	*to charge at sb, to dash for sth*
Il a foncé **sur** moi.	*He charged at me.*
Ils ont foncé **sur** la sortie.	*They dashed for the exit.*
influer **sur** qn/qch	*to have an influence on sb/sth*

insister **sur** qch	*to insist on sth, to stress sth*
interroger qn **sur** qch	*to question sb about sth*
s'interroger **sur** qch	*to wonder about sth*
jeter un coup d'œil **sur**	*to glance at*
juger qn **sur** qch	*to judge sb by sth*
Ne jugez pas les gens **sur** leurs apparences.	*Don't judge people by their appearance.*
jurer **sur** qn/qch	*to swear on sb/sth*
Je le jure **sur** la tête de ma mère.	*I swear it on my mother's life.*
se lamenter **sur** (or: **de**) qch	*to moan about sth*
lésiner **sur** qch	*to be stingy with/skimp on sth*
ne pas lésiner **sur** qch	*to be liberal with sth* [money, etc.]
ne pas lésiner **sur** la dépense	*to spare no expense*
se méprendre **sur** qch	*to be wrong/mistaken about sth*
mettre l'accent **sur** qch	*to emphasize sth*
mettre la main **sur** qch	*to confiscate/lay one's hand on sth*
miser **sur** [un cheval/le rouge/le dix]	*to (place a) bet on* [a horse/red/ten]
(s')ouvrir **sur** qch	*to open on to sth*
Cette porte (s')ouvre **sur** le jardin.	*This door opens on to the garden.*
parier **sur** qch	*to bet on sth*
se pencher **sur** qch	*to bend over sth, to look into sth*
Il s'est penché **sur** ce problème.	*He looked into this problem.*
pleurer **sur** qch	*to shed tears over sth*
porter (un) jugement **sur** qn	*to pass judgment on sb*
poser des questions **sur** qn/qch	*to ask questions about sb/sth*
se précipiter **sur** qn/qch	*to throw oneself on sb, to rush at/toward sth*
prendre exemple **sur** qn	*to follow the example of sb*
Prenez exemple **sur** lui.	*Follow his example.*
prendre le pas **sur** qn/qch	*to override/take the lead over sb/sth*
questionner qn **sur** qch	*to ask sb about sth*
se rabattre **sur** qch	*to make do with/settle for sth*
raconter qch **sur** qn	*to say sth about sb*
Elle est très au courant de ce qu'on raconte **sur** elle.	*She is very well informed about what one says about her.*
réfléchir **sur** (or: **à**) qch	*to think about sth*
J'ai réfléchi **sur** ce problème.	*I thought about this problem.*

renchérir **sur** qn/qch	*to outdo sb/sth*
Elle renchérit **sur** son frère.	*She outdoes her brother.*
se renseigner **sur** qn/qch	*to inquire about sb/sth, to ask for/ get information about sb/sth*
Je voudrais me renseigner **sur** les caméscopes.	*I would like to get some information about camcorders.*
renseigner qn **sur** qch	*to inform sb about sth*
se retourner **sur** qn	*to turn to look at sb*
Elle est si belle que tous les hommes se retournent **sur** elle.	*She is so beautiful that all men turn to look at her.*
revenir **sur** qch	*to go back on sth* [decision, promise...]
Il ne va pas revenir **sur** sa décision/ promesse/déclaration.	*He is not going to go back on his decision/promise/declaration.*
se ruer **sur** qn/qch	*to pounce on sb/sth*
savoir qch **sur** (or: **de**) qn/qch	*to know sth about sb/sth*
Elle sait peu de choses **sur** ce poème.	*She knows little about this poem.*
Il ne sait rien **sur** moi.	*He knows nothing about me.*
se taire **sur** qch	*to keep quiet about sth*
tirer **sur** qn	*to shoot/fire at sb*
tirer un trait **sur** qch	*to put sth behind one*
tomber **sur** qch/qn	*to come across sth, to run into sb*
travailler **sur** qch	*to work on sth*
se tromper **sur** qch	*to be mistaken about sth*
veiller **sur** qn/qch	*to watch over sb/sth*

7. sur is part of the following expressions

faire **sur** mesure	*to make to order*
un complet fait **sur** mesure	*a custom-made suit*
C'est **sur** mon chemin.	*It's on my way.*
s'inscrire **sur** des listes électorales	*to register to vote*
marcher **sur** pile	*to run on batteries*
mettre **sur** orbite	*to put into orbit, to launch*
naviguer **sur** le net	*to surf on the net*
noter qch **sur** son carnet	*to note sth in one's notebook*
appeler qn **sur** son portable[1]	*to call sb on one's cellphone*

---

1. But: parler **au** téléphone = *to speak* ***on*** *the phone*

regarder **sur** le bottin	*to look in the phonebook*

8. **sur** is part of the following nouns

une assurance **sur** la vie	*life insurance*
l'impôt **sur** le revenu/**sur** la fortune	*income/wealth tax*
des œufs **sur** le plat	*scrambled eggs*
le hockey **sur** glace	*ice hockey*
le **sur**nom	*the nickname*
des médicaments vendus **sur** ordonnance	*prescription drugs*

9. **sur** expresses 'from' in the following expressions

sur le plan [+ adj.]	***from*** *a* [+ adj.] *point of view*
sur le plan professionnel	***from*** *a professional point of view*
sur le plan de [+ article + nom]	***from*** *the point of view of, as far as...is concerned*
sur le plan de la nourriture/de l'efficacité	*as far as food/efficiency is concerned*

10. **sur** expresses 'in' with the following expressions

sur la photo/**sur** l'image	***in*** *the picture*
sur l'arbre	***in*** *the tree*
sur la chaise	***in*** *the chair*
sur le parking	***in*** *the parking lot*
sur la banquette arrière	***in*** *the back seat*
sur la voie de droite/de gauche	***in*** *the right/left lane*
laisser la clé **sur** la porte/**sur** la serrure	*to leave the key* ***in*** *the door/****in*** *the keyhole*

11. **sur** expresses 'by' in the expression

sur rendez-vous	***by*** *appointment*

12. **sur** expresses 'upon', 'at' in the following expressions

sur demande	***upon*** *request*
sur la demande de	***at*** *the request of*

Sayings and idioms

C'est la cerise **sur** le gâteau.	*It's the icing on the cake.*
Je l'ai **sur** le bout de la langue.	*It's on the tip of my tongue.*
avoir pignon **sur** rue	*to be well-established* [business]
avoir qch **sur** le cœur	*to have sth on one's heart*
avoir le coeur **sur** la main	*to be open-handed, to be kindhearted*
avoir/garder les pieds **sur** terre	*to have/keep one's feet firmly on the ground, to be down to earth*
ne pas avoir les pieds **sur** terre	*to be a dreamer*
se compter **sur** les doigts d'une seule main	*not to be very numerous*
Mes amis intimes se comptent **sur** les doigts d'une seule main.	*I have few close friends.*
s'endormir/se reposer **sur** ses lauriers	*to rest on one's laurels*
être **sur** des charbons ardents	*to be on pins and needles*
être **sur** le bon chemin/**sur** la bonne voie	*to be on the right track, to be heading in the right direction*
être/rester **sur** ses gardes	*to be/remain on one's guard*
être **sur** la même longueur d'onde	*to be on the same wave-length*
être **sur** les genoux (fam.)	*to be on one's last legs/very tired*
être **sur** le pavé	*to be without a job/out on the street*
être **sur** le point de (faire qch)	*to be about to (do sth)*
être **sur** le qui-vive	*to be on the look-out/on the alert*
être **sur** le sentier de la/**sur** le pied de guerre	*to be on the warpath/a war footing*
être **sur** son trente-et-un (fam.)	*to be dressed up to the nines*
jeter/verser de l'huile **sur** le feu	*to add fuel to the fire*
ne pas savoir **sur** quel pied danser	*not to know what to do*
manger **sur** le pouce	*to grab a bite, to eat in a hurry*
parler **sur** un ton irrité/aimable	*to speak in an irritated/friendly voice*
Ne me parlez pas **sur** ce ton!	*Don't speak to me in that tone!*
prendre sa revanche **sur** qn	*to get even with sb, to take one's revenge*
se replier **sur** soi-même	*to become withdrawn, to shut one-self off from the rest of the world*

revenir/retourner **sur** ses pas	*to retrace one's steps*
rouler **sur** l'or	*to be rolling in money*
taper **sur** les nerfs de qn	*to get on sb's nerves*
Tu me tapes **sur** les nerfs.	*You get on my nerves.*
trier **sur** le volet	*to handpick*
vivre **sur** un grand pied	*to live like a lord*
sur ce	*upon which, thereupon, and now*
sur le coup	*instantly, on the spot*
sur le chemin du retour	*on the way back*
sur la pointe des pieds	*on tiptoe*
marcher **sur** la pointe des pieds	*to tiptoe*
sur le tard	*late in life*
sur toute la ligne	*all along the line*
sur le vif	*candid (photo), on the spot, live*
C'est écrit/marqué noir **sur** blanc.	*It's there in black and white.*
Elle va **sur** ses 50 ans.	*She is in her late forties.*

Translation difficulties

Frequently, English 'on' is *not* translated with **sur**, but with other prepositions.

- **on** is translated with **à** (+ def. article) in the following expressions

on TV	**à la** télé
on the radio	**à la** radio
on the news	**aux** informations
on Valentine's Day	**à la** Saint-Valentin
on page five	**à la** page cinq
on the test	**à l'**examen
on New Year's Eve	**à la** Saint-Sylvestre
on All Saint's Day	**à la** Toussaint
on Mother's Day	**à la** Fête des Mères

- **on** is translated with **dans** in expressions such as[1]

on the (intercity) bus	**dans** le car
on the train	**dans** le train

---

1. For a more detailed list of these expressions see p. 128 #14

- **on** is translated with **de** in the expression

on the other side	**de** l'autre côté
on the other side of the border	**de** l'autre côté de la frontière

- **on** is translated with **pour** in the expression

to spend money **on** sth	dépenser de l'argent **pour** qch

- **on** is *not* translated with weekdays[1] and dates

on Sunday	dimanche
on the second of January	le deux janvier

Mistakes to avoid

Incorrect	*Correct*	*English meaning*
~~sur~~ lundi	lundi	*on Monday*
~~sur~~ le week-end	**le** week-end	*on the weekend*
~~sur~~ le trois mars	**le** trois mars	*on the third of March*
Nous avons mangé ~~sur~~ l'avion/le train.	Nous avons mangé **dans**[2] l'avion/le train.	*We ate **on** the plane/train.*

I The preposition **sous**

1. **sous** indicates a *location* expressing 'under', 'underneath'

Le chat est **sous** le canapé.	*The cat is under the sofa.*
Ils se sont abrités **sous** un arbre.	*They took shelter under a tree.*

2. **sous** refers to a *time period under a ruler*

sous (le règne de) Louis XIV	*under (the reign of) Louis XIV*
sous (la présidence de) de Gaulle	*under (the presidency of) de Gaulle*
sous Mitterrand	*under Mitterrand*

---

1. 'le' expresses 'on' before a weekday when a repetition of the weekday is indicated: **le** samedi = **on** Saturdays

2. But: **sur** le vol = *on the flight*

3. **sous** is part of numerous nouns

la **sous**-alimentation	*the malnutrition*
le **sous**-bois	*the undergrowth*
le **sous**-directeur	*the assistant manager*
le **sous**-emploi	*the under-employment*
le **sous**-entendu	*the innuendo*
le **sous**-locataire	*the subtenant*
le **sous**-main	*the desk blotter*
le **sous**-marin	*the submarine*
le **sous**-sol	*the basement*
le **sous**-titre	*the subtitle*
le **sous**-vêtement	*the undergarment*

4. **sous** is part of certain adjectives

sous-alimenté	*malnourished*
sous-développé	*underdeveloped*
sous-équipé	*underequipped*
sous-rémunéré	*underpaid*
sous-titré	*subtitled*
sous-peuplé	*underpopulated*

5. **sous** is part of certain verbs

sous-entendre	*to imply*
sous-estimer	*to underestimate*
sous-louer	*to sublet, to sublease*
sous-payer	*to underpay*
sous-traiter	*to subcontract, to contract out*
sous-utiliser	*to underuse*

6. **sous** is used in the following expressions

sous certaines conditions	*on certain conditions*
sous l'influence de	*under the influence of*
sous prétexte [+ de + inf.]	*on the pretext of*
avoir qch **sous** la main	*to have sth at hand*
As-tu un stylo **sous** la main?	*Do you have a pen at hand?*
avoir qch **sous** les yeux	*to have sth before one's eyes*
sous peine de [+ noun]	*under penalty of, at the risk of*
Défense de fumer **sous** peine d'amende.	*If you smoke, you have to pay a fine.*

sous les verrous	*under lock and key*
sous peu	*shortly, before long*
ne rien avoir à se mettre **sous** la dent	*to have nothing to eat*
être né **sous** une bonne étoile	*to have been born under a lucky star*
(mentir, déclarer) **sous** serment	*(to lie, to declare) under oath*
(voir qch) **sous** un jour favorable	*(to see sth) in a favorable light*
Je ne vois pas les choses **sous** le même jour que vous.	*I don't see things in the same light as you.*
mettre qch **sous** clef	*to lock sth up*
sous réserve de qch	*subject to sth*
sous réserve de disponibilité	*subject to availability*

7. **sous** translates 'in' in expressions such as[1]

sous la neige	***in*** *the snow*
sous un temps ensoleillé	***in*** *sunny weather*
sous ces latitudes	***in*** *these latitudes*
sous toutes les latitudes	***in*** *all parts of the world*
dormir **sous** la tente	*to sleep* ***in*** *a tent*
sous forme de	***in*** *the form of*

J. The preposition **avec**

1. **avec** expresses 'with'

- indicating the *means*

Il allume la cigarette **avec** une allumette.	*He lights the cigarette with a match.*
Nous voyons **avec** les yeux et nous entendons **avec** les oreilles.	*We see with the eyes and we hear with the ears.*

- indicating an *accompaniment*

Je travaille **avec** lui.	*I work with him.*
J'ai amené ma fille **avec** moi.	*I brought my daughter with me.*
Elle sort **avec** son fiancé ce soir.	*She goes out with her fiancé tonight.*

---

1. For more expressions translating 'in' by 'sous', see p. 131

2. avec can have the meaning of 'malgré' (= *in spite of*)

Avec tout son argent, il n'est pas heureux.	*In spite of all his money, he is not happy.*

3. avec + noun (without article) often replaces an *adverb of manner* or is used in place of an adverb when no adverb exists

avec courage (= courageusement)	*courageously*
avec passion (= passionnément)	*passionately*
avec plaisir	*gladly*
avec enthousiasme	*enthusiastically*
avec prudence (= prudemment)	*carefully*
avec impatience (= impatiemment)	*impatiently*
avec soin (= soigneusement)	*carefully*
avec joie (= joyeusement)	*joyfully*

4. avec introduces the object in the following expressions

aller de pair **avec** qch	*to go hand in hand with sth*
avoir qch à voir **avec**	*to have sth to do with*
Qu'est-ce que ça a à voir **avec**...?	*What does this have to do with...?*
Ça n'a rien à voir **avec** ça.	*This has nothing to do with that.*
causer **avec** qn	*to chat with sb*
communiquer **avec** qn	*to communicate with sb*
comparer qn/qch **avec** (or: **à**) qch	*to compare sb/sth to sb/sth*
correspondre **avec** qn	*to correspond with sb*
coucher **avec** qn	*to sleep/have sex with sb*
divorcer d'**avec** qn	*to divorce sb*
Il a divorcé d'**avec** sa deuxième femme.	*He divorced his second wife.*
s'entendre bien **avec** qn	*to get along well with sb*
entrer en collision **avec** qch	*to collide with sth*
s'entretenir **avec** qn	*to talk to sb, to converse with sb*
être/se mettre d'accord **avec** qn	*to agree/come to an agreement with [sb*
Je suis d'accord **avec** vous.	*I agree with you.*
être en opposition **avec** qn/qch	*to be in opposition to sb/sth*
se fâcher **avec** qn[1]	*to fall out with sb*
être fâché **avec** qn	*to have fallen out with sb*

---

1. But: se fâcher **contre** qn = *to get angry* ***with*** *(= mad at) sb*

être familiarisé **avec** qch	*to be familiar with sth*
être fiancé **avec** qn	*to be engaged to sb*
être froid **avec** (or: **envers**) qn	*to be cold toward sb*
être gentil/sympa/méchant **avec** qn	*to be nice/mean to sb*
Soyez gentil **avec** moi!	*Be nice to me!*
être incompatible **avec** qn/qch	*to be incompatible with sb/sth*
être marié **avec** (or: **à**) qn	*to be married to sb*
se familiariser **avec** qch	*to familiarize oneself with sth*
finir **avec** qch	*to put an end to sth*
s'identifier **avec** qn/qch	*to identify with sb/sth*
se marier/se fiancer **avec** qn	*to get married/engaged to sb*
parler **avec** qn	*to speak with sb*
rivaliser **avec** qn	*to rival/compete with sb*
rompre **avec** qn	*to break up with sb*
sympathiser **avec** qn	*to sympathize with sb*

5. In informal French, **avec** expresses 'in' in the following expressions

avec cette chaleur/ce froid	***in*** *this heat/cold*
avec ce verglas	***in*** *this icy weather*

Proverbs, sayings, and idioms

Il ne faut pas jouer **avec** le feu.	*One must not play with the fire.*
Il faut hurler **avec** les loups.[1]	*When you are in Rome, do as the Romans do.*
jeter le bébé **avec** l'eau du bain (fam.)	*to throw the baby out with the bath water*
se lever **avec** le jour	*to get up at daybreak*
téléphoner **avec** préavis	*to call person to person*
avec des glaçons	*on the rocks* [drink]
Et **avec** ceci, Monsieur/Madame?	*Anything else, Sir/Madam?*
avec les années	*over the years*

1. lit.: *One must howl with the wolves.*

Translation difficulties

Frequently, 'with' is *not* translated with **avec**, but with other prepositions

- **de** means 'with' after the following verbs, adjectives and past participles[1]

être/tomber amoureux **de**	*to be/fall in love **with***
être content/ mécontent **de**	*to be pleased/unsatisfied **with***
Es-tu content **de** ta chambre?	*Are you pleased **with** your room?*
faire qch **de** qn/qch	*to do sth **with** sb/sth*
Qu'est-ce que je vais faire **de** toi?	*What am I going to do **with** you?*
Qu'est-ce que j'ai fait **de** mes clés?	*What did I do **with** my keys?*
couvert **de**	*covered **with***
rempli **de**	*filled **with***

- **contre** means 'with' in the following expressions

se fâcher **contre** qn/qch	*to get angry **with** sb/sth*
être fâché **contre** qn/qch	*to be angry **with** sb/sth*
être furieux **contre** qn	*to be furious **with** sb*
se mettre en colère **contre** qn/qch	*to get angry **with** sb/sth*

- **à** means 'with' when a physical feature of a person is indicated[2]

la dame **aux** cheveux cendrés	*the lady **with** the ashblond hair*
un homme **aux** pommettes saillantes	*a man **with** the high cheekbones*
Don Quichotte est le chevalier **à** la triste figure.	*Don Quixote is the knight **with** the sad face.*

- **chez** means 'with' when the home of a person is referred to

Elle habite **chez** ses parents.	*She lives **with** her parents.*

---

1. See also p. 50-51, p. 55 #7, p. 57-58 #12 and p. 64 #22
2. See also p. 29

K. The preposition **sans**

1. **sans** expresses 'without'

Elle est venue **sans** ses enfants.	*She came without her children.*
Pourquoi es-tu parti **sans** moi?	*Why did you leave without me?*
Buvez-vous votre café avec ou **sans** sucre?	*Do you drink your coffee with or without sugar?*
un jus d'orange **sans** glaçons	*an orange juice without ice*
un chèque **sans** provision[1]	*a bad check*
un escargot **sans** coquille	*a snail without shell*

2. **sans** is used in the following expressions

sans arrêt	*incessantly, constantly*
sans but	*aimlessly*
sans ça	*otherwise*
sans cesse	*incessantly, continuously*
C'est **sans** danger.	*It's safe.*
sans difficulté	*without difficulty*
sans doute	*without doubt*
sans égard pour	*without regard for*
C'est **sans** espoir.	*It's hopeless.*
sans faute	*without fail, definitely*
sans fin	*endless*
sans importance	*unimportant*
sans intérêt	*uninteresting*
sans lendemain	*shortlived*
sans pitié	*merciless*
sans plus	*that's all, nothing more*
sans préjugés	*unprejudiced, unbiased*
sans réserve	*without any reservations*
être **sans** le sou	*to be broke, to be penniless*
sans suite	*discontinued*

---

1. lit.: *a check without funds*

3. sans is used with a following infinitive

Je ne crois pas qu'on puisse vraiment connaître un pays **sans** savoir sa langue.	*I don't believe that one can get to know a country well without knowing its language.*
Je n'irai pas **sans** être invité.	*I will not go without being invited.*

4. sans is part of the following nouns

un **sans**-abri	*a homeless person*
le **sans**-culotte[1]	*the sans-culotte*
les **sans** domicile fixe (= les SDF)	*the homeless*
un **sans**-gêne	*an ill-mannered person*
un **sans**-papiers	*an illegal immigrant*
les **sans**-emploi	*the unemployed*

Proverbs, sayings, and idioms

Il n'y a pas de fumée **sans** feu.	*Where there is smoke, there is fire.*
Il n'y a pas de roses **sans** épines.	*There is no rose without thorns.*
On ne fait pas d'omelette **sans** casser des œufs.	*One can't make an omelette without breaking eggs.*
Un repas **sans** vin est comme un jour **sans** soleil. (Brillat-Savarin)	*A meal without wine is like a day without sunshine.*
Ça va **sans** dire.	*That goes without saying.*
sans façon	*casual* [meal], *without fuss*
un dîner **sans** façon	*an informal dinner*
Il a accepté **sans** façon notre offre.	*He accepted our offer without fuss.*
(Non) merci, **sans** façon.	*No thank you, honestly/really.*
ne pas être **sans** savoir que...	*to know very well that...*
Vous n'êtes pas **sans** savoir que...	*You know very well that...*
sans rime ni raison	*without rhyme or reason*
sans blague! (fam.)	*no kidding!*

1. Name given to those Parisian revolutionaries who wore striped pants instead of the 'culotte' (= knee-breeches), which was a symbol of the 'Ancien Regime', i.e. the monarchy before the French Revolution of 1789.

L. The preposition **avant**

1. avant expresses 'before' in time

Venez **avant** midi!	*Come before noon!*
avant la guerre	*before the war*
avant le dîner	*before dinner*
en l'an 50 **avant** Jésus-Christ	*in the year 50 BC*

2. avant can express 'before' in space in some instances

juste **avant** le pont	*just before the bridge*
J'étais **avant** vous.	*I was before you.*
On met les pronoms **avant** le verbe.	*One puts the pronouns before the verb.*

3. avant + *determiner* + *noun* frequently replaces the conjunction *avant que* + subordinate clause

avant ta naissance (= avant que tu sois né)	*before you were born*
avant son départ (= avant qu'il soit parti)	*before he left*

4. avant is followed by 'de' when used with an infinitive

Il faut réfléchir **avant de** prendre une décision.	*One must think before making a decision.*

5. avant is part of the following *nouns, adverbs* and *adjectives*

l'**avant**-bras (m)	*the forearm*
l'**avant**-propos (m)	*the foreword*
l'**avant**-veille (f)	*two days before*
avant-hier	*the day before yesterday*
l'**avant**-dernier chapitre (m)	*the next to the last chapter*
les signes **avant**-coureurs	*early warning signs*

6. **ne...pas avant** expresses '**not** until' when the beginning of an action is marked (see p. 158-159)

Il **n'**est **pas** rentré **avant** minuit.	*He **didn't** come home **until** midnight.*
N'ouvrez **pas** le cadeau **avant** Noël!	*Don't open the gift **until** Christmas!*

7. **avant** translates 'by' before time expressions

Il faut que ce travail soit fini **avant** jeudi.	*This work must be finished **by** Thursday.*
La dissertation est à remettre **avant** le vingt janvier.	*The paper must be handed in **by** the twentieth of January.*

Proverbs, sayings, and idioms

Il ne faut pas mettre la charrue **avant** les bœufs.	*Don't put the cart before the horse.*
Ne vendez pas la peau de l'ours **avant** de l'avoir tué.	*Don't count your chickens before they are hatched.*
C'est le calme **avant** la tempête.	*It's the calm before the storm.*
avant tout	*above all*
avant toute chose	*first and foremost*
avant peu	*before long*

M. The preposition **après**

1. **après** expresses 'after' in time

Je suis libre **après** le déjeuner.	*I am free after lunch.*
en 300 **après** Jésus-Christ	*in 300 AD*
Après vous, Madame!	*After you, Madam!*

2. **après** can express 'after' in space in some instances

Tournez à droite **après** le feu rouge.	*Turn right after the red light.*

En français, la plupart des adjectifs sont placés **après** le nom. — *In French, most adjectives are placed after the noun.*

3. après is part of the *prepositional expression*

d'après — *according to, (film) based on, (person) named after*

un film **d'après** un roman de Balzac — *a movie based on a novel by Balzac*
D'après lui, il va pleuvoir demain. — *According to him, it is going to rain tomorrow.*

and of the expressions

après tout — *after all*
après cela — *after that*
après quoi — *after which*
année **après** année — *year after year*
jour **après** jour — *day after day, day in day out*
livre **après** livre — *book after book*

4. après is used with the *past infinitive* (see p. 18)

Après *avoir déjeuné,* ils sont sortis. — *After eating/having eaten lunch, they went out.*

5. après + *determiner* + *noun* frequently replaces the conjunction *après que* + subordinate clause

après son départ — *after he left*
après la sortie de son livre — *after his book came out*

6. après is part of the following nouns

l'**après**-guerre (m) — *the postwar period*
l'**après**-midi (m *or* f) — *the afternoon*
l'**après**-ski (m) — *après-ski*

7. après is used after the verb 'courir'

courir **après** qn/qch — *to chase after sb/sth*

Il court **après** le succès. — *He chases after success.*
Ils courent **après** cette personne. — *They are chasing after this person.*

Proverbs

Après la pluie le beau temps.	*Every cloud has a silver lining.*

N. The preposition **jusque** (before vowel: **jusqu'**)

1. **jusque** marks a *limit in time* and *space* expressing

'until', 'till' and 'as far as', 'to'

Il travaille **jusque** tard la nuit.	*He works until late at night.*
jusque vers sept heures	*until about seven o'clock*
jusque dans les années trente	*until the thirties*
jusqu'ici	*so far, up to now, as far as here*
Jusqu'ici, tout a bien marché.	*So far, everything worked well.*
Avance **jusqu'**ici.	*Advance as far as here.*
jusque là	*until then, up to that time, as far as there*
Jusque là, tout s'était bien passé.	*Until then, everything had gone well.*
jusqu'alors	*until then*
jusqu'en 1870	*until/up to 1870*
Mon passeport est valable **jusqu'**en juin.	*My passport is valid until June.*
jusqu'**en** été	*until summer*
Il m'a accompagné **jusqu'**en Australie.	*He accompanied me all the way to (= as far as) Australia.*
Ils m'ont suivi **jusque** chez moi.	*They followed me to my home.*

Note:

jusque (indicating a *limit in time* and *space*) is mostly followed by **à**

jusqu'à aujourd'hui/demain/hier	*until today/tomorrow/yesterday*
jusqu'à quand?	*until when? how long?*
Jusqu'à quand restez-vous?	*How long are you staying?*
jusqu'à dimanche	*until Sunday*
jusqu'à la fin du mois	*until the end of the month*
jusqu'à maintenant	*until now*
jusqu'à présent	*until now, up to now, so far*

jusqu'à la mort	*until death*
du début **jusqu'à** la fin	*from beginning to end*
jusqu'à fin janvier	*until the end of January*
jusqu'à la mi-octobre	*until the middle of October*
jusqu'à il y a un an	*until a year ago*
jusqu'à minuit	*until midnight*
Je t'attendrai **jusqu'à** huit heures.	*I will wait for you until 8 o'clock.*
En Amérique, on travaille **jusqu'à** (l'âge de) 65 ans.	*In America, people work until they are 65.*
Il a vécu **jusqu'à** quatre-vingts ans.	*He lived till he was eighty years old.*
N'attendez pas **jusqu'à** la dernière minute pour...	*Don't wait until the last minute to...*
jusqu'au[1] dernier moment	*up to/until the last moment*
jusqu'au moment où...	*until (the moment when...)*
jusqu'au 24 mai (inclus)	*until the 24th of May (included)*
jusqu'au mois dernier	*until last month*
du matin **jusqu'au** soir	*from morning till night*
jusqu'aux[1] années cinquante	*until the fifties*
jusqu'aux examens	*until (the) exams*
Le train va **jusqu'à** Marseille.	*The train goes as far as Marseille.*
Je vais t'accompagner **jusqu'à** la gare.	*I am going to accompany you to (= as far as) the train station.*
Je vous suivrai **jusqu'au** bout du monde.	*I will follow you to the end of the world.*

2. **jusqu'à** can give the upper limit expressing 'up to' *(= as much as)*, or the lower limit expressing 'down to' *(= as little as)*

Ça peut coûter **jusqu'à** 3000 euros.	*That can cost up to 3000 euros.*
Il peut soulever **jusqu'à** vingt kilos.	*He can lift up to twenty kilos.*
L'euro peut descendre **jusqu'à** 0,8 dollars.	*The euro can fall down to 0.8 dollars.*

---

1. Note that
jusqu'à + *le* contracts to **jusqu'au**
jusqu'à + *les* contracts to **jusqu'aux**

3. **jusqu'à** + *determiner* + *noun* frequently replaces the conjunction *jusqu'à ce que* + subordinate clause

Restez ici **jusqu'à** mon retour. (= Restez ici *jusqu'à ce que* je revienne.)	*Stay here until I get back.*
jusqu'à sa mort	*until he/she dies*

Sayings and idioms

aller **jusqu'à** [+ inf.] Il va **jusqu'à** nier son origine.	*to go as far as to* *He goes as far as denying his origin.*
aller/se battre **jusqu'au** bout	*to go/fight all the way/to the end*
être ému **jusqu'aux** larmes	*to be moved to tears*
être trempé **jusqu'aux** os	*to be soaked to the skin*
jusqu'à nouvel ordre	*until further notice*
jusqu'à preuve du contraire	*until proven otherwise*
jusqu'où **Jusqu'où** irons-nous?	*how far* *How far will we go?*
J'en ai **jusque** là.	*I am sick and tired of it.*

Translation difficulties

Since **jusqu'à** can*not* be used in a *negative* sentence when it marks the *beginning* of an action or state, *not until* is generally translated with **ne...pas avant**

*This will **not** be ready **until** Monday.*	Ce **ne** sera **pas** prêt **avant** lundi.
*In France, young people can**not** have their driver's licence **until** they are eighteen.*	En France, les jeunes **ne** peuvent **pas** avoir leur permis de conduire **avant** dix-huit ans.
*I did **not** receive your letter **until** this morning.*	Je **n**'ai **pas** reçu ta lettre **avant** ce matin.

But:

When 'not until' indicates that an action or situation will *not* last *until* a certain time, i.e. when it marks the *end* of an action, '**ne...pas jusqu'à**' translates 'not until'.

*Today, I will **not** stay here **until** midnight* (= not as long as midnight).	Aujourd'hui, je **ne** vais **pas** rester ici **jusqu'à** minuit.

Mistakes to avoid		
Incorrect	*Correct*	*English meaning*
Je *ne* peux *pas* venir vous voir ~~jusqu'à~~ mardi.	Je *ne* peux *pas* venir vous voir **avant** mardi.	*I cannot visit you* ***until*** *Tuesday.*

O. The preposition **contre**

1. contre expresses *close contact* or *opposition (*English: *against)*

Il pousse la chaise **contre** la porte. — *He pushes the chair against the door.*
J'ai appuyé l'échelle **contre** le mur. — *I leaned the ladder against the wall.*
nager **contre** le courant — *to swim against the current*

2. contre indicates a *disease* with *remedies*

un sirop **contre** (or: **pour**) la toux — *a cough syrup*
un vaccin **contre** la grippe — *a flu vaccine*

3. contre expresses 'to' between numbers in votes, bets, etc.

Il a été élu directeur par six voix **contre** quatre. — *He was elected director by six votes* ***to*** *four.*
La mesure a été approuvé dix **contre** un. — *The measure was approved ten* ***to*** *one.*

4. contre expresses 'on' in the expression

un attentat **contre** qn — *an attempt* ***on*** *someone's life*

5. contre introduces the complement after the following verbs and expressions

s'appuyer **contre** qn/qch — *to lean against sb/sth*
Je me suis appuyé **contre** le mur. — *I leaned against the wall.*

s'assurer **contre** [le vol/l'incendie] — *to insure oneself against* [theft/fire]

avoir qch **contre** qn/qch — *to have sth against sb/sth*
Je n'ai rien **contre** cela/lui. — *I have nothing against that/him.*
Il a quelque chose **contre** moi. — *He has something against me.*

avoir un préjugé **contre** qn/qch	*to have a prejudice against sb/sth*
se cogner **contre** qch	*to bump into/bang against sth*
échanger/troquer qch **contre** qch	*to exchange/trade/swap sth for sth*
s'écraser **contre** qch	*to crash into sth*
être **contre** qch Je suis **contre** la peine de mort.	*to be against sth* *I am against the death penalty.*
être/se mettre en colère **contre** qn/qch	*to be/get angry with/mad at sb/sth*
se fâcher/être fâché **contre** qn/qch	*to get/be angry with sb/sth*
être furieux **contre** qn	*to be furious with sb*
se heurter **contre** qch	*to bump into/to collide with sth*
s'indigner **contre** (or: **de**) qch	*to be outraged by*
jouer **contre** qn	*to play against sb* [sport]
lutter **contre** qn/qch Ils luttent **contre** l'illettrisme.	*to fight against sb/sth* *They fight against illiteracy.*
mettre qn en garde **contre** qn/qch	*to warn sb against sb/sth*
porter plainte **contre** qn	*to sue sb in court*
se prémunir **contre** qch	*to protect oneself from/against sth*
se prononcer **contre** qch	*to declare oneself against sth*
protéger qn/qch **contre** (or: **de**) qn/qch	*to protect sb/sth from sb/sth*
protester **contre** qch	*to protest against sth*
se retourner **contre** qn Ses intrigues se sont retournées **contre** lui.	*to turn against sb, to backfire on sb* *His intrigues backfired on him.*
voter **contre** qn/qch	*to vote against sb/sth*

Sayings and idioms

faire **contre** mauvaise fortune bon cœur	*to make the best of it, to put on a brave face, to grin and bear it*
contre vents et marées	*come hell or high water, against all odds, despite all the obstacles*
un royaume **contre** un cheval	*a kingdom for a horse*
contre toute attente	*against all expectations*
par **contre**	*on the other hand*
contre le gré de qn **contre** mon/notre/leur gré	*against someone's will* *against my/our/their will*

Translation difficulties

- **against** is *not* translated with 'contre' in the expression

*It's **against** the law.*	C'est **contraire** à la loi.

- English 'to' is translated with **contre** in the following expressions

*to drive along bumper **to** bumper*	rouler pare-chocs **contre** pare-chocs
*ten votes **to** six*	dix voix **contre** six

P. The preposition **dès**

1. **dès** is followed by a *time point* or *period* and expresses 'as early as', 'from...on', emphasizing the starting point of an action

Il a été malade **dès** (l'âge de) huit ans.	*He was ill from the age of eight.*
Je vais m'y mettre **dès** demain.	*I am going to put myself to work from tomorrow on.*

Also in the expressions

dès aujourd'hui	*from today on*
dès le début (= **dès** le départ)	*right from the start, from the beginning*
dès le matin	*from the morning on*
dès le premier abord	*from the very first*
dès maintenant	*from now on*
dès lors	*from then on*

2. **dès** + *determiner* + *noun* frequently replaces the conjunction *dès que* + subordinate clause

dès votre arrivée	*as soon as you arrive*
dès son retour	*as soon as he returns*
dès la rentrée	*as soon as the new school year starts, as soon as fall arrives*

3. **dès** can also be followed by a *place* meaning 'from...onwards'

Vous devez vous attendre à des bouchons **dès** la banlieue.	*You have to expect traffic jams from the suburbs onwards.*

Q. The prepositional phrase **à partir de**

1. **à partir de** indicates a *starting point in time* expressing 'starting', 'from...onward'

Je serai chez moi **à partir de** cinq heures.	*I will be at home from five o'clock on.*
A partir de ce jour-là, il se sentit mieux.	*From that day on, he felt better.*
A partir d'aujourd'hui, tout changera.	*From today on, everything will change.*
à partir de maintenant/demain	*from now/tomorrow on*
à partir du quinze février	*from the 15th of February onwards*
On peut boire le Beaujolais Nouveau[1] le troisième jeudi de novembre **à partir de** zéro heure (locale).	*One can drink the Beaujolais Nouveau on the third Thursday of November from midnight on.*
Le gouvernement français a décidé de réduire le temps de travail à 35 heures **à partir de** l'an 2000.	*The French government decided to reduce the working hours to 35 from the year 2000.*

2. **à partir** indicates a *starting point in space* expressing 'from...on'

Il y a des embouteillages **à partir de** Lyon.	*There are traffic jams from Lyon onwards.*
C'est le deuxième bouton **à partir du** bas.	*It's the second button from the bottom.*
C'est la troisième porte **à partir de** la droite.	*It's the third door from the right.*
Il est paralysé **à partir de** la taille.	*He is paralyzed from the waist down.*

3. **à partir de** can also indicate an *amount*

Les chèques sont acceptés **à partir de** 50 euros.	*Checks are accepted for 50 euros or more.*

---

1. Red wine from the Beaujolais region (area east of the Massif Central, between the Loire and the Saône).

R. The preposition **depuis**

1. **depuis** means 'since' when followed by a *precise moment of time*[1] and when used before '*quand*'; it means 'for' when followed by a *time period*[2] and when used before '*combien de temps*'

Depuis quand le connais-tu?	***Since*** *when have you known him?*
Je le connais **depuis** Noël.	*I have known him* ***since*** *Christmas.*
Elle joue du piano **depuis** l'âge de quatre ans.	*She has played the piano* ***since*** *she was four.*
Je suis levé **depuis** six heures du matin.	*I have been up* ***since*** *six in the morning.*
Depuis combien de temps est-ce que vous êtes marié?	(***For***) *how long have you been married?*
Je suis marié[3] **depuis** dix ans.	*I have been married* ***for*** *ten years.*
Nous sommes amis **depuis** longtemps.	*We have been friends* ***for*** *a long time.*
Il vit ici **depuis** des années.	*He has lived here* ***for*** *years.*

2. **depuis** can also mean *from* (often in combination with 'jusqu'à') referring to *time* or *space*

depuis le matin jusqu'au soir	***from*** *morning till night*
L'avenue des Champs-Elysées s'étend **depuis** la Place de la Concorde jusqu'à la Place de l'Etoile.	*The Champs-Elysées extend* ***from*** *Concord Square to Etoile Square.*
Il a écrit à sa mère **depuis** sa prison.	*He wrote to his mother* ***from*** *his prison.*

3. **depuis** is part of the following idiomatic expression

depuis peu	*lately, not long ago*

---

1. such as: *yesterday, Tuesday, the third of April, Easter, etc.*
2. such as: *three weeks, four months, five hours, six years, etc.*
3. See also p. 118

Note the use of *tenses* with 'depuis':

In sentences where **depuis** is used to express 'for' or 'since'

- the verb is in the *present tense* when the action started in the past and continues in the present
[English: '*...have/has been doing*' or: '*...have/has done...for/since...*']

Ils le ***savent*** *depuis* des lustres.	*They* ***have known*** *it for ages.*

- the verb is in the *passé composé* when a **negative** statement is made, i.e. when an action is described that was **not** going on for a certain time in the past up to the present, but which has changed or can change in the present
[English: '*...have/has* ***not*** *done...for/since...*']

Je *ne* vous **ai** *pas* **vu** *depuis* longtemps.	*I* ***haven't seen*** *you for a long time.* (But now I see you.)
Ce *n'***est** *pas* **arrivé** *depuis* plusieurs années/*depuis* 1985.	*This* ***hasn't happened*** *for several years/since 1985.*

- the verb is in the *imperfect tense* when the action started in the past and was going on until a certain moment in the past when another action set in
[English: '*...had been doing...for/since...*']

Je **regardais** la télé *depuis* une heure quand il est arrivé.	*I* ***had been watching*** *TV for an hour when he arrived.*

- the verb is in the *pluperfect* when a **negative** action started in the past and continued until a certain moment in the past when another action set in
[English: '*...had* ***not*** *done...for/since...*']

Je *n'***avais** *pas* **parlé** avec Jean *depuis* Pâques quand je l'ai vu au cinéma.	*I* ***had not spoken*** *to John since Easter when I saw him at the movies.*

Mistakes to avoid

Incorrect	*Correct*	*English meaning*
J'~~ai habité~~ à Portland *depuis* neuf mois.	J'**habite**[1] à Portland *depuis* neuf mois.	***I have lived*** *in Portland for nine months.* (And I still do.)

---

1. See also p. 118 (footnote)

S. The preposition **pendant**

1. **pendant** expresses 'during'

Qu'est-ce que tu as fait **pendant** les vacances de printemps?	*What did you do during spring break?*
Ils ont tout perdu **pendant** la guerre.	*They lost everything during the war.*
pendant la nuit	*during the night*
pendant toute l'année	*throughout/during the whole year*

2. **pendant** expresses 'for' when referring to the duration of an action completed in the past[1]

Pendant combien de temps avez-vous travaillé en France?	*(For) how long did you work in France?*
J'ai travaillé à Lyon **pendant** un an.	*I worked in Lyon for one year.*

Do not confuse 'pendant' (= for) and 'depuis' (= for).[2]

Compare:

• Je t'ai attendu **pendant** des heures.	*I waited for you **for** hours.* (But I am no longer waiting.)
Je t'attends **depuis** des heures.	*I have waited for you **for** hours.* (And I am still waiting.)
• **pendant** longtemps	*for a long time*[3]
depuis longtemps	*for a long time*[4]

T. The prepositional phrase **à cause de**

à cause de expresses 'because **of**'

Je n'entends rien **à cause du** bruit.	*I hear nothing because **of** the noise.*
Nous ne sommes pas sortis **à cause de** la pluie.[5]	*We didn't go out because **of** the rain.*

---

1. See also p. 119
2. See also p. 118-119
3. The action or situation is no longer going on, it was completed in the past.
4. The action or situation is still going on.
5. But: Nous ne sommes pas sortis **parce qu'**il pleuvait. (*...because it was raining.*)

Do not confuse the preposition **à cause de** with the conjunction **parce que** (= car). One uses **à cause de** when a *noun* or *stressed pronoun* follows, and **parce que** when a *subordinate clause* follows.

Mistakes to avoid

Incorrect	*Correct*	*English meaning*
Il ne vient pas ~~parce que~~ la neige.	Il ne vient pas **à cause de** la neige.	*He doesn't come* ***because of*** *the snow.*

U. The prepositional phrase **au bout de**

1. au bout de followed by a *time period* expresses 'at the end of', 'after'

Il est revenu **au bout d'**un an.	*He came back after a year.*
au bout de quelques minutes	*after a few minutes*
au bout d'une semaine	*after a week*
au bout d'un certain temps	*after a while*
au bout d'un moment	*after a moment*
au bout de 24 heures	*after 24 hours*

Note:

au bout de + *time period* replaces 'à la fin de' + *time period* when the period of time is accompanied by a number or another expression of quantity

Compare:

- *à la fin du* mois — *at the end of the month*
  au bout de trois mois — *at the end of three months*
- *à la fin de* l'année — *at the end of the year*
  au bout de plusieurs années — *at the end of several years*

2. au bout de can be followed by a *place*

Les toilettes sont **au bout du** couloir/**au bout de** la rue.	*The restroom is at the end of the hallway/at the end of the street.*
à l'autre bout du monde	*on the other end of the world*

Sayings and idioms

au bout du compte	*ultimately, in the end*
être **au bout du** fil	*to be on the line* [telephone]
Madame Duval est **au bout du** fil.	*Mrs. Duval is on the phone.*
être **au bout de** ses forces	*to be exhausted*
Je suis **au bout de** mes forces.	*I am exhausted.*
être **au bout du** rouleau (fam.)	*to be at one's wit's end*

V. The preposition **entre**

1. entre expresses 'between' (usually referring to two elements)

Le parc se trouve **entre** l'église et la poste.	*The park is located between the church and the post office.*
Elle a **entre** trente et quarante ans.[1]	*She is in her thirties.*
Il faut savoir lire **entre** les lignes.	*One must know how to read between the lines.*

2. In some instances, **entre** expresses 'among', referring to more than two elements

Nous sommes **entre** amis.	*We are among friends.*
entre nous	*among ourselves, just between us*
entre vous	*among yourselves*
Ils peuvent s'arranger **entre** eux.	*They can work it out among themselves.*

3. d'entre (meaning 'of') is used before a disjunctive pronoun

- after a number

l'un **d'entre** vous	*one of you*

- after expressions of quantity (*beaucoup, la plupart, peu,* etc.)

plusieurs/beaucoup **d'entre** elles	*several/many of them*
la plupart/la moitié **d'entre** eux	*most/half of them*

1. lit.: *She is between thirty and forty years old.*

- after an indefinite pronoun (*quelques-uns, certains, chacun*)

chacun **d'entre** nous	*each of us, everyone of us*

- after a negative expression (*aucun...ne, personne...ne*)

aucun **d'entre** eux	*none of them*
personne **d'entre** elles	*nobody of them*

- after a demonstrative pronoun (*ceux, celles*)

ceux **d'entre** vous	*those of you*

- after an interrogative expression

qui **d'entre** vous?	*who of you?*
combien **d'entre** eux?	*how many of them?*

- after a superlative

Marie était la plus sympathique **d'entre** elles.	*Mary was the nicest of them.*

4. **entre** expresses 'in' in the following expressions

entre guillemets	***in** quotation marks*
Mettez le mot **entre** parenthèses.	*Put the word **in** brackets.*
L'avenir est **entre** vos mains.	*The future is **in** your hands.*
être **entre** de bonnes mains	*to be **in** good hands*
tomber **entre** les mains de qn	*to fall **in** sb's hands*
entre les deux	***in** between*

Sayings and idioms

entre la poire et le fromage [1]	*at the end of the meal, over coffee*
être **entre** l'enclume et le marteau [2]	*to be between the devil and the deep blue sea*
entre autres	*among others*
entre autres choses	*among other things*
entre chien et loup	*at twilight, at dusk*

1. lit.: *between the pear and the cheese*
2. lit.: *between the anvil and the hammer*

parler **entre** ses dents (= dans sa barbe)	*to mumble*
être **entre** la vie et la mort	*to hover between life and death*
être partagé **entre**	*to be torn between*

W. The preposition **parmi**

parmi expresses 'among' referring to more than two elements

Y a-t-il **parmi** vous quelqu'un qui s'intéresse à cela?	*Is there someone among you who is interested in that?*
Il était **parmi** les invités.	*He was among the guests.*
Parmi ces livres vous trouverez l'encyclopédie que vous cherchez.	*Among these books you will find the encyclopedia you are looking for.*

X. The preposition **vers**

1. **vers** indicates a *direction* ['toward(s)'] (literally or figuratively)

se diriger **vers** Elle se dirige **vers** la porte.	*to walk toward, to be heading for* *She walks toward the door.*
se précipiter **vers** Ils se sont précipités **vers** la sortie.	*to rush toward* *They rushed toward the exit.*
se tourner **vers** Il se tourne **vers** elle.	*to turn toward* *He turns toward her.*
la ruée **vers** l'or	*the gold rush*
des appels **vers** l'étranger	*phone calls abroad*

2. **vers** expresses 'at about', 'around' with *clock time* and *dates*

vers le 4 juillet	*around the 4th of July*
Venez **vers** six heures.	*Come at about six o'clock.*
Il arrivera **vers** minuit.	*He will arrive around midnight.*

Except after 'il est' and 'à' where 'environ' must be used to express 'about'

Il est **environ** deux heures. à **environ** trois heures	*It's about two o'clock.* *at about three o'clock*

Y. The preposition **envers**

envers expresses 'toward' when referring to *persons* in a figurative sense

Sois respectueux **envers** tes parents.	*Be respectful toward your parents.*
Ne sois pas ingrat **envers** tes professeurs.	*Don't be ungrateful toward your teachers.*
Le professeur s'est montré indulgent **envers** les étudiants.	*The teacher was lenient toward the students.*
être attentionné **envers** (or: **pour**) qn	*to be attentive/considerate toward sb*

===================================

Summary

The following frequently used expressions contain prepositions which are different from their English counterparts.

Si j'étais **à** votre (ta, sa...) place...	*If I was **in** your (his, her...) place...*
C'est très gentil/bien aimable **à** vous.	*That's very nice **of** you.*
à l'âge des ordinateurs	***in** the computer age*
Je l'ai reconnu **à** sa voix.	*I recognized him **by** his voice.*
à mon avis	***in** my opinion*
passer **à** la douane	*to pass **through** customs*
tenir un stylo **à** la main	*to hold a pen **in** one's hand*
au téléphone	***on** the phone*
à la page 50	***on** page 50*
au soleil	***in** the sun*
à l'ombre	***in** the shade*
à la télé	***on** TV*
Quand j'étais **dans** l'avion/le train...	*When I was **on** the plane/train...*
dans son dos	***behind** his back*
dans l'escalier	***on** the stairs*
dans l'assiette	***on** the plate*
dans l'espoir de	***with** the hope of*
dans l'intention de	***with** the intention of*

de l'autre côté	***on*** *the other side*
Je le connais **de** vue/**de** nom.	*I know him* ***by*** *sight/****by*** *name.*
être **de** bonne/**de** mauvaise humeur	*to be* ***in*** *a good/****in*** *a bad mood*
de la même façon/manière	***in*** *the same way*
trembler **de** peur	*to tremble* ***with*** *fear*
de mon temps	***in*** *my time*
être couvert/rempli/chargé **de**	*to be covered/filled/loaded* ***with***
Merci **de** (or: **pour**) votre gentillesse/**de** votre coopération/**de** votre attention.	*Thanks* ***for*** *your kindness/****for*** *your cooperation/****for*** *your attention.*
être **en** vacances	*to be* ***on*** *vacation*
par cette chaleur	***in*** *this heat*
par exemple	***for*** *example*
regarder **par** la fenêtre	*to look* ***out of*** *the window*
par terre	***on*** *the floor*
par ordre alphabétique/chronologique	***in*** *alphabetical/chronological order*
sous la pluie	***in*** *the rain*
avoir qch **sous** la main	*to have sth* ***at*** *hand*
sous la douche	***in*** *the shower*
sous le choc	***in*** *shock*
sur la demande de	***at*** *the request of*
sur la photo	***in*** *the picture*

Mistakes to avoid

Incorrect	*Correct*	*English meaning*
~~sur~~ l'autre côté de la rue	**de** l'autre côté de la rue	***on*** *the other side of the street*
Il y a un bel arbre ~~dans~~ la photo.	Il y a un bel arbre **sur** la photo.	*There is a beautiful tree* ***in*** *the picture.*

Chapter 6

Prepositions in Verb + Noun Constructions

This chapter deals with the use of prepositions between verbs (or verbal expressions) and the following complement (noun or stressed pronoun).
In French, as in English, many verbs take a preposition before adding on a complement. Frequently, the preposition required between a verb and an object is the same in French and English.

Le livre est **à** moi.	*The book belongs* ***to*** *me.* (**à** = *to*)
Il a peur **de** son professeur.	*He is afraid* ***of*** *his teacher.* (**de** = *of*)
Je compte **sur** vous.	*I count* ***on*** *you.* (**sur** = *on*)

In some instances however, the use of prepositions in French differs from the use of prepositions in English. Some verbs require a preposition before the following object in English but not in French, or vice versa. Some verbs take a different preposition in French than in English. Following are the most common examples of each of these cases.

A. Verbs that take a preposition before a complement in English but not in French[1]

attendre	*to wait* ***for***
chercher	*to look* ***for***
demander	*to ask* ***for***
écouter	*to listen* ***to***
payer[2]	*to pay* ***for***
regarder	*to look* ***at***

---

1. In French, these verbs are followed by a **direct object**. A *direct object* is added to the verb *without* a preposition.
2. But: **pour** is used after 'payer' when a sum of money is mentioned or when a person is paid for.

Elle a payé 100 euros **pour** la robe.	*She paid 100 euros for the dress.*
Il a payé **pour** moi.	*He paid for me.*

J'attends l'autobus.	*I am waiting **for** the bus.*
Je cherche mes clés.	*I am looking **for** my keys.*
Nous avons demandé l'addition.	*We asked **for** the bill.*
Ils écoutent la radio.	*They are listening **to** the radio.*
Elle doit payer la voiture.	*She has to pay **for** the car.*
Ils regardent les photos.	*They are looking **at** the pictures.*

Mistakes to avoid

Incorrect	*Correct*	*English meaning*
Je cherche ~~pour~~ une pharmacie.	Je cherche une pharmacie.	*I am looking **for** a pharmacy.*
Nous écoutons ~~au~~ professeur.	Nous écoutons le professeur.	*We are listening **to** the teacher.*
Il attend ~~pour~~ son ami.	Il attend son ami.	*He is waiting **for** his friend.*

Also:

aller/venir chercher qn	*to pick **up** sb (from airport, etc.)*
allumer qch	*to switch/turn **on** sth*
(dés)approuver qch	*to (dis)approve **of** sth*
s'avérer qch	*to turn **out** to be sth*
avoir fini qch	*to be finished **with** sth*
baisser qch	*to turn **down** sth* [radio, TV]
bousculer qn/qch	*to bump **into** sb/sth*
cambrioler qch	*to break **into** sth*
commenter qch	*to comment **on** sth*
compenser qch	*to make **up**/compensate **for** sth*
concurrencer qn/qch	*to compete **with** sb/sth*
coudre qch	*to sew **on** sth*
dénoncer qn	*to turn sb **in** (for doing sth wrong)*
déposer qn	*to drop **off** sb*
descendre qch	*to go **down** sth, to take **down** sth*
déterrer qch	*to dig **up** sth*
disputer qch	*to participate **in** sth* [sport event]
distinguer qn/qch et qn/qch	*to distinguish **between** sb/sth and sb/sth*
écraser qn/qch	*to run **over** sb/sth* [a person or animal]
envoyer chercher qn	*to send **for** sb*
espérer qch	*to hope **for** sth*
essayer qch	*to try **on** sth* [clothing, shoes, etc.]
éteindre qch	*to switch/turn **off** sth*
éviter qn/qch	*to stay away **from** sb/sth*

faire sauter qch	*to blow* ***up*** *sth*
faire venir qn	*to send* ***for*** *sb*
fixer qn/qch	*to stare* ***at*** *sb/sth*
fuir qn/qch	*to flee* ***from*** *sb/sth*
garder qn/qch	*to look* ***after*** *sb/sth* [house, child, animal]
gronder qn	*to tell sb* ***off***
heurter qn/qch	*to run* ***into*** *sb/sth, to collide* ***with*** *sb/sth*
inventer une histoire	*to make* ***up*** *a story*
jalouser qn	*to be jealous* ***of*** *sb*
jeter qch	*to throw* ***out*** *sth*
lacer (des chaussures)	*to tie* ***up*** *(shoes)*
loger qn	*to put sb* ***up***
longer qch	*to go/drive* ***along*** *sth*
marier qn[1]	*to marry sb* ***off***
monter qch	*to go* ***up*** *sth, to take* ***up*** *sth*
ôter (= enlever) qch	*to take* ***off*** *sth*
percuter qch/qn	*to run/crash* ***into*** *sth/sb*
plaindre qn	*to feel sorry* ***for*** *sb (= to pity sb)*
pleurer qn	*to mourn/weep* ***for*** *sb*
postuler (un emploi)	*to apply* ***for*** *(a job)*
préparer un examen	*to study* ***for*** *a test*
ramasser qch	*to pick* ***up*** *sth*
ranger qch	*to tidy* ***up*** *sth*
rattraper qch	*to make* ***up (for)*** *sth* [lost time]
rattraper qn	*to catch* ***up with*** *sb*
remettre qch	*to hand* ***in*** *sth* [a paper, an essay, etc.]
remplir qch	*to fill* ***in*** *sth*
rencontrer qn	*to meet* ***with*** *sb*
rendre qch	*to give sth* ***back***
renverser qn/qch	*to run* ***over*** *(and injure) sb, to knock sth* ***over***
sentir qch	*to smell* ***like*** *sth*
servir qn	*to wait* ***on*** *sb*
sortir qch	*to take* ***out*** *sth*
tirer la langue	*to stick* ***out*** *the tongue*
tomber [+ jour ou date]	*to fall* ***on*** [+ name of a day or date]
tromper qn	*to cheat* ***on*** *sb*
viser qn/qch	*to aim/be aimed* ***at*** *sb/sth*
vivre qch	*to live* ***through*** *sth*

---

1. Do not confuse *marier qn* with *se marier* ***avec*** *qn* (= to marry sb) [see p. 194].

Je *vais chercher* mes parents à la gare.	*I am going to pick* ***up*** *my parents from the trainstation.*
Pourrais-tu *allumer* la télé?	*Could you switch* ***on*** *the TV?*
Cela *s'avérait* une affaire compliquée.	*This turned* ***out*** *to be a complicated affair.*
Ils ont *cambriolé* la maison.	*They broke* ***into*** *the house.*
Ils vont *compenser* leurs pertes par...	*They are going to compensate* ***for*** *their losses by...*
Ils veulent *concurrencer* les Américains.	*They want to compete* ***with*** *the Americans.*
Je peux vous *déposer* quelque part?	*Can I drop you* ***off*** *somewhere?*
Nous *descendons* les Champs-Elysées. Pourriez-vous *descendre* la poubelle?	*We go* ***down*** *the Champs-Elysées.* *Could you take* ***down*** *the garbage?*
Ils ont *disputé* les tournois de Wimbledon.	*They participated* ***in*** *the tournaments of Wimbledon.*
Il faut *distinguer* deux domaines bien différents.	*We must distinguish* ***between*** *two very different fields.*
Espérons le meilleur.	*Let's hope* ***for*** *the best.*
Je vais *éteindre* la lumière.	*I am going to switch* ***off*** *the light.*
Ils ont *fait venir* le médecin.	*They sent* ***for*** *the doctor.*
As-tu *fini* ton travail?	*Are you finished* ***with*** *your work?*
Il *fuit* ses créanciers.	*He flees* ***from*** *his creditors.*
Qui *garde* votre chat?	*Who's looking* ***after*** *your cat?*
Il a *heurté* un camion.	*He collided* ***with*** *a truck.*
Nous avons *longé* la Seine.	*We went* ***along*** *the Seine.*
Il *monte* l'escalier.	*He goes* ***up*** *the stairs.*
Il a *ôté* son chapeau.	*He took* ***off*** *his hat.*
La voiture a *percuté* un camion. Il a *percuté* un policier.	*The car ran* ***into*** *a truck.* *He ran* ***into*** *a policeman.*
Je le *plains*.	*I feel sorry* ***for*** *him.*
Il a *rattrapé* les autres étudiants.	*He caught up* ***with*** *the other students.*
Nous avons *rattrapé* le temps perdu.	*We made* ***up*** *for lost time.*
Je dois *remplir* ce formulaire.	*I have to fill* ***in*** *this form.*
Il faut *remettre* les copies au professeur avant la fin de la semaine.	*We must hand* ***in*** *the papers to the teacher by the end of the week.*
La caissière *rend* la monnaie aux clients.	*The cashier gives* ***back*** *the change to the customers.*

Ce parfum *sent* la vanille.	*This perfume smells* ***like*** *vanilla.*
La vendeuse *sert* les clients.	*The saleslady waits* ***on*** *the clients.*
Il a *sorti* la voiture du garage.	*He took the car* ***out of*** *the garage.*
Si un jour férié *tombe* un mardi ou un jeudi, on fait le pont.	*If a holiday falls* ***on*** *a Tuesday or Thursday, one takes a long week-end.*
Pâques *tombe* le 20 avril cette année.	*Easter falls* ***on*** *April 20th this year.*
Cette mesure *vise* les locataires.	*This measure is aimed* ***at*** *the tenants.*
Il a *vécu* une période difficile.	*He lived* ***through*** *a difficult time.*

Note also that the English equivalents of the following intransitive or intransitively used French verbs (i.e. verbs which cannot take an object) contain a preposition as well.

décoller	*to take* ***off*** *(airplane)*
céder	*to give* ***in****, to back* ***down***
finir	*to end* ***up***
passer	*to drop* ***by***
ralentir	*to slow* ***down***
reculer	*to back* ***up***
renoncer (= laisser tomber)	*to give* ***up***
rompre	*to break* ***up***
signaler	*to point* ***out***
sortir	*to go* ***out***
s'assoupir	*to doze* ***off***
s'asseoir	*to sit* ***down***
se calmer	*to calm* ***down***
s'entendre (bien) avec qn	*to get* ***along*** *(well) with sb*
s'évanouir	*to pass* ***out***
s'inscrire	*to sign* ***up***
se lever	*to get* ***up***
se rattraper	*to make* ***up*** *for it, to catch* ***up***
se retirer	*to pull* ***out***
se sauver	*to run* ***away***

L'avion *décolle.*	*The plane takes* ***off.***
Fais-le *céder*!	*Make him give* ***in!***
C'est trop dur pour moi. Je *renonce*!	*That is too hard for me. I give* ***up!***
Les peluches vont *finir* sur une étagère.	*The teddy bears are going to end* ***up*** *on a shelf.*
Est-ce que je peux *passer* ce soir?	*Can I drop* ***by*** *tonight?*
Ils ont *rompu.*	*They broke* ***up.***
Asseyez-vous!	*Sit* ***down!***
Tout à coup, elle *s'est évanouie.*	*She suddenly passed* ***out.***
Je *me lève* à sept heures.	*I get* ***up*** *at seven o'clock.*
On peut toujours *se rattraper.*	*One can always make* ***up*** *for it.*

B. Verbs which require a preposition before a complement in French but not in English

- Verbs which require the preposition **à** before their complement

aller (bien) **à** qn	*to fit sb (well)*
assister **à** qch	*to attend sth*[1] [wedding, concert, etc.]
s'attendre **à** qch	*to expect sth*
convenir **à** qn	*to suit sb*
demander **à** qn[2]	*to ask sb*
échapper **à** qch[3]	*to escape sth* [death, danger, etc.]
échouer **à** un examen	*to fail a test*
enseigner **à** qn	*to teach sb*
s'entraîner **à** qch	*to practice sth*
s'exercer **à** qch	*to practice sth*
faire confiance **à** qn	*to trust sb*
faire front **à** qch	*to face sth*
faire mal **à** qn	*to hurt sb*
faire peur **à** qn	*to frighten sb*
faire pitié **à** qn	*to fill sb with pity*
faire plaisir **à** qn	*to please sb*
se fier **à** qn/qch	*to trust sb/sth*
goûter **à** qch [un aliment]	*to try sth* [food or drink]
grimper **à** qch	*to climb sth*
s'initier **à** qch	*to start learning sth*
jouer **à** qch[4]	*to play* [a sport or game]
nuire **à** qn/qch	*to harm sb/sth*
(dés)obéir **à** qn/qch	*to (dis)obey sb/sth*
s'opposer **à** qch	*to oppose sth*
pardonner **à** qn	*to forgive sb*
parvenir **à** qch	*to achieve/reach sth*
(dé)plaire **à** qn[5]	*to (dis)please sb*
s'en prendre **à** qn/qch	*to blame sb/sth*
remédier **à** qch	*to remedy sth*

---

1. But: to attend sth regularly = *aller à* Il *va à* l'université = *He attends college.*
2. Don't confuse *demander **à** qn* with *demander qn/qch* (to ask **for** sb/sth) [see p. 193]
3. But: s'échapper **de** qch (to escape ***from*** sth) [see p. 81].
4. See p. 33-34
5. See p. 195

rendre visite **à** qn[1] (= aller voir qn)	*to visit sb*
répondre **à** qn/qch	*to answer sb/sth*
résister **à** qn/qch	*to resist sb/sth*
ressembler **à** qn/qch	*to resemble sb/sth*
réussir **à** un examen	*to pass an exam*
subvenir **à** qch	*to meet* [a need]
suffire **à** qn	*to suffice sb*
succéder **à** qn/qch	*to succeed sb/sth, to follow sb/sth*
survivre **à** qn/qch	*to survive sb/sth*
téléphoner **à** qn	*to call sb* [on the phone]
tenir **à** qch/qn	*to value sth/sb*
toucher **à** qn/qch	*to touch sb/sth*

Cette robe *va* très bien **à** ma mère.	*This dress fits my mother really well.*
Nous avons *assisté* **à** la réunion.	*We attended the meeting.*
Il faut *s'attendre* **au** pire.	*One must expect the worst.*
Je vais *demander* **à** mon père.	*I am going to ask my father.*
Ils ont *échappé* **à** la mort.	*They escaped death.*
Il s'est *entraîné* **au** tir.	*He practiced shooting.*
Il *s'exerce* **à** la plongée.	*He practices diving.*
Il *fait pitié* **à** ses parents.	*His parents feel sorry for him.*
Il ne faut pas *se fier* **aux** apparences.	*One must not trust appearances.*
Vous pouvez vous *fier* **à** lui.	*You can trust him.*
Elle s'est *initiée* **à** la langue russe.	*She started learning Russian.*
Je *manque* **à** mes parents.	*My parents miss me.*
Ce produit peut *nuire* **à** votre santé.	*This product can harm your health.*
Obéissez-vous **à** vos parents?	*Do you obey your parents?*
Ils se sont *opposés* **à** son mariage.	*They opposed his marriage.*
Ça n'a pas *plu* **à** mon père.	*My father didn't like that.*
On ne peut pas *plaire* **à** tout le monde.	*One cannot please everybody.*
Il est *parvenu* **à** son but.	*He reached his goal.*
Comment allons-nous *remédier* **à** ce problème?	*How are we going to remedy this problem?*
Répondez **à** la question!	*Answer the question!*
Je ne peux pas *résister* **à** la tentation.	*I cannot resist the temptation.*

---

1. Note that ***rendre visite à*** is only used when **people** are visited. When a **place** is being visited, one uses the verb ***visiter*** followed by a direct object.
Nous **visitons** le musée. *We visit the museum.*

Il faut *subvenir* **aux** besoins des clients.	*We must meet the needs of the customers.*
Ça devrait *suffire* **à** ton ami.	*That should suffice your friend.*
Napoléon *succède* **à** Louis XVI.	*Napoleon succeeds Louis XVI.*
J'ai *survécu* **à** deux ouragans.	*I survived two hurricanes.*
Je *tiens* **à** elle/**à** mon indépendance.	*I value her/my independence.*
Touche pas **à** mon pote![1]	*Hands off my pal!*
Ne *touchez* **à** rien.	*Don't touch anything.*

Mistakes to avoid

Incorrect	*Correct*	*English meaning*
Demande ~~le~~ professeur!	Demande **au** professeur!	*Ask the teacher!*
J'ai ~~visité~~ mes parents.	J'ai **rendu visite à** mes parents.	*I visited my parents.*
J'ai téléphoné ma mère.	J'ai téléphoné **à** ma mère.	*I called my mother.*

Some verbs can take two objects and require **à** before the person(s).

apprendre qch **à** qn	*to teach sb sth*
conseiller qch **à** qn	*to advise sb sth*
défendre qch **à** qn	*to forbid sb sth*
demander qch **à** qn	*to ask sb for sth*
devoir qch **à** qn	*to owe sb sth*
dire qch **à** qn	*to tell sb sth*
enseigner qch **à** qn	*to teach sb sth*
interdire qch **à** qn	*to forbid sb sth*
offrir qch **à** qn	*to offer sb sth*
pardonner qch **à** qn	*to forgive sb sth*
passer qch **à** qn	*to pass sb sth*
permettre qch **à** qn	*to allow sb sth*
poser une question **à** qn	*to ask sb a question*
prêter qch **à** qn	*to loan sb sth*
procurer qch **à** qn	*to get sb sth*
promettre qch **à** qn	*to promise sb sth*
raconter qch **à** qn	*to tell sb sth*
rappeler qch **à** qn	*to remind sb of sth*
refuser qch **à** qn	*to refuse sb sth*
remonter le moral **à** qn	*to cheer sb up*
reprocher qch **à** qn	*to reproach sb sth/blame sb for sth*
souhaiter qch **à** qn	*to wish sb sth*

---

1. Slogan of *SOS Racisme*, an organization for the integration of immigrants.

Il a *appris* l'italien **à** ses enfants.	*He taught his children Italian.*
As-tu *prêté* la voiture **à** ton fils?	*Did you lend your son the car?*
Il a *raconté* une histoire **aux** élèves.	*He told the students a story.*
Nous avons *rappelé* la promesse **au** professeur.	*We reminded the teacher of his promise.*
J'ai *souhaité* bonne chance **à** mon ami.	*I wished my friend good luck.*

- Verbs and verbal expressions which require the preposition **de** before their complement

abuser **de** qn/qch	*to abuse/overuse sb/sth*
s'apercevoir **de** qch	*to notice sth*
(s') approcher **de** qn/qch	*to approach sb/sth*
avoir besoin **de** qn/qch	*to need sb/sth*
avoir horreur **de** qn/qch	*to abhor/loathe/hate sb/sth*
changer **de** qch[1]	*to change sth*
discuter/débattre **de** qch	*to discuss sth*
divorcer **d'avec** qn	*to divorce sb*
se doter **de** qch	*to acquire sth*
se douter **de** qch	*to suspect sth, to guess sth*
s'emparer **de** qch	*to seize sth*
faire abstraction **de** qch	*to disregard sth*
faire la connaissance **de** qn	*to meet sb* (for the first time)
faire (le) don **de** qch (à qn)	*to donate sth (to sb)*
faire l'éloge **de** qn/qch	*to praise sb/sth*
faire l'expérience **de** qch	*to experience sth*
faire part **de** qch à qn	*to announce sth to sb*
faire preuve **de** qch	*to show sth* [a quality or virtue]
hériter **de** qch	*to inherit sth*
jouer **de** qch[2]	*to play sth* [a musical instrument]
jouir **de** qch	*to enjoy sth*
manquer **de** qch[3]	*to lack sth*
médire **de** qn	*to slander sb*
se méfier **de** qn/qch	*to distrust sb/sth*
partir **de** qch	*to leave sth*
redoubler **de** qch	*to double sth*

---

1. See p. 192 2. See p. 49-50 3. See p. 193

se rendre compte **de** qch	*to realize sth*
se repentir **de** qch	*to regret sth*
se servir **de** qch	*to use sth*
se souvenir **de** qn/qch	*to remember sb/sth*
témoigner **de** qch	*to show/prove sth*
se tromper **de** qch	*to have the wrong* [+ noun]
traiter qn **de** [+ pejorative noun]	*to call sb sth* [pejorative]
user **de** qch	*to use sth*
ne pas vouloir **de** qn/qch	*not to want sb/sth*

Ils ont *abusé* **de** moi/**de** ma bonté.	*They abused me/my kindness.*
Il s'est *aperçu* **de** votre absence.	*He noticed your absence.*
Elle s'est *approchée* **de** moi.	*She approached me.*
As-tu *besoin* **de** quelque chose?	*Do you need something?*
J'*ai horreur* **des** menteurs.	*I hate liars.*
Changeons **de** sujet.	*Let's change the subject.*
Nous avons *discuté* **des** prix.	*We discussed the prices.*
La ville s'est *dotée* **d'**une université.	*The city acquired a university.*
Je *me doute* **de** ses sentiments.	*I can guess his feelings.*
Le général a *fait l'éloge* **des** soldats.	*The general praised the soldiers.*
Il m'a *fait part* **de** ses intentions.	*He announced his intentions to me.*
Faites-moi *part* **de** vos pensées.	*Let me know your thoughts.*
Les pompiers ont *fait preuve* **de** courage.	*The firemen showed courage.*
Ils ont *hérité* **d'**une fortune.	*They inherited a fortune.*
Il *jouit* **d'**une bonne réputation.	*He enjoys a good reputation.*
Il *manque* **de** savoir-vivre.	*He lacks good manners.*
Il a *redoublé* **d'**efforts.	*He doubled his efforts.*
Je me *rends compte* **de** mon erreur.	*I realize my mistake.*
Il s'est *repenti* **de** son action.	*He regretted his action.*
Je ne me *souviens* pas **de** cette dame.	*I don't remember that lady.*
Ça *témoigne* **de** leur courage.	*That proves their courage.*
Elle m'a *traité* **de** tous les noms.	*She called me all sorts of names.*
Il s'est *trompé* **d'**adresse/**de** numéro.	*He had the wrong address/number.*
Il n'a pas *voulu* **du** cadeau que je lui avais offert.	*He didn't want the gift I had given to him.*

- Verbs and verbal expressions which require other prepositions before their complement

s'acharner **sur** qn	*to hound sb*
appuyer **sur** qch	*to press sth*
avoir confiance **en** qn/qch	*to trust sb/sth*
s'embarquer **sur** un vol	*to board a flight*
l'emporter **sur** qn	*to beat/defeat sb*
l'emporter **sur** qch	*to surpass/outweigh sth*
enquêter **sur** qch	*to investigate sth*
entrer **dans** qch[1]	*to enter sth*
grimper **sur** qch	*to climb sth*
insister **sur** qch	*to stress sth*
se marier **avec** qn[2] (= épouser qn)	*to marry sb*
mettre l'accent **sur** qch	*to emphasize sth*
mettre la main **sur** qch	*to confiscate sth*
renchérir **sur** qn/qch	*to outdo sb/sth*
sortir **avec** qn	*to date sb*
tirer **sur** qn/qch	*to shoot sb/sth*

Il faut appuyer **sur** le bouton.	*You have to press the button.*
Il l'emporta **sur** les autres joueurs.	*He beat the other players.*
Les enfants grimpent **sur** l'arbre.	*The children climb the tree.*
Le professeur insistait **sur** la nécessité de faire ses devoirs.	*The teacher stressed the need to do one's homework.*
Elle s'est mariée **avec** un médecin.	*She married a doctor.*
Il a tiré **sur** le président.	*He shot the president.*

Mistakes to avoid

Incorrect	*Correct*	*English meaning*
Elle ~~a marié~~ Paul.	Elle **s'est** mariée **avec** Paul.	*She married Paul.*

---

1. But: *entrer **à*** [+ institution] (see p. 125)
2. But: *marier qn* (to marry sb **off**)

C. Verbs and expressions which take one preposition in French and a different one in English

accabler qn **de** qch	*to overburden sb **with** sth*
accoucher **de** qn	*to give birth **to** sb*
acheter qch **à** qn	*to buy sth **for/from** sb*
s'apitoyer **sur** qn	*to feel sorry **for** sb*
arracher qch **à** qn	*to snatch/grab sth **from** sb*
aspirer **à** qch	*to yearn **for** sth*
assister qn **de** qch	*to help sb **with** sth*
attirer l'attention de qn **sur** qch	*to draw someone's attention **to** sth*
avoir affaire **à** qn	*to be dealing **with** sb*
avoir l'air **de** qn/qch	*to look **like** sb/sth*
avoir de l'aversion **pour** qn/qch	*to have an aversion **to** sb/sth*
avoir le coup de foudre **pour** qn	*to fall head over heels in love **with** sb*
avoir droit **à** qch	*to be eligible **for** sth*
avoir égard **à** qch	*to have consideration **for** sth*
avoir des égards **pour** qn	*to be considerate **toward** sb*
avoir envie **de** qch	*to feel **like** (having) sth*
avoir un goût **de** qch	*to taste **like** sth*
avoir l'habitude **de** qch	*to be used **to** sth*
en avoir assez/marre (fam.) **de** qch	*to be fed up **with** sth*
avoir une bonne mémoire **de** qch	*to have a good memory **for** sth*
avoir la passion **de** qch	*to have a passion **for** sth*
avoir pitié **de** qn	*to feel sorry **for**/to have pity **on** sb*
avoir/assumer la responsabilité **de**	*to have/take responsibility **for** sth*
cacher qch **à** qn	*to hide sth **from** sb*
choisir **parmi** qn/qch	*to choose **from** sb/sth*
commencer **par** qch	*to begin **with** sth*
ne rien comprendre/connaître **à** qch	*to understand/know nothing **about** sth*
se confier **à** qn	*to confide **in** sb*
consister **en** qch	*to consist **of** sth*
se contenter **de** qch	*to be satisfied **with** sth*
convenir **de** qch	*to agree **on** sth* [price, date]
copier **sur** qn	*to copy **from** sb*
couvrir qn/qch **de** qch	*to cover sb/sth **with** sth*
croire **à** qch	*to believe **in** sth*
déborder **de** qch	*to be overflowing **with** sth*
décider **de** qch	*to decide **on** sth*
se déguiser **en** qn/qch	*to disguise **as** sb/sth*
dépendre **de** qn/qch	*to depend **on** sb/sth*
dépenser de l'argent **pour** qch	*to spend money **on** sth*

se désintéresser **de** qch/qn	*to lose interest **in** sth/sb*
se diriger **vers**	*to head **for***
se disputer **pour** qch	*to argue **over** sth*
donner **sur** qch	*to look **out** on sth*
doter qn/qch **de** qch	*to equip/endow sb/sth **with** sth*
douter **de** qch/qn	*to have one's doubts **about** sth/sb*
échanger qch **contre** qch	*to exchange sth **for** sth*
s'écraser **sur** (or: **contre**)	*to crash **into***
s'émerveiller **de** qch	*to marvel **at** sth*
s'empiffrer/se goinfrer **de** qch (fam.)	*to stuff oneself **with** sth*
emprunter qch **à** qn	*to borrow sth **from** sb*
s'enquérir **de** qch	*to inquire **about** sth*
enquêter **sur** qch	*to carry out an investigation **into** sth*
entendre parler **de** qn/qch	*to hear **about** sb/sth*
s'entretenir **avec** qn (**de** qch)	*to speak **to** sb (**about** sth)*
s'éprendre **de** qn	*to fall in love **with** sb*
équiper qn **de** qch	*to equip sb **with** sth*
s'étonner **de** qch	*to be surprised **at/by** sth*
s'excuser (**auprès de** qn) **de** qch	*to apologize (**to** sb) **for** sth*
se fâcher **contre** qn	*to get angry **with**/mad **at** sb*
faire l'amour **avec** qn	*to make love **to** sb*
faire concurrence **à** qn	*to compete **with** sb*
faire une demande **de** qch	*to apply **for** sth*
faire face **à** qch	*to cope **with** sth*
faire partie **de** qch	*to belong **to** sth*
faire qch **de** qch/qn	*to do sth **with** sth/sb*
farcir qch **de** qch	*to stuff sth **with** sth*
féliciter qn **de** (or: **pour**) qch	*to congratulate sb **on** sth*
se féliciter **de** qch	*to be pleased **about** sth*
se fiancer **avec** qn	*to get engaged **to** sb*
fourmiller **de** qn/qch	*to be swarming/bustling **with** sb/sth*
hésiter **sur** qch	*not to be sure **about** sth*
se heurter **contre** (or: **à**) qch/qn	*to bump **into** sth/sb*
s'identifier **à** (or: **avec**) qn/qch	*to identify **with** sb/sth*
s'illustrer **dans** qch	*to become famous **through** sth*
s'incliner **devant** qn/qch	*to bow **to** sb/sth*
inculper qn **de** qch	*to charge sb **with** sth*
informer qn **de** qch	*to inform sb **about** sth*
s'informer **de** qch	*to inquire **about** sth*
s'inquiéter **pour** (or: **de**) qn/qch	*to worry **about** sb/sth*
s'inscrire **à** qch	*to register **for** sth, to enroll **in** sth*

s'intéresser **à** qn/qch	*to be interested **in** sb/sth*
s'irriter **de** qch	*to get annoyed **about** sth*
se lamenter **sur** (or: **de**) qch	*to moan **about** sth*
lésiner **sur** qch	*to be stingy / sparing **with** sth*
se marier **avec** qn	*to get married **to** sb*
se mêler **de** qch	*to meddle **in** / stick one's nose **in** sth*
se méprendre **sur** qch	*to be wrong **about** sth*
se mettre en colère **contre** qn	*to get angry **with** / mad **at** sb*
monter **dans** qch	*to get **on** sth* [a train, bus, etc.]
munir qn **de** qch	*to provide sb **with** sth*
se munir **de** qch	*to equip oneself **with** sth*
nourrir qn **de** (or: **avec**) qch	*to feed sb **with** sth*
se nourrir **de** (or: **avec**) qch	*to live **on** / feed oneself **with** sth*
s'occuper **de** qn/qch	*to look **after** (= take care of) sb/sth*
opérer qn **de** qch	*to operate sb **on** sth*
orner qch **de** qch	*to decorate sth **with** sth*
parler **de** qch/qn	*to speak / talk **about** sth/sb*
participer **à** qch	*to participate **in**, to take part **in** sth*
passer **à** qch	*to pass / drop / stop **by** sth* [a place]
passer **devant** qch	*to go **by** sth*
se passer **de** qn/qch	*to do **without** sb/sth*
penser **à** qn/qch[1]	*to think **of** (or: **about**) sb/sth*
se plaindre **de** qch	*to complain **about** sth*
se précipiter **sur** qn	*to rush **toward** sb*
prendre garde **à**	*to watch out **for***
prendre qch **à** qn	*to take sth **from** sb*
s'en prendre **à** qn/qch	*to put the blame **on** sb/sth*
prendre parti **pour** qn	*to side **with** sb*
prendre sa revanche **sur** qn	*to get even **with** sb*
prendre soin **de** qn/qch	*to look **after** sb/sth*
se préparer **à** qch[2]	*to prepare **for** sth, to get ready **for** sth*
presser qn **de** qch	*to overwhelm sb **with** sth*
prévenir qn **de** qch	*to inform sb **about** sth*
se priver **de** qch	*to do **without** sth*
qualifier qn/qch **de** qn/qch	*to describe sb/sth **as** sb/sth*
raffoler **de** qn/qch	*to be crazy **about** sb / keen **on** sth*
se rapprocher **de** qn/qch	*to get closer **to** sb/sth*
récompenser qn **de** (or: **pour**) qch	*to reward sb **for** sth*

1. For the difference between *penser à* and *penser de*, see p. 194.
2. But: se préparer **pour** un examen = *to prepare / study **for** an exam*

réfléchir **à** (or: **sur**) qch	*to think* ***about*** */ to reflect* ***on/upon*** *sth*
regorger **de** qch	*to be packed* ***with*** */abound* ***in*** *sth*
se réjouir **de** qch	*to be happy* ***about*** *sth*
remercier qn **de** (or: **pour**) qch	*to thank sb* ***for*** *sth*
remplir qch **de** qch	*to fill sth* ***with*** *sth*
renoncer **à** qch	*to give* ***up*** *sth*
se renseigner **sur** qch	*to inquire* ***about*** *sth*
renseigner qn **sur** qch	*to inform sb* ***about*** *sth*
répondre **de** qn/qch	*to account/ vouch* ***for*** *sb/sth*
reporter qch **à**	*to postpone sth* ***until***
ressembler **à** qn/qch	*to look* ***like*** *sb/sth*
retirer qch **à** qn	*to take sth away* ***from*** *sb*
rire **de** qn/qch	*to laugh* ***at/about*** *sb/sth*
se ruer **sur** qn/qch	*to rush* ***at*** *sb /* ***to*** *sth*
saisir qch **à** qn	*to seize sth* ***from*** *sb*
servir **de** qch	*to be good* ***for*** *sth, to serve* ***as*** *sth*
songer **à** qn/qch	*to think* ***of*** *sb/sth*
se soucier **de** qn/qch	*to worry* ***about*** *sb/sth*
substituer qn/qch **à** qn/qch	*to substitute sb/sth* ***for*** *sb/sth*
subvenir **à** [un besoin]	*to provide* ***for*** [a need]
tenir **de** qn	*to take* ***after*** *sb*
tenir compte **de** qch	*to take sth* ***into*** *account*
tenir lieu (à qn) **de** qch	*to serve (sb)* ***as*** *sth*
tenir qn pour responsable **de** qch	*to hold sb responsible* ***for*** *sth*
tirer **sur** qn/qch	*to shoot* ***at*** *sb/sth*
tomber amoureux **de** qn/qch	*to fall in love* ***with*** *sb/sth*
tomber **sur** qn	*to run* ***into*** *sb (= meet sb accidentally)*
tomber **sur** qch	*to come* ***across*** *sth*
traiter qn **de** [+ nom péjoratif]	*to treat sb* ***like*** [+ pejorative noun]
traiter **de** qch	*to be* ***about*** *sth, to deal* ***with***
triompher **de** qn/qch	*to triumph* ***over*** *sb/sth*
se tromper **sur** qn	*to be wrong* ***about*** *sb*
troquer qch **contre** qch	*to trade/ swap sth* ***for*** *sth*
trouver à redire **à** qch	*to find fault* ***with*** *sth*
se vanter **de** qn/qch	*to brag* ***about*** *sb/sth*
veiller **à** qch	*to look* ***after*** *sth*
veiller **sur** qn/qch	*to watch* ***over*** *sb/sth*
se venger **de** qn/qch	*to take revenge* ***on*** *sb/sth*
vivre **de** qch	*to live* ***on*** *sth*
voler qch **à** qn	*to steal sth* ***from*** *sb*
en vouloir **à** qn **de** qch	*to hold a grudge* ***against*** *sb* ***for*** *sth*

Il nous a *accablés* **de** reproches.	*He crushed us* ***with*** *reproaches.*
Elle a *accouché* **d'**une petite fille.	*She gave birth* ***to*** *a little girl.*
Assistez-le **de** vos conseils!	*Help him* ***with*** *your advice!*
Nous *avons affaire* **à** des terroristes.	*We are dealing* ***with*** *terrorists.*
Il *a l'air* **d'**un avocat.	*He looks* ***like*** *a lawyer.*
J'en *ai assez* **de** tes mensonges.	*I am fed up* ***with*** *your lies.*
J'*ai envie* **de** ce travail.	*I feel* ***like*** *(having) this job.*
Ayons égard **à** son âge.	*Let's have consideration* ***for*** *his age.*
Ayez des *égards* **pour** ces gens.	*Be considerate* ***toward*** *these people.*
Il *a l'habitude* **de** ce temps.	*He is used* ***to*** *this weather.*
Elle *a* une *mémoire* phénoménale **des** visages et **des** noms.	*She has a phenomenal memory* ***for*** *faces and names.*
Il *a* la *passion* **des** voyages.	*He has a passion* ***for*** *travel.*
Ayez pitié **de** moi!	*Have pity* ***on*** *me!*
J'*ai pitié* **de** vous.	*I feel sorry* ***for*** *you.*
Ils ont *choisi* leur représentant **parmi** plusieurs candidats.	*They chose their representative* ***from*** *several candidates.*
Je vais *commencer* **par** une expression idiomatique.	*I am going to begin* ***with*** *an idiomatic expression.*
Je ne *comprends* rien **aux** maths.	*I understand nothing* ***about*** math.
Ils ne *connaissent* rien **à** l'histoire du cinéma.	*They know nothing* ***about*** *the history of the cinema.*
Je me *contenterai* **du** reste.	*I will be satisfied* ***with*** *the rest.*
Elle a *couvert* la table **d'**une nappe.	*She covered the table* ***with*** *a tablecloth.*
Il a *couvert* son visage **de** ses mains.	*He covered his face* ***with*** *his hands.*
Il *croit* **aux** revenants.	*He believes* ***in*** *ghosts.*
Cet homme *déborde* **d'**enthousiasme.	*This man overflows* ***with*** *enthusiasm.*
Il *décide* **de** la politique de son pays.	*He decides* ***on*** *his country's politics.*
Je me suis *déguisée* **en** bergère.	*I disguised myself* ***as*** *a shepherdess.*
Ça *dépend* **de** toi.	*That depends* ***on*** *you.*
La fenêtre de sa chambre *donne* **sur** le jardin.	*The window of her/his room looks* ***out*** *on the yard.*
Je *doute* **de** sa sincérité.	*I have doubts* ***about*** *his honesty.*
Je commence à *douter* **de** lui.	*I am beginning to have doubts* ***about*** *him.*
J'ai *échangé* le pull **contre** un autre.	*I exchanged the sweater* ***for*** *another one.*

Il s'est *émerveillé* **de** mon exploit.	*He marvelled* ***at*** *my accomplishment.*
J'ai beaucoup *entendu parler* **de** vous.	*I heard a lot* ***about*** *you.*
Il s'est *épris* **d'**elle.	*He fell in love* ***with*** *her.*
Nous nous sommes longtemps *entretenus* **des** problèmes.	*We talked a long time* ***about*** *the problems.*
Pourquoi vous *étonnez*-vous **de** cette nouvelle?	*Why are you surprised* ***by*** *this piece of news?*
Il s'est *excusé* **auprès d'**elle **de** l'erreur qu'il avait faite.	*He apologized* ***to*** *her* ***for*** *the error he had made.*
Que *faire* **d'**un enfant qui ne veut pas apprendre?	*What should one do* ***with*** *a child who doesn't want to learn?*
Nous allons *faire* un avocat **de** lui.	*We are going to make a lawyer* ***out of*** *him.*
Il a *fait une demande* **de** bourse.	*He applied* ***for*** *a scholarship.*
Il *fait partie* **de** ce groupe.	*He belongs* ***to*** *this group.*
On *farcit* la dinde **de** marrons.	*One stuffs the turkey* ***with*** *chestnuts.*
Je vous *félicite* **de** votre réussite.	*I congratulate you* ***on*** *your success.*
Il se *félicite* **de** l'issue du procès.	*He is pleased* ***with*** *the outcome of the trial.*
Ce livre *fourmille* **d'**anecdotes.	*This book is swarming* ***with*** *anecdotes.*
Il *hésite* **sur** la décision à prendre.	*He is not sure* ***about*** *which decision to make.*
Il *s'est heurté* **contre** un mur.	*He bumped* ***into*** *a wall.*
L'acteur s'*identifie* **à** son rôle.	*The actor identifies* ***with*** *his role.*
On l'a *inculpé* **d'**homicide.	*He was charged* ***with*** *homicide.*
Il m'a *informé* **de** son arrivée.	*He informed me* ***about*** *his/her arrival.*
Ne vous *inquiétez* pas **pour** moi!	*Don't worry* ***about*** *me.*
Il *s'inquiète* **du** retard de l'avion.	*He is worried* ***about*** *the plane being late.*
Je vais *m'inscrire* **à** ce cours.	*I am going to register* ***for*** *this course.*
Il *s'intéresse* **à** tout.	*He is interested* ***in*** *everything.*
Elle s'est *irritée* **de** cette réponse.	*She got annoyed* ***about*** *this answer.*
Ne vous *mêlez* pas **de** mes affaires.	*Don't stick your nose* ***in*** *my business.*
Mêle-toi **de** ce qui te regarde.	*Stick your nose* ***in*** *your own business.*
Je *me mettrai en colère* **contre** lui.	*I will get angry* ***with*** *him.*
Nous avons *muni* les enfants **de** provisions.	*We provided the children* ***with*** *food.*

Je me suis *muni* **de** devises.	*I equipped myself* ***with*** *foreign currency.*
Il se *nourrit* **de** légumes.	*He lives* ***on*** *vegetables.*
On l'a *opéré* **du** cœur.	*They operated* ***on*** *his heart.*
Je *passerai* **à** votre bureau.	*I will stop* ***by*** *your office.*
Il est *passé* **devant** la bibliothèque.	*He went* ***by*** *the library.*
Au baccalauréat, les élèves doivent *se passer* **de** dictionnaire.	*At the bac exam, the students must do* ***without*** *a dictionary.*
Est-ce que tu *penses* **à** tes vacances?	*Do you think* ***of*** *your vacation?*
Elle s'est *plainte* **de** moi.	*She complained* ***about*** *me.*
Il a *pris le parti* **de** Pierre.	*He agreed/sided* ***with*** *Peter.*
Préparez-vous **au** départ/**au** pire!	*Prepare* ***for*** *departure/****for*** *the worst!*
Prévenez-nous **de** votre visite.	*Inform us* ***about*** *your visit.*
La colonne d'Austerlitz a été faite avec le bronze des canons *pris* **aux** Autrichiens et **aux** Russes.	*The Austerlitz column was made with the bronze of the cannons taken* ***from*** *the Austrians and the Russians.*
Elle s'*en est prise* **à** lui.	*She put the blame* ***on*** *him.*
Il m'a *pressé* **de** questions.	*He bombarded me* ***with*** *questions.*
Ils *se sont privés* **de** tout.	*They gave* ***up*** *everything.*
Il m'a *qualifié* **de** menteur.	*He described me* ***as*** *(= called me) a liar.*
Les enfants *raffolent* **des** céréales.	*Children are crazy* ***about*** *cereal.*
On l'a *récompensé* **de** son travail.	*He was rewarded* ***for*** *his work.*
Ils *réfléchissent* **à** l'avenir.	*They think* ***about*** *the future.*
La France *regorge* **de** trésors cachés.	*France is packed* ***with*** *hidden treasures.*
Je me *réjouis* **de** cette nouvelle.	*I am happy* ***about*** *this piece of news.*
Je vous *remercie* **de** votre attention.	*I thank you* ***for*** *your attention.*
Il *remplit* la bouteille **d'**eau.	*He fills the bottle* ***with*** *water.*
Cela m'a *rempli* **d'**espoir.	*That filled me* ***with*** *hope.*
J'ai dû *renoncer* **à** ce projet.	*I had to give* ***up*** *this plan.*
On a *reporté* la visite **à** un autre jour.	*They postponed the visit* ***until*** *another day.*
Elle *ressemble* **à** un mannequin.	*She looks* ***like*** *a fashion model.*
Ne *riez* pas **de** moi!	*Don't laugh* ***at*** *me!*
Il *sert* **de** bouc émissaire.	*He serves* ***as*** *a scapegoat.*
Cela me *servira* **de** leçon.	*That will serve me* ***as*** *a lesson.*

Les allocations familiales sont destinées à *subvenir* **aux** enfants.	*The family allowances are intended to provide* ***for*** *the children.*
Il *tient* **de** son père.	*He takes* ***after*** *his father.*
Cet instrument leur *tenait lieu* **de** marteau.	*This instrument served them* ***as*** *a hammer.*
Elle est *tombée amoureuse* **de** lui.	*She fell in love* ***with*** *him.*
Il m'a *traité* **de** menteur/**d'**imbécile.	*He treated me* ***like*** *a liar/****like*** *an idiot.*
Ce livre *traite* **de** l'histoire de France.	*This book deals* ***with*** *the history of France.*
Il a *triomphé* **de** tous les obstacles.	*He triumphed* ***over*** *all obstacles.*
Elle *trouve à redire* **à** tout.	*She finds fault* ***with*** *everything.*
Il se *vante* **de** son courage.	*He brags* ***about*** *his courage.*
Il *veille* **à** vos intérêts.	*He looks* ***after*** *your interests.*
Veille **sur** ton frère.	*Watch* ***over*** *your brother.*
Je vais *me venger* **de** vous.	*I am going to take revenge* ***on*** *you.*
Je lui *en veux* **de** son impatience.	*I am angry with him* ***for*** *his impatience.*

Mistakes to avoid

Incorrect	*Correct*	*English meaning*
Ça dépend ~~sur~~ la circulation.	Ça dépend **de** la circulation.	*That depends* ***on*** *the traffic.*

Do not confuse

♦ **apprendre** qch — *to learn sth*

Nous apprenons le français. — *We learn French.*

apprendre qch ***de*** (or: **par**) qn — *to learn/find out sth from sb*

J'ai appris cela **d'**un ami. — *I learned that from a friend.*

apprendre qch ***à*** qn — *to teach sb sth*

Il apprend la grammaire **aux** élèves. — *He teaches the students grammar.*

♦ **aspirer** qch — *to suck sth up, to vacuum sth*

On aspire la poussière avec un aspirateur. — *One sucks up the dust with a vacuum cleaner.*

aspirer ***à*** qch — *to yearn for sth*

Il aspirait **à** la gloire. — *He yearned for glory.*

♦ **assister** qn — *to help sb*
Ils ont assisté les pauvres. — *They helped the poor.*

assister qn ***de*** qch — *to help sb with sth*
On les a assistés **de** nos conseils. — *We helped them with our advice.*

assister *à* qch — *to attend sth*
Nous avons assisté **à** la messe de minuit. — *We attended midnight Mass.*

♦ **attendre** qn/qch — *to wait for sb/sth*
Ils attendent le tramway. — *They are waiting for the light-rail.*

attendre qch ***de*** qn — *to expect sth from sb*
Qu'est-ce que tu attends **de** moi? — *What do you expect from me?*

s'attendre *à* qch — *to expect sth*
Je m'attendais **à** tout, sauf **à** cela. — *I expected everything, except that.*

♦ **changer** qn/qch — *to change sb/sth* ***(by altering)***
On ne peut pas changer les gens. — *One cannot change people.*
Il a changé son comportement. — *He changed his behavior.*

changer *de* qch — *to change sth* ***(by replacing it)***
As-tu changé **d'**adresse? — *Did you change your address?*
J'ai dû changer **de** train/**d'**avion. — *I had to change trains/planes.*

changer qch ***en*** qch — *to change sth into sth*
Il a changé 100 dollars ***en*** euros. — *He changed 100 dollars into euros.*

♦ **conduire *à*** — *to lead to*
Ce chemin conduit **à** l'église. — *This road leads to the church.*

conduire qn ***à*** qch — *to lead sb to sth*
Ces événements l'ont conduit **au** suicide. — *These events led him to (commit) suicide.*

conduire qn ***à*** [un endroit] — *to drive sb to* [a place]
Je vais vous conduire **à** l'hôtel. — *I am going to drive you to the hotel.*

♦ **convenir *à*** qn — *to suit sb, to be suitable for sb*
Cette date ne convient pas **à** mon père. — *This date doesn't suit my father.*

convenir *de* qch — *to agree on sth*
Ils ont convenu **du** prix de la maison. — *They agreed on the price of the house.*

♦ **croire** qn/qch — *to believe sb/sth*
Nous croyons le professeur. — *We believe the teacher.*
Je ne crois pas cette histoire. — *I don't believe this story.*

croire *à* qn/qch — *to believe in sb/sth*
Les enfants croient **au** Père Noël. — *Children believe in Santa Claus.*

croire *en* qn — *to (fully) believe in sb*
Les chrétiens croient **en** Dieu. — *Christians believe in God.*

♦ **demander** qn/qch — *to ask for sb/sth*
On demande Paul au téléphone. — *They're asking for Paul on the phone.*
Ils demandent des dommages-intérêts. — *They are asking for damages.*

demander *à* qn — *to ask sb*
J'ai demandé **à** la dame. — *I asked the lady.*
Demande **au** patron! — *Ask the boss!*

demander qch ***à*** qn — *to ask sb for sth/request sth from sb*
Je lui ai demandé son avis. — *I asked him for his opinion.*
Demandons l'heure **au** monsieur. — *Let's ask the gentleman for the time.*

demander [+ prix] **de** qch — *to charge/ask* [+ price] *for sth*
Il demande 300 000 euros **de** la maison. — *He asks 300 000 euros for the house.*

♦ **descendre** qn — *to shoot/kill sb*
On l'a descendu d'un coup de revolver. — *He was shot with a gun.*

descendre qch — *to go down sth, to carry sth down*
Ils ont descendu l'escalier. — *They went down the stairs.*
As-tu descendu les bagages au rez-de-chaussée? — *Did you carry down the luggage to the first floor?*

descendre *de* qch — *to get off/out of* [a vehicle]
Ils sont descendus **de** la voiture/**du** train/**de** l'avion. — *They got out of the car/off the train/off the plane.*

descendre *de* qn — *to be descended from sb*
Il descend **de** Louis XIV. — *He is descended from Louis XIV.*

♦ **jouer *à*** qch[1] — *to play sth* [a sport or game]
Elle joue **au** tennis. — *She plays tennis.*

jouer *de* qch[2] — *to play sth* [a musical instrument]
Je joue **du** piano. — *I play the piano.*

♦ **manquer** qch — *to miss sth* [a train, a bus, a plane, an opportunity, or an event]
Ne manque pas l'avion! — *Don't miss the plane!*
Il a manqué l'école. — *He missed school.*

manquer *de* qch — *to lack sth*
Ils manquent **de** patience/**d'**aliments. — *They lack patience/food.*

manquer *à* qn[3] — *to be missed by sb*
Paris manque **à** ma sœur. — *My sister misses Paris.*

---

1. See p. 33-34 2. See p. 49-50 3. See p. 195

♦ **marier** qn	*to marry sb off, to unite sb in marriage*
Elle a encore une fille à marier.	*She still has a daughter to marry off.*
Le prêtre a marié le couple.	*The priest married the couple.*
se marier ***avec*** qn	*to marry sb*
Il s'est marié **avec** Chantal.	*He married Chantal.*
♦ **monter** qch	*to go up sth, to carry sth up*
J'aime monter les Champs-Elysées.	*I like to go up the Champs-Elysées.*
J'ai monté les valises au grenier.	*I carried the suitcases up to the attic.*
monter ***dans*** qch	*to get in/on* [a vehicle]
Nous sommes montés **dans** le train.	*We got on the train.*
Il est monté **dans** la voiture.	*He got in the car.*
♦ **penser** ***à*** qn/qch	*to think of/about sb/sth* = to have one's thoughts with sb/sth
Je pense **à** mon voyage/**à** mon ami.	*I think about my trip/of my friend.*
penser ***de*** qn/qch	*to think of/about sb/sth* = to have an **opinion** of sb/sth
Que pensez-vous **de** ce problème?	*What do you think of this problem?* (= What is your opinion?)
Je te dirai ce que je pense **d'**elle.	*I will tell you what I think of her.*
♦ **répondre** ***à*** qn/qch	*to answer sb/sth*
Elle a répondu **à** la lettre.	*She answered the letter.*
répondre ***de*** qn/qch	*to account/vouch for sb/sth*
Je réponds **de** lui.	*I vouch for him.*
Il doit répondre **de** son rôle dans la guerre.	*He must account for his role in the war.*
répondre ***par*** qch	*to reply with sth*
Il a répondu **par** des injures.	*He replied with insults.*
♦ **servir** qn/qch	*to serve sb/sth*
Elle sert le dîner.	*She serves dinner.*
servir ***à***	*to be good for, to be used for*
Cela ne sert **à** rien.	*It's not used/good for anything.*
servir ***de*** qn/qch	*to serve as sth, to act as sb*
Il sert **d'**interprète.	*He acts as an interpreter.*
Ce couteau sert **de** coupe-papier.	*This knife serves as a letter opener.*
se servir ***de*** qch	*to use sth*
Les Chinois se servent **de** baguettes pour manger le riz.	*The Chinese use chopsticks to eat rice.*

♦ **sortir** qch — *to take sth out*
Je dois sortir la poubelle. — *I must take out the garbage can.*
sortir *de* qch — *to go out of sth*
Il est sorti **du** bâtiment. — *He went out of the building.*

♦ **tenir** qch/qn — *to hold/keep sb/sth*
Il a tenu sa promesse. — *He kept his promise.*
tenir *à* qn/qch — *to value/care about sb/sth*
Je tiens beaucoup **à** la vie/**à** mes amis. — *I value life/my friends a lot.*
tenir *de* qn — *to take after sb*
Elle tient **de** sa mère. — *She takes after her mother.*

♦ **user** qch — *to wear sth out*
Il a usé ses chaussures. — *He wore out his shoes.*
user *de* qch — *to use sb/sth*
Il use et abuse **de** ses enfants. — *He uses and abuses his children.*

♦ **veiller *à*** qch — *to look after sth*
Il veille **à** mon bien-être. — *He looks after my well-being.*
veiller *sur* qn/qch — *to watch over sb/sth*
Nous veillons **sur** les enfants. — *We watch over the children.*

Translation difficulties

1. to miss

When the verb ***to miss*** expresses regret about the absence of something or someone, it is translated into French with *manquer **à***.

His parents miss him. — Il manque **à** ses parents.[1]

Note that the *object* of the English sentence (*him*) becomes the *subject* of the French sentence (*il*), and the *subject* of the English sentence (*his parents*) becomes the ***indirect object*** of the French sentence (***à** ses parents*).

2. to like

The verb ***to like*** is frequently translated into French with *plaire **à**.*

The students like the book. — Le livre plaît **aux** élèves.[2]

Note that, as with 'manquer à', the *object* of the English sentence becomes the *subject* of the French sentence, and the *subject* of the English sentence becomes the ***indirect object*** of the French sentence.

---

1. lit.: *He lacks **to** his parents.*
2. lit.: *The book pleases **to** the students.*

3. The English preposition **about** has several equivalents in French

- **to be about** referring to the subject matter of a film, book, article, play, etc. is translated with **s'agir de**

What is this novel **about**?	De quoi **s'agit**-il **dans** ce roman?[1]
This book is **about** the war.	**Dans** ce livre, **il s'agit** de la guerre.[2]
What is it **about**?	**De** quoi s'agit-il?[3]

Mistakes to avoid

Incorrect	*Correct*	*English meaning*
~~Cette pièce s'agit~~ de...	**Dans** cette pièce, **il** s'agit de...	*This play is about...*

- **about** is translated with **sur** in the following instances

a book/movie **about**...	un livre/film **sur**...
He read/wrote a book **about** France.	Il a lu/écrit un livre **sur** la France.
It's a play **about** love.	C'est une pièce **sur** l'amour.
to agree **about** sth	être/se mettre d'accord **sur** qch
They agreed **about** the price.	Ils se sont mis d'accord **sur** le prix.
to alert sb **about** sth	alerter qn **sur** qch
to ask a question **about** sth	poser une question **sur** qch
She asked questions **about** this wine.	Elle a posé des questions **sur** ce vin.
to give one's opinion **about** sth/sb	donner son avis/opinion **sur** qch/qn
What is your opinion **about** this book?	Quelle est votre opinion **sur** ce livre?
I ask you for your opinion **about** her.	Je vous demande votre avis **sur** elle.
to inform sb **about** sth/sb	renseigner qn **sur** qch/qn
Can you give us some information **about** him?	Pouvez-vous nous renseigner **sur** lui?
to inquire **about** sb/sth	se renseigner **sur** qn/qch
We inquired **about** the train schedule.	On s'est renseigné **sur** les horaires des trains.

---

1. Also: **De** quoi parle ce roman?
2. Also: Ce livre traite **de**/parle **de** la guerre.
3. Or: C'est **à** quel sujet?

to keep quiet **about** sth	se taire **sur** qch
to know sth **about** sb/sth	savoir qch **sur** (or: **de**) qn/qch
I would like to know more **about** this person.	Je voudrais savoir plus **sur** cette personne.
I don't know much **about** him.	Je ne sais pas beaucoup **sur** lui.
He knows everything **about** this car.	Il sait tout **sur** cette voiture.
To know more **about** this story...	Pour en savoir plus **sur** cette histoire...
to question sb **about** sth	interroger/questionner qn **sur** qch
to read sth **about** sth/sb	lire qch **sur** qch/qn
I read all **about** her.	J'ai tout lu **sur** elle.
to say/tell sth **about** sb/sth	dire/raconter qch **sur** qn/qch
He says nice things **about** her.	Il dit des choses gentilles **sur** elle.
That's all one can say **about** this castle.	C'est tout ce qu'on peut dire **sur** ce château.
to tell the truth **about** sth/sb	dire la vérité **sur** qn/qch
I am fed up with all one says **about** me.	J'en ai marre de tout ce qu'on raconte **sur** moi.
to be strict **about** sth	être strict **sur** qch
to think/reflect **about** sth	réfléchir **sur** (or: **à**) qch
to wonder **about** sth	se poser des questions **sur** qch, s'interroger **sur** qch
I wonder **about** my future.	Je m'interroge **sur** mon avenir.
to write **about** sth/sb	écrire **sur** (= *au sujet de*) qch/qn
She wrote an article **about** Morocco.	Elle a écrit un article **sur** le Maroc.
to be wrong/mistaken **about** sth	se tromper/avoir tort **sur** qch
I was wrong **about** that.	J'avais tort **sur** ce point.
How do you feel **about**...?	Quel est votre sentiment **sur**...?
How do you feel **about** these events?	Quel est votre sentiment **sur** ces événements?
information **about** sth	des informations **sur** qch
The newspaper gave the latest information **about** this conflict.	Le journal a donné les dernières informations **sur** ce conflit.

a conversation **about** sb/sth	une conversation **sur** qn/qch
rumors **about** sth/sb	des rumeurs **sur** qch/qn

• **about** is translated with **de** with the following verbs and expressions

to be **about** sth [book, article, etc.] This book is **about** violence.	traiter **de** qch Ce livre traite **de** la violence.
to be angry **about** sth	être fâché **de** qch
to be certain **about** sth	être certain **de** qch
to be crazy **about** sth/sb She is crazy **about** luxury. She is crazy **about** dancing/chocolate.	être fou **de** qch/qn, raffoler **de** qch Elle est folle **du** luxe. Elle raffole **de la** danse/**du** chocolat.
to be delighted **about** sth	être ravi **de** qch
to be disappointed **about** sth	être déçu **de** qch
to be happy **about** sth I was happy **about** this promotion. I am very happy **about** that.	être content/heureux **de** qch, se réjouir **de** qch J'étais content **de** cette promotion. Je suis très heureux **de** ça.
to be passionate **about** sth	être passionné **de** qch
to be pleased **about** sth	se féliciter **de** qch
to be sad **about** sth	être triste **de** qch
to be sorry **about** sth I am sorry **about** that misunderstanding.	être désolé **de** (or: **pour**) qch Je suis désolé **de** ce malentendu.
to be sure **about** sth Are you sure **about** his honesty?	être sûr **de** qch Etes-vous sûr **de** son honnêteté?
to be sure **about** oneself He is sure **about** himself.	être sûr **de** soi Il est sûr **de** lui.
to be uncertain **about** sth	être incertain **de** qch
to be worried **about** sb/sth	être inquiet **de** (or: **pour**) qn/qch

to brag **about** sth	se vanter **de** qch
to complain **about** sb/sth	se plaindre **de** qn/qch
The students complain **about** the exams.	Les élèves se plaignent **des** examens.
to dream **about**	rêver **de**
to feel good **about** sth	être satisfait **de** qch
to get annoyed/irritated **about** sth	s'irriter **de** qch
to hear **about** sb/sth	entendre parler **de** qn/qch
I heard **about** this problem.	J'ai entendu parler **de** ce problème.
to inform sb **about** sth	informer/prévenir qn **de** qch
to inquire **about** sth	s'informer **de** qch, s'enquérir **de** qch
He inquired **about** your health.	Il s'est enquis **de** votre santé.
to know sth **about** sb/sth	savoir qch **de** (or: **sur**) qn/qch
That's all I know **about** her.	C'est tout ce que je sais **d'**elle.
What do you know **about** France's geography?	Qu'est-ce que vous savez **de** la géographie de la France?
I know nothing **about** them.	Je ne sais rien **d'**eux.
to know **about** sth[1]	être au courant **de** qch
He knew **about** the conspiracy.	Il était au courant **de** la conspiration.
I don't know (anything) **about** it.	Je ne suis pas au courant.
to laugh **about** sb/sth	rire **de** qn/qch
He laughs **about** my jokes.	Il rit **de** mes plaisanteries.
to say sth **about** sb/sth	dire qch **de** (or: **sur**) qn/qch
I want to know what one says **about** me.	Je veux savoir ce qu'on dit **de** moi.
She says bad things **about** everything.	Elle dit du mal **de** tout.
to speak/talk/tell **about** sb/sth	parler **de** qn/qch, s'entretenir **de** qch
He talks **about** his children.	Il parle **de** ses enfants.
What are you talking **about**?	**De** quoi parles-tu?
Tell me **about** your family.	Parlez-moi **de** votre famille.
We talked **about** one thing or another.	On a parlé **de** choses et **d'**autres.

---

1. But: 'to know much **about** sth' = 's'y connaître **en** qch' (see p. 201)
'to know nothing **about** sth' = 'ne rien connaître **à** qch' (see p. 200)

to think **about** (= *to have an opinion*)	penser **de**[1]
What do you think **about** him?	Qu'est-ce que vous pensez **de** lui?
to worry **about** sb/sth	s'inquiéter **de** (or: **pour**) qn/qch, se soucier **de** qn/qch

- **about** is translated with **pour** in the following expressions

to argue **about** sth	se disputer **pour** qch
They argued **about** money.	Ils se sont disputés **pour** des questions d'argent.
to worry **about** sb/sth	s'inquiéter **pour** (or: **de**) qn, se faire du souci **pour** qn, être inquiet **pour** (or: **de**) qn/qch,
They worry **about** their health.	Ils sont inquiets **pour** leur santé.
I worry a lot **about** him.	Je suis très inquiet **pour** lui.
He worries **about** you.	Il se fait du souci/s'inquiète **pour** toi.
to be lazy **about** doing sth	être paresseux **pour**
He is lazy **about** writing.	Il est paresseux **pour** écrire.
to not be very excited **about** sth	ne pas être très courageux **pour** qch
She is not very excited **about** studying.	Elle n'est pas très courageuse **pour** les études.

- **about** is translated with **à** in the following expressions

to care **about** sth[2]	tenir **à** qch, s'intéresser **à** qch, être sensible **à** qch
She doesn't care **about** scarves.	Elle ne tient pas/ne s'intéresse pas **aux** écharpes.
They care **about** our problems.	Ils sont sensibles **à** nos problèmes.
to know nothing **about** sb/sth	ne rien connaître **à** qn/qch
We know nothing **about** the world that surrounds us.	Nous ne connaissons rien **au** monde qui nous entoure.
I know nothing **about** computers.	Je ne connais rien **aux** ordinateurs.

---

1. But:
   What/whom are you thinking **about**? = **A** quoi/**à** qui pensez-vous?
   For the difference between 'penser **de**' and 'penser **à**' (to think **about**) see p.194.
2. But: *to care **about** sb* = aimer qn → *She cares **about** him.* = Elle l'aime.

to think **about** sb/sth (= to have one's thoughts with sb/sth)	penser **à** qn/qch
I am thinking **about** my parents.	Je pense **à** mes parents.
to think (reflect) **about** sth	réfléchir **à** (or: **sur**) qch
I am going to think **about** it.	Je vais réfléchir **à** ça.
He seriously thinks **about** this option.	Il réfléchit sérieusement **à** cette option.
to understand nothing **about** sth	ne rien comprendre **à** qch
He understands nothing **about** the United States.	Il ne comprend rien **aux** Etats-Unis.

- **about** is translated with **en** in the expression

to know much **about** sth	s'y connaître **en** qch
She knows much **about** philosophy.	Elle s'y connaît **en** philosophie.
Do you know much **about** flowers?	Tu t'y connais **en** fleurs?

- **about** is translated with **chez** when a person's character or looks is referred to

What do you like **about** her?	Qu'est-ce que tu aimes **chez** elle?
What I like **about** him is his frankness.	Ce que j'aime **chez** lui, c'est sa franchise.

- **about** is translated with **par** in the following expression

to be enthusiastic/excited **about** sth	être enthousiasmé **par** qch
They weren't very enthusiastic **about** this marriage.	Ils n'ont pas été très enthousiasmés **par** ce mariage.

- **about** meaning *concerning* is translated with **au sujet de** or with **à propos de**

What is it **about**?	C'est **à** quel **sujet**?
It's **about** my daughter.	C'est **à propos de** ma fille.
It's **about** the trip to Europe.	C'est **au sujet du** voyage en Europe.
He said nothing **about** this problem.	Il n'a rien dit **au sujet de** ce problème.
I would like to ask you some questions **about** your son.	Je voudrais vous poser quelques questions **au sujet de** votre fils.

We were fighting **about** my brother.	Nous nous sommes disputés **au sujet de** mon frère.
to have nightmares **about** sth	faire des cauchemars **à propos de** qch

- **about** is translated with **dans** in

to be confident **about** sth	être confiant/avoir confiance **dans** (or: **en**) qch

---

Note:

When **about** indicates *approximation* it is an *adverb* and is rendered in the following manner:

♦ The *adverbs* **environ**, and **à peu près** are generally used with numbers, quantity and duration of time

There are **about** 400 cheeses in France.	Il y a **environ** (= **à peu près**) 400 fromages en France.
France has a population of **about** 61 million.	La France a une population d'**à peu près** 61 millions.
I have **about** three dollars.	J'ai **à peu près** deux dollars.
He is **about** 20.	Il a **environ** 20 ans.

♦ **vers** (= aux environs de) is used before clock time to express '*at about*'

Come ***at*** **about** 3 o'clock.	Viens **vers** (les) trois heures.
I went to bed ***at*** **about** 11 o'clock.	Je me suis couché **vers** 11 heures. (or: **à environ** 11 h)
We ought to be in Paris ***at*** **about** three o'clock.	Nous devrions être à Paris **aux environs** (= aux alentours) **de** trois heures.

♦ an approximate number (= cardinal number + **-aine**: **une dizaine**, etc.) is used when the numbers 10, 20, 30, 40, 50, 60 and 100 are approximated

about twenty years ago	il y a **une** vingt**aine d'**années
About a hundred students came.	**Une** cent**aine d'**étudiants sont venus.
She is **about** 50.	Elle a **une** cinquant**aine d'**années.

Chapter 7

Prepositions in Verb + Verb Constructions

This chapter deals with the use of prepositions between a (conjugated) verb and the following infinitive[1]. There are three possibilities when linking an infinitive to the preceding verb:

- There is *no preposition* between the main verb and the infinitive

  J'adore *parler* français. *I adore speaking French.*

- The *preposition **à*** links the two verbs

  J'apprends **à** *parler* français. *I learn to speak French.*

- The *preposition **de*** links the two verbs

  J'essaie **de** *parler* français. *I try to speak French.*

The verb preceding the infinitive determines whether there is a preposition between the two verbs and if so, whether it is **à** or **de**. There can be more than one infinitive in a sentence. In this case, the preceding verb which is closest to the infinitive (even if it is an infinitive itself) determines how the two verbs are linked.

J'aime *aider* ma mère **à** *faire* la cuisine. *I like to help my mother to cook.*
J'ai envie **d'***arrêter* **de** *fumer*. *I feel like stopping to smoke.*

---

1. When two verbs follow each other with no conjunction (such as 'que') between them, the first verb is conjugated and the second verb is in its infinitive form. In English, these infinitive constructions are rendered in three ways, depending on the expression used.

   - **that + subordinate clause**
     Il dit l'avoir vu. *He says **(that)** he saw her.*
     Il a estimé devoir ouvrir le débat. *He felt **(that)** he had to open the debate.*
   - **the infinitive**
     J'aime voyager. *I like **to travel**.*
   - **(preposition) + ... -ing**
     Je rêve d'aller en France. *I dream **of going** to France.*

Nous commençons **à** *regretter* **d'***être venus.*	*We start to regret to have come.*
Je veux *apprendre* **à** me *servir* d'un ordinateur.	*I want to learn how to use a computer.*
J'ai renoncé **à** *essayer* **de** vous *faire* plaisir.	*I have given up trying to please you.*
J'espère *pouvoir* le *convaincre* **de** *venir* avec nous.	*I hope to be able to convince him to come with us.*
Il m'a demandé **de** l'*aider* **à** *résoudre* un problème.	*He asked me to help him solve a problem.*
En France, les enfants commencent **à** *apprendre* **à** *écrire* à l'âge de six ans.	*In France, children start learning to write at the age of six.*

A. No **preposition is required before the infinitive after**

• **verbs of perception** (seeing, hearing, feeling)

apercevoir	*to notice, to see*
écouter	*to listen to*
entendre	*to hear*
observer	*to observe*
regarder	*to watch*
sentir	*to feel*
voir	*to see*

J'*entends* le bébé pleurer.	*I hear the baby cry.*
Je t'ai *entendu* venir.	*I heard you coming.*
J'ai *entendu* parler[1] de l'inondation.	*I heard about the flood.*
J'ai *entendu* dire[1] que ton père est malade.	*I heard that your father is ill.*
Elle *regarde* le soleil se coucher.	*She watches the sun set.*
Ils *regardent* la neige tomber.	*They are watching the snow fall.*
Elle *sent* la terre bouger.	*She feels the earth moving.*
Il *sent* ses cheveux se dresser sur sa tête.	*He feels his hair stand on end.*
J'ai *vu* l'autobus passer.	*I saw the bus pass by.*

---

1. to hear = entendre
   to hear **about** sb/sth = entendre **parler de** qn/qch
   to hear **that** (+ subordinate clause) = entendre **dire que** (+ subordinate clause)

Sayings and idioms

On entendrait une mouche voler.	*You could hear a pin drop.*
Il s'écoute parler.	*He likes to hear himself speak.*
On ne voit pas le temps passer.	*Time passes quickly.*
Je n'ai pas vu le temps passer.	*Time flew by.*

• verbs of wishing, hoping, liking and disliking

adorer	*to adore*
aimer	*to like*
aimer mieux	*to like better, to prefer*
désirer	*to desire, to want*
détester	*to detest, to dislike, to hate*
espérer	*to hope*
préférer	*to prefer*
souhaiter[1]	*to wish*
vouloir	*to want*

J'*adore* aller au théâtre.	*I adore going to the theatre.*
Il *aime* aider les gens.	*He likes to help people.*
Elle n'*aime* pas être en retard.	*She doesn't like to be late.*
J'*aimerais* mieux ne pas en parler.	*I'd rather not talk about it.*
Je *désire* ne pas être dérangé.	*I wish not to be disturbed.*
Je *déteste* me lever tôt.	*I hate to get up early.*
J'*espère* me tromper.	*I hope that I am wrong.*
J'*espère* avoir bientôt de vos nouvelles.	*I hope to hear from you soon.*
Nous *préférons* ne pas sortir.	*We prefer not to go out.*
Que *souhaitez*-vous boire?	*What do you wish to drink?*
Ils *souhaitent* avoir des enfants.	*They wish to have children.*
Je ne *veux* pas dire de bêtises.	*I don't want to talk nonsense.*
Il *veut* partir en vacances.	*He wants to go on a vacation.*
Veux-tu prendre Joseph pour mari?	*Do you want to take Joseph as a husband?*
Je *voudrais* m'asseoir.	*I would like to sit down.*

1. But: souhaiter à qn **de** = *to wish sb to* (see p. 250)

Mistakes to avoid

Incorrect	*Correct*	*English meaning*
J'espère ~~de~~ vous voir bientôt.	J'espère vous voir bientôt.	*I hope to see you soon.*

• verbs of movement

aller[1]	*to be going to, to go and* (do)
s'en aller	*to go away*
amener	*to bring* (a person)
courir	*to run and* (do)
descendre	*to go down, to come down*
entrer	*to enter*
emmener	*to take* (a person somewhere)
envoyer	*to send*
mener	*to lead*
monter	*to go up*
partir	*to leave*
passer	*to go by, to come by*
rentrer	*to go home, to come home*
retourner	*to go back, to return*
sortir	*to go out*
venir	*to come*
revenir	*to come back*

J'*allais* t'écrire.[2]	*I was going to write to you.*
J'*irai* voir ma tante.	*I will visit my aunt.*
Va te changer.	*Go and change (your clothes).*
Va voir si le facteur est déjà passé.	*Go and see whether the mailman came by already.*
Courez ouvrir la porte.	*Run and open the door.*
Il est *descendu* chercher son courrier.	*He went down to get his mail.*
J'ai *emmené* les enfants jouer au parc.	*I took the children to play in the park.*
Je t'*emmène* dîner.	*I take you out to dinner.*
Elle est *montée* se coucher.	*She went up to go to bed.*

---

1. Also 'être' with the meaning of 'aller':
   Nous avons été cueillir des roses. — *We went and picked roses.*
2. For the use of 'aller' + infinitive to express the *close future*, see p. 245.

Il est juste *parti* déjeuner.	*He just left to have lunch.*
Nous sommes *rentrés* lui dire au revoir.	*We went home to say good-bye to him/her.*
Je *retourne* le chercher.	*I return to look for him.*
Il est *sorti* acheter du lait	*He went out to buy some milk.*
Venez nous rejoindre.	*Come and join us.*
Je *viens* m'excuser.	*I (have) come to apologize.*

Idioms

aller/venir chercher qch/qn	*to (go/come and) get sth, to pick sb up*
Je vais chercher de l'eau.	*I am going to get some water.*
Je viendrai te chercher à l'aéroport.	*I will pick you up at the airport.*
aller/venir voir qn	*to visit (a person)*
Il est allé voir ses parents.	*He visited his parents.*
envoyer chercher qn	*to send for sb*
Ils ont envoyé chercher le médecin.	*They sent for the doctor.*
envoyer promener qn (fam.)	*to send sb packing*
Ils m'ont envoyé promener.	*They sent me packing.*
passer prendre qn	*to pick sb up*
Je passe te prendre vers huit heures.	*I pick you up at about eight o'clock.*

• verbs of thinking, believing, saying, and verbs expressing an intention*

admettre	*to admit*
affirmer	*to claim*
assurer	*to assure*
avouer	*to admit, to confess*
compter	*to intend, to plan*
confesser	*to confess*
confirmer	*to confirm*

---

* Note that many of these verbs are usually followed by the past infinitive.

Le coupable avoue **avoir commis** le crime. *The culprit confesses having committed the crime.*

croire	*to believe, to think*
déclarer	*to declare*
démentir	*to deny*
dire	*to say*
estimer	*to reckon, to consider*
se figurer	*to imagine*
s'imaginer	*to imagine*
jurer[1]	*to swear (= to declare under oath)*
nier	*to deny*
prétendre	*to pretend, to claim*
penser	*to intend, to plan, to think*
raconter	*to tell*
se rappeler	*to remember*
reconnaître	*to recognize, to admit*
supposer	*to suppose*

L'accusé *affirme* être innocent.	*The accused claims to be innocent.*
Qu'est-ce que tu *comptes* faire?	*What do you plan to do?*
Je *compte* déménager.	*I plan to move.*
Il *croyait* me faire plaisir.	*He believed that he pleased me.*
Je *crois* l'avoir reconnu.	*I believe that I recognized him.*
J'ai *cru* rêver.	*I thought I was dreaming.*
Le témoin a *déclaré* avoir vu l'accident.	*The witness declared that he saw the accident.*
Il *dit* l'avoir appris hier soir.	*He says that he learned it last night.*
J'*estime* avoir fait assez pour lui.	*I feel that I did enough for him.*
Elle *s'imagine* être intelligente.	*She imagines that she is intelligent.*
Il *jure* avoir dit la vérité.	*He swears that he told the truth.*
Il *nie* avoir préparé l'assassinat.	*He denies having prepared the murder.*
Que *pensez*-vous faire pendant les vacances?	*What do you plan to do during the vacation?*
Je ne *pensais* pas être à l'heure.	*I didn't think I would be on time.*
Il *prétend* avoir trouvé le porte-monnaie.	*He pretends to have found the wallet.*
Je *me rappelle* avoir habité ici.	*I remember having lived here.*
Il *reconnaît* avoir entendu les enfants.	*He admits having heard the children.*

---

1. But: jurer **de** + inf. = *to swear (promise) to* [see p. 248]

• the following impersonal expressions

il faut	*it is necessary, one must*
il fait bon	*it does good*
il semble	*it seems*
il vaut mieux	*it is better, it is preferable*

Il *faut* travailler pour réussir.	*One must work to succeed.*
Il *fallait* s'y attendre.	*It was to be expected.*
Il *va falloir* passer la nuit dans le train.	*It will be necessary to spend the night on the train.*
Il *fait bon* se promener au soleil.	*It does good to walk in the sun.*
Il *semble* faire plus froid ce soir.	*It seems to be colder tonight.*
Il *vaut mieux* rester que de partir.	*It is better to stay than to leave.*

Proverbs and sayings

Il faut battre le fer pendant qu'il est chaud.	*Strike the iron while it is hot.*
Il ne faut pas brûler la chandelle par les deux bouts.	*One must not burn the candle at both ends.*
Il ne faut pas tenter le diable.	*One must not ask for trouble.*
Il vaut mieux faire envie que pitié.	*It is better to be envied than pitied.*
Mieux vaut prévenir que guérir.	*An ounce of prevention is worth a pound of cure.*

• the following verbs

daigner[1]	*to deign, to condescend*
devoir[2]	*to have to, to be supposed to*
faire	*to have (sth done), to make (sb do sth)*
laisser	*to let, to allow*
oser	*to dare (= to have the courage to)*
paraître	*to appear, to seem*
pouvoir	*to be able*
savoir	*to know (how to do sth)*
sembler	*to seem*

1. But: dédaigner **de** = *to disdain (doing)*
2. But: devoir à qn **de** = *to owe it to sb to*

Il n'a pas *daigné* nous répondre.	*He didn't deign to answer us.*
Elle *doit* faire la lessive.	*She must do the laundry.*
Je *dois* avoir tort.	*I must be wrong.*
Tu *dois* avoir faim.	*You must be hungry.*
Il *doit* y avoir une pharmacie.	*There must be a pharmacy.*
Le train *doit* arriver d'un instant à l'autre.	*The train must arrive any minute now.*
Il *doit* se retourner dans sa tombe.	*He must turn over in his grave.*
Tu *devrais* travailler plus.	*You ought to work more.*
J'*ai dû* attraper la grippe.	*I must have caught the flu.*
J'*aurais dû* suivre son conseil.	*I should have followed his advice.*
Louis XIV a *fait* construire Versailles.	*Louis XIV had Versailles built.*
Si vous avez besoin de quelque chose, *faites*-le-moi savoir.	*If you need something, let me know.*
Ça *fait* grossir.	*That is fattening.*
Je me suis *fait* rouler. (fam.)	*I had myself (= was) cheated.*
Il s'est *fait* écraser.	*He got run over.*
Laissez-moi dire quelque chose.	*Let me say something.*
Les voitures *laissent* passer les piétons.	*The cars let the pedestrians pass.*
Laisse-les faire!	*Leave it to them! Let them do it!*
Pourquoi te *laisses*-tu aller comme ça?	*Why do you let yourself go like that?*
Ne vous *laissez* pas décourager.	*Don't let yourself be discouraged.*
Je n'*ose* pas le déranger.	*I don't dare to disturb him.*
Si j'*ose* dire.	*If I may say so, if I dare say.*
Il *paraît* dire la vérité.	*He appears to tell the truth.*
Je *peux* vous aider?	*Can I help you?*
Vous *pouvez* disposer.	*You may go now.*
Si ça *peut* te consoler.	*If that can be of any comfort to you.*
Je ne *peux* pas le sentir.	*I cannot stand him.*
Pourriez-vous me dire où est la gare?	*Could you tell me where the train station is?*
Elle *semble* s'ennuyer.	*She seems to be bored.*
Vous ne *semblez* pas me comprendre.	*You don't seem to understand me.*
Elle *sait* jouer du piano.	*She can play the piano.*
Je ne *saurais* jamais vous remercier.	*I would never know how to thank you.*

Idioms

faire venir	*to send for*
Nous avons fait venir le médecin.	*We sent for the doctor.*
faire voir	*to show*
Fais-voir!	*Show me!*
se laisser faire	*to let oneself be pushed around*
Elle ne se laisse pas faire.	*She won't be pushed around.*
laisser/faire tomber	*to drop*
Elle a laissé tomber le paquet.	*She dropped the package.*

• the following expressions

avoir beau faire qch	*to do sth in vain*
Tu *as beau* pleurer, il ne t'entend pas.	*You cry in vain, he doesn't hear you.*
être censé/supposé faire qch	*to be supposed to do sth*
Est-ce que je *suis censé* faire tout?	*Am I supposed to do everything?*
Le jade *est supposé* porter bonheur.	*Jade is supposed to bring (you) luck.*
faillir faire qch[1]	*to almost do sth*
J'*ai failli* avoir un accident.	*I almost had an accident.*
ne faire que + inf.	*to only do sth, to do nothing but*
Je *ne fais que* passer.	*I am only passing through.*
Ça *ne fait que* commencer.	*It has only just begun.*
verbe + de quoi + inf.	*verb + enough/something to*
Avez-vous *de quoi* vivre?	*Do you have enough to live?*
Apportez *de quoi* lire!	*Bring something to read!*
il y a de quoi + inf.	*there is (good) reason to*
Il y a de quoi se fâcher.	*There is (good) reason to get angry.*
il n'y a pas de quoi + inf.	*there is no reason to*
Il n'y a pas de quoi rire.	*There is no reason to laugh.*
Also:	
à quoi bon + inf.	*What's the use of...-ing, what good does it do to...*
A quoi bon arrêter les bandits?	*What's the use of arresting the bandits?*

1. *faillir faire qch* is only used in the passé composé. See *manquer **de** faire qch* p. 225.

B. The preposition à is required before the infinitive

• after the following verbs

accoutumer qn **à**	*to get sb used to*
s'accoutumer **à** (= s'habituer **à**)	*to get used to*
s'acharner **à**	*to persist in*
aider qn **à**	*to help sb to*
aimer **à** (literary)	*to like to*
amener qn **à**	*to get/lead/prompt sb to*
s'amuser **à**	*to have a good time/fun (doing)*
appeler qn **à**	*to call on sb to*
s'appliquer **à**	*to apply oneself, to take care to*
apporter qch **à**	*to bring sth to*
apprendre **à**	*to learn (how) to*
apprendre à qn **à**	*to teach sb (how) to*
s'apprêter **à**	*to get ready to, to prepare to*
arriver **à** (= réussir **à**, parvenir **à**)	*to succeed in, to be able to*
aspirer **à**	*to aspire to, to desire to*
astreindre qn **à**	*to compel/force sb to*
s'astreindre **à**	*to force oneself to*
s'attarder **à**	*to take one's time (doing)*
s'attendre **à**	*to expect to*
attraper qn **à**	*to catch sb (doing)*
autoriser qn **à**	*to authorize sb to*
avoir (qch) **à**	*to have (sth) to*
se borner **à**	*to restrict/limit oneself to*
chercher **à**	*to seek to, to try to*
commencer **à**[1] (= se mettre **à**)	*to begin to*
concourir **à**	*to help to, to contribute to*
condamner qn **à**	*to condemn sb to*
condescendre **à**	*to condescend to*
conduire qn **à**	*to lead sb to, to bring sb to*
se consacrer **à**	*to devote oneself to (doing)*
consentir **à**	*to consent to, to agree to*
consister **à**	*to consist in (doing)*
conspirer **à**	*to conspire to*
continuer **à**[2]	*to continue to*
contraindre qn **à** (= forcer qn **à**)	*to force sb to*
contribuer **à**	*to contribute to*
convier qn **à**	*to suggest that sb (does)*

---

1. Also: ***commencer de*** (see p. 223)

2. Also: ***continuer de*** (see p. 223)

décider qn **à**	*to persuade sb to*
se décider **à** (= se résoudre **à**)[1]	*to decide/make up one's mind to*
demander **à**	*to ask/ask permission/request to*
désapprendre **à**	*to unlearn, to forget to*
destiner **à**	*to destine to, to devote to*
se destiner **à**	*to decide on (doing)*
déterminer qn **à**	*to cause/induce sb to*
se déterminer **à**	*to make up one's mind to*
se disposer **à**	*to prepare/get ready to*
donner à qn qch **à**	*to give sb sth to*
dresser (un animal) **à**	*to train (an animal) to*
échouer **à**	*to fail to*
encourager qn **à**[2]	*to encourage sb to*
engager qn **à**	*to urge/advise sb to*
s'engager **à**	*to promise/commit oneself to*
s'ennuyer **à**	*to be/get bored (doing)*
enseigner à qn **à**	*to teach sb to*
s'entendre **à**	*to be an expert at (doing)*
s'entêter **à**	*to persist in (doing)*
entraîner qn **à**	*to train/encourage sb to*
s'entraîner **à**	*to practice (doing)*
s'épuiser **à**	*to exhaust oneself (doing)*
s'essayer **à**[3]	*to try one's hand at (doing)*
s'évertuer **à**	*to try one's best to*
exceller **à**	*to excel in (doing)*
s'exercer **à**	*to practice (doing)*
exhorter qn **à**	*to urge sb to*
s'exposer **à**	*to run the risk of (doing)*
se fatiguer **à**	*to tire oneself out (doing)*
forcer qn **à** (= obliger qn **à**)	*to force sb to*
se forcer **à**	*to force oneself to*
habituer qn **à**[4]	*to get sb used to (doing)*
s'habituer **à** (= s'accoutumer **à**)[5]	*to get used to (doing)*
hésiter **à**	*to hesitate to*
inciter qn **à**	*to encourage/urge/incite sb to*
incliner **à**	*to be inclined to*

1. But: décider/résoudre **de** = *to decide to*
2. But: **dé**courager qn **de** = *to **dis**courage sb to*
3. But: essayer **de** = *to try to*
4. But: **dés**habituer qn **de** = *to get sb out of the habit of (doing)*
5. But: se **dés**habituer **de** = *to get out of the habit of (doing)*

incliner qn **à**	*to encourage sb to*
induire qn **à**	*to induce sb to*
s'ingénier **à**	*to do one's utmost to*
s'intéresser **à**	*to be interested in (doing)*
inviter qn **à**	*to invite/ask sb to*
jouer **à**	*to play (doing)*
mettre [un certain temps] **à** (or: **pour**)	*to take* [+ time period] *to*
se mettre **à** (= commencer **à**)	*to begin/start (doing)*
motiver qn **à**	*to motivate sb to*
obliger qn **à** (= contraindre qn **à**)	*to force sb to*
s'obstiner **à**	*to persist in (doing)*
s'occuper **à**	*to spend one's time (doing)*
s'offrir **à**[1]	*to offer/volunteer to*
passer [un certain temps] **à**	*to spend* [+ time period] *(doing)*
parvenir **à** (= réussir **à**, arriver **à**)	*to succeed in (doing)*
pencher **à**	*to be inclined to*
penser **à**	*to think about/remember (doing)*
persévérer **à**	*to persevere in (doing)*
persister **à**	*to persist in (doing)*
se plaire **à**	*to take pleasure in (doing)*
porter qn **à**	*to lead sb to*
pousser qn **à**	*to urge/prompt sb to*
préparer qn **à**	*to prepare sb to*
se préparer **à**	*to get ready/prepare oneself to*
provoquer qn **à**	*to incite sb to*
recommencer **à**	*to start over (doing)*
réduire qn **à**	*to compel/reduce sb to*
se refuser **à**[2]	*to decline/refuse to*
se remettre **à**	*to start (doing) again*
renoncer **à**	*to give up (doing)*
répugner **à**[3]	*to be reluctant/loath to*
se résigner **à**	*to resign oneself to*
se résoudre **à** (= se décider **à**)	*to decide to*
rester **à**	*to remain to (be done)*
réussir **à** (= parvenir **à**, arriver **à**)	*to succeed in (doing)*
servir **à**	*to be good/useful for (doing)*
songer **à**	*to think/dream of (doing)*

---

1. But: offrir **de** = *to offer to*
2. But: refuser **de** = *to refuse to*
3. But: il me répugne **de** = *I hate to, I am loath to*

suffire **à**	*to be enough to*
surprendre qn **à**[1]	*to surprise/catch sb* (doing)
se surprendre **à**	*to catch/find oneself* (doing)
tarder **à**	*to delay/be slow in* (doing)
tendre **à**	*to tend/have a tendency to*
tenir **à**	*to be anxious to/insist on* (doing)
travailler **à**	*to work on* (doing)
trouver qch **à**	*to find sth to*
se tuer **à**	*to kill oneself by* (doing)
veiller **à**	*to make/be sure to*
venir **à**	*to happen to* (do)
en venir **à**	*to come/get to the point where*
viser **à**	*to aim at* (doing)

Ils *aident* leurs parents **à** financer les études.	*They help their parents pay for the tuition.*
Veux-tu que je t'*aide* **à** faire tes devoirs?	*Do you want me to help you do your homework?*
Ils l'ont *amené* **à** le faire.	*They prompted/got him to do it.*
Il *apprend* **à** monter à vélo.	*He learns to ride a bike.*
Ma mère m'a *appris* **à** cuisiner.	*My mother taught me to cook.*
Ils s'*apprêtent* **à** partir.	*They are getting ready to leave.*
Il n'*arrive* pas **à** s'acclimater.	*He is unable to adapt.*
Je n'*arrive* pas **à** y croire.	*I cannot believe it.*
Elle *aspire* **à** être une actrice célèbre.	*She desires to be a famous actress.*
Je ne m'*attendais* pas **à** vous voir.	*I didn't expect to see you.*
Le médecin l'a *autorisé* **à** sortir.	*The doctor authorized him to go out.*
J'*ai* une dissertation **à** écrire.	*I have a paper to write.*
J'*ai* un grand service **à** te demander.	*I have a big favor to ask you.*
J'*ai* quelque chose **à** vous dire.	*I have something to tell you.*
Je n'*ai* pas de temps **à** perdre.	*I have no time to waste.*
Tu n'*as* pas **à** t'excuser.	*You don't have to apologize.*
Vous n'*avez* rien **à** craindre.	*You have nothing to fear.*
Il *cherche* **à** nous nuire.	*He tries to harm us.*
Je *commençais* **à** me faire du souci.	*I was beginning to worry.*
Je *commence* **à** avoir un petit creux. *(fam.)*	*I am beginning to feel a little hungry.*

1. But: être surpris **de** = *to be surprised to* (see p. 268 and footnote p. 269)

Sisyphe fut *condamné* **à** rouler une grosse pierre au sommet d'une montagne d'où elle retombait sans cesse.	*Sisyphus was condemned to roll a big stone up a mountain down which it fell incessantly.*
Il a *condescendu* **à** nous écouter.	*He condescended to listen to us.*
Ça a *conduit* le tribunal **à** annuler le procès.	*This led the court to cancel the trial.*
Consentez-vous **à** prendre pour épouse Mlle X?	*Do you agree to take Mlle X as a spouse?*
Le bonheur *consiste* **à** rendre heureux les autres.	*Happiness consists in making others happy.*
Il *continue* **à** (or: **de**) pleuvoir.	*It continues to rain.*
L'euro a *contribué* **à** faire monter les prix.	*The euro contributed to the rise of prices.*
Qu'est-ce qui t'a *décidé* **à** partir en vacances?	*What persuaded you to go on a vacation?*
Elle *s'est décidée* **à** rester.	*She decided to stay.*
Il *demande* **à** être entendu.	*He requests to be heard.*
Je *me disposais* **à** partir quand vous avez téléphoné.	*I was getting ready to leave when you called.*
Donnez-lui quelque chose **à** manger.	*Give him something to eat.*
On m'a *donné* des formulaires **à** remplir.	*They gave me forms to fill out.*
Ils ont *échoué* **à** saisir cette chance.	*They failed to seize this chance.*
Le professeur a *encouragé* les élèves **à** participer.	*The teacher encouraged the students to participate.*
Les participants *s'engagent* **à** ne parler que le français.	*The participants promise to only speak French.*
Je *m'ennuie* **à** attendre.	*I am bored waiting.*
Il lui a *enseigné* **à** se défendre.	*He taught him to defend himself.*
Il *s'entend* **à** berner les gens.	*He is an expert at fooling people.*
Elle *s'est entêtée* **à** rester au lit.	*She persisted in staying in bed.*
Il a *entraîné* son camarade **à** commettre le crime.	*He encouraged his friend to commit the crime.*
Ils *s'entraînent* **à** jouer du violon.	*They practice playing the violin.*
Il *s'essaie* **à** conduire un camion.	*He tries his hand at driving a truck.*

Il *excelle* **à** peindre des portraits.	*He excels in painting portraits.*
Ils nous ont *exhortés* **à** rester.	*They urged us to stay.*
Il *se fatigue* **à** nous expliquer cela.	*He gets tired explaining this to us.*
On l'a *forcé* **à** démissionner.	*He was forced to resign.*
Je *me suis forcé* **à** manger ce gâteau.	*I forced myself to eat this cake.*
Il faut l'*habituer* **à** obéir.	*One must get him used to obeying.*
Elle ne peut *s'habituer* **à** vivre seule.	*She cannot get used to living alone.*
J'*hésite* **à** vous poser cette question.	*I hesitate to ask you this question.*
Si tu as besoin de moi, n'*hésite* pas **à** le[1] dire.	*If you need me, don't hesitate to say so.*
Le gouvernement français accorde de l'aide financière aux familles afin de les *inciter* **à** avoir plus d'enfants.	*The French government grants financial aid to families in order to urge them to have more children.*
J'*incline* **à** penser que...	*I am inclined to think that...*
Sa bonne conduite a *incliné* les juges **à** lui accorder des circonstances atténuantes.	*His good behavior led the judges to grant him mitigating circumstances.*
Il m'a *invité* **à** prendre un verre.	*He invited me to have a drink.*
J'ai *mis* une heure **à** m'endormir.	*It took me one hour to go to sleep.*
Rien ne vous *oblige* **à** accepter ça.	*Nothing forces you to accept that.*
Il *s'obstine* **à** se taire.	*He persists in saying nothing.*
Il *s'est offert* **à** transporter le blessé à l'hôpital.	*He offered to take the wounded to the hospital.*
Je suis *parvenu* **à** m'échapper.	*I suceeded (= managed) to escape.*
Nous avons *passé* 30 minutes **à** chercher un parking.	*We spent 30 minutes looking for a parking place.*
Il a *passé* la journée **à** jouer au golf.	*He spent the day playing golf.*
Je *penche* **à** croire qu'il est innocent.	*I am inclined to think that he is innocent.*
As-tu *pensé* **à** poster la lettre?	*Did you remember to mail the letter?*
Il se *plaît* **à** contredire tout le monde.	*He enjoys contradicting everyone.*
Tout nous *porte* **à** croire qu'il a raison.	*Everything leads us to believe that he is right.*
Qu'est-ce qui t'a *poussé* **à** faire cela?	*What prompted you to do that?*
Cela les a *poussés* **à** agir.	*That made them act.*

1. Note that the preposition à does *not* contract with **le** or **les** when *le* or *les* are object pronouns.

Préparez-le **à** entendre cette nouvelle.	*Prepare him to hear this piece of news.*
Elle se *prépare* **à** faire un stage.	*She gets ready to do an internship.*
Son frère l'a *provoqué* **à** faire cela.	*His brother incited him to do that.*
Il les a *réduits* **à** mendier.	*He reduced them to begging.*
Quand te *remettras*-tu **à** travailler?	*When will you start working again?*
Je *renonce* **à** t'expliquer la situation.	*I give up explaining the situation to you.*
Il ne *répugne* pas **à** mentir.	*It doesn't bother him to lie.*
Beaucoup *reste* **à** faire.	*Much remains to be done.*
Ils ont *réussi* **à** s'échapper.	*They managed to escape.*
Ce couteau *sert* **à** trancher la viande.	*This knife is good for slicing meat.*
Il ne *songe* pas **à** aller habiter ailleurs.	*He doesn't think of living elsewhere.*
Il ne *songe* qu'**à** gagner de l'argent.	*He only thinks of earning money.*
Cinq euros *suffisent* **à** le motiver.	*Five euros suffice to motivate him.*
Je l'ai *surpris* **à** voler.	*I caught him stealing.*
Il *se surprit* **à** pleurer.	*He found himself crying.*
L'aide *tarde* **à** venir.	*Help is slow in coming.*
Il ne *tardera* pas **à** arriver.	*It will not be long before he is here.*
Il y a des choses qui *tendent* **à** nous compliquer la vie.	*There are things that tend to complicate our lives.*
Je *tiens* **à** vous raccompagner.	*I insist on taking you home.*
Ils ont *tenu* **à** venir.	*They insisted on coming.*
Je *tiens* **à** vous remercier pour votre gentillesse.	*I would like to thank you for your kindness.*
Il *travaille* **à** améliorer sa prononciation.	*He works on improving his pronunciation.*
Tu *trouveras* quelque chose **à** boire dans le frigidaire.	*You will find something to drink in the refrigerator.*
Elle *se tue* **à** travailler.	*She kills herself (by) working.*
Veillez **à** fermer la porte à clé.	*Make/be sure to lock the door.*
S'il *venait* **à** mourir, elle...	*If he should (happen to) die, she...*
Il *en vint* **à** la détester.	*He got to the point of hating her.*
Cette émission *vise* **à** changer les opinions.	*This program aims at changing opinions.*

Sayings and idioms

J'ai d'autres chats **à** fouetter.[1]	*I have other fish to fry.*
avoir qch **à** voir (avec)	*to have sth to do (with)*
Ça n'a rien **à** voir avec la religion.	*That has nothing to do with religion.*
n'avoir qu'**à** + inf.	*to only have to, all somebody has to do is...*
Si vous n'êtes pas content, vous n'avez qu'**à** le dire.	*If you are unhappy, all you have to do is say so.*
Je n'ai qu'**à** m'en prendre à moi-même.	*I only have myself to blame.*
avoir du chemin **à** faire	*to have a long way to go*
On a encore du chemin **à** faire.	*We still have a long way to go.*
donner à qn du fil **à** retordre	*to give sb a lot of trouble*
Il lui a donné du fil **à** retordre.	*He gave her/him a lot of trouble.*
Cela donne **à** réfléchir.	*That's food for thought.*
Cela leur donne **à** réfléchir.	*That gives them sth to think about.*
s'ennuyer **à** mourir	*to be bored to death*
Reste **à** savoir si...	*It remains to be seen whether...*
trouver **à** redire (à qch)	*to find fault (with sth)*
Il y a toujours des gens qui trouvent quelque chose **à** redire.	*There are always people who find fault with something.*
Je ne trouve rien **à** redire à cet ouvrage.	*I find no fault with this work.*

• after the following verbal expressions

avoir de la difficulté **à**	*to have a hard time (doing)*
avoir des difficultés **à**	*to have difficulty in (doing)*
Il avait de grandes difficultés **à** me suivre.	*He had a lot of trouble following me.*
avoir (tout) intérêt **à**	*to be in sb's (best) interest to*
Tu aurais intérêt **à** ne pas dépenser tant d'argent.	*It would be in your interest not to spend so much money.*

1. lit.: *I have other cats to whip. (= I have more important things to do.)*

avoir du mal **à**	*to have trouble (doing)*
J'ai du mal **à** vous entendre.	*I have trouble hearing you.*
J'ai toujours eu du mal **à** refuser.	*I have always had trouble refusing.*
J'ai beaucoup de mal **à** joindre les deux bouts.	*I have a hard time making ends meet.*
avoir un mal fou **à** (fam.)	*to have terrible trouble to*
J'ai eu un mal fou **à** m'y habituer.	*I had terrible trouble to get used to it.*
avoir (de la) peine **à**	*to find it hard/difficult to*
J'ai de la peine **à** croire que tu puisses l'aider.	*I find it hard to believe that you can help him.*
avoir (du) plaisir **à**	*to enjoy/take pleasure in (doing)*
J'ai du plaisir **à** être avec vous.	*I enjoy being with you.*
avoir tendance **à**	*to have the tendency/tend to*
J'ai tendance **à** m'endormir quand je lis le soir.	*I have the tendency to fall asleep when I read at night.*
être **à**	*to be + passive infinitive* [= *is/are to be + past participle*]
Ces gens sont **à** plaindre.	*These people are to be pitied.*
C'était **à** ne pas manger.	*It was not to be eaten (= inedible).*
Le pire est **à** craindre.	*The worst is to be feared.*
Ce n'est pas **à** dédaigner.	*That is not to be sneezed at.*
Des retards sont **à** prévoir.	*Delays are to be expected.*
C'est **à** espérer.	*It's to be hoped for.*
Il est **à** espérer que...	*It's to be hoped that...*
C'est **à** souhaiter.	*It's to be wished for.*
La maison est **à** louer.	*The house is for rent. (= to be rented)*
en être **à**	*to be at/get to the point where*
J'en suis **à** me demander si...	*I am beginning to wonder whether...*
J'en étais **à** ne plus entendre les gens.	*I got to the point where I no longer heard the people.*
faire attention **à** (or: **de**)	*to be careful (not) to*
Faites attention **à** ne pas lui faire de peine.	*Be careful not to hurt his feelings.*

passer son temps **à** — *to spend one's time (doing)*

Il passe son temps **à** ne rien faire. — *He spends his time doing nothing.*

Elle passe le plus clair de son temps **à** téléphoner. — *She spends most of her time talking on the phone.*

Au Moyen Age, les moines passaient leur existence **à** recopier les livres à la main. — *In the Middle Ages, the monks spent their lives copying books by hand.*

perdre du/son temps **à** — *to waste (one's) time (doing)*

Je ne perdrai pas mon temps **à** essayer de proposer des améliorations. — *I will not waste my time trying to suggest improvements.*

ne pas perdre de temps **à** — *to be quick to*

Il n'a pas perdu de temps **à** nous condamner. — *He was quick to condemn us.*

prendre (du) plaisir **à** — *to take/find pleasure in (doing)*

Je prends du plaisir **à** faire des courses. — *I find pleasure in going shopping.*

prendre garde **à** — *to be careful to*

Prenez garde **à** ne pas trop vous engager. — *Be careful not to commit yourself too much.*

trouver son profit **à** — *to find it to one's advantage to*

Il trouve son profit **à** flatter les professeurs. — *He finds it to his advantage to flatter the teachers.*

• after the following impersonal expressions

il (me, lui...) reste **à** — *there is/are...left (for me, for him...) to*

Il reste des obstacles **à** surmonter. — *There are obstacles left to overcome.*

Il reste du travail **à** faire. — *There is work left to do.*

Qu'est-ce qu'il nous reste **à** manger? — *What is there left for us to eat?*

Il ne me reste plus qu'**à** vous souhaiter une bonne journée. — *All there is left for me to do is wish you a good day.*

il y a...**à** — *there is...to, there are...to*

Est-ce qu'il y a quelque chose de bon **à** boire? — *Is there something good to drink?*

Il n'y a rien **à** faire. — *There is nothing one can do.*

Qu'est-ce qu'il y a **à** manger? — *What is there to eat?*

Sayings and idioms

C'est **à** prendre ou **à** laisser.[1]	*Take it or leave it.*
Ça laisse beaucoup **à** désirer.	*That leaves a lot to be desired.*
Ce n'est pas la mer **à** boire.[2]	*It's not such a big deal. It's not the impossible.*
Si c'était **à** refaire...[3]	*If I had to do it all over again...*
Il y a fort **à** parier que...	*It's a safe bet that...*
Il n'y a pas **à** s'inquiéter.	*There is no reason to worry.*
C'est **à** devenir fou.	*That could drive you crazy.*
C'est **à** désespérer.	*That could drive one to despair.*
C'est **à** voir.[4]	*That remains to be seen.*
C'est **à** ne pas manquer.[5]	*That is a must. Don't miss it.*
C'est **à** s'y méprendre.	*It's hard not to make a mistake.*
C'est **à** mourir d'ennui.	*It's enough to bore you stiff.*
C'est **à** mourir de rire.	*You could laugh yourself sick.*
C'est **à** pleurer.	*It's enough to make you cry.*
C'est **à** hurler de rire.	*It's enough to make you roar with laughter.*
C'est **à** s'arracher les cheveux.	*It's enough to make you pull your hair out.*
C'était **à** mourir de honte.	*I could have died with shame.*
Le plus dur est **à** venir.	*The hardest is (yet) to come.*

---

1. lit.: *It's to be taken or left.*
2. lit.: *It's not the ocean to drink.*
3. lit.: *If it was to be redone...*
4. lit.: *That's to be seen.*
5. lit.: *It's not to be missed.*

C. The preposition de is required before the infinitive

• after the following verbs

s'abstenir **de**	*to abstain/refrain from (doing)*
accepter **de**	*to accept to, to agree to*
accorder à qn **de**	*to grant sb permission to*
accuser qn **de**	*to accuse sb of (doing/having done)*
achever **de**	*to finish, to complete (doing)*
admettre **de**	*to admit (doing), to admit that*
admirer qn **de**	*to admire sb for (doing)*
affecter **de**	*to pretend to*
s'affliger **de**	*to be distressed about (doing)*
s'agir **de**	*to be a question of (doing)*
appréhender **de**	*to dread (doing)*
(s')arrêter **de**	*to stop, to quit (doing)*
attendre **de**	*to wait till*
avertir qn **de**	*to warn sb to*
s'aviser **de**	*to dare to, to think one can (do)*
blâmer qn **de**	*to blame sb for (doing/having done)*
brûler **de**	*to long to, to be eager to*
cesser **de**	*to stop, to cease, to quit (doing)*
ne (pas)[1] cesser **de**	*to keep (doing), to continually (do)*
charger qn **de**	*to give sb the job/responsibility of (doing), to ask sb to*
se charger **de**	*to take it upon oneself to*
choisir **de**	*to choose to*
commander à qn **de**	*to order/command sb to*
conjurer qn **de**	*to beg/entreat sb to*
conseiller à qn **de**	*to advise sb to*
consoler qn **de**	*to console sb to*
se consoler **de**	*to get over (doing)*
se contenter **de**	*to be satisfied with (doing)*
continuer **de**[2]	*to continue to*
convaincre qn **de**	*to convince sb to*
convenir **de**	*to agree to (doing)*

---

1. Note that *pas* can be omitted with the verbs 'cesser', 'pouvoir', 'savoir' and 'oser'.
   Il ne cesse **de** pleuvoir. *It keeps (on) raining.*
2. Also: continuer **à**
   Note that ***commencer*** and ***continuer*** can be used with either **à** or **de** before an infinitive; *commencer* is more frequently used with **à** whereas *continuer* can be found more and more with **de**.

craindre **de**	*to fear, to be afraid of (doing)*
crier à qn **de**	*to scream at sb to*
décider **de** (= résoudre **de**)[1]	*to decide to*
déconseiller à qn **de**	*to advise sb not to*
décourager qn **de**[2]	*to discourage sb from (doing)*
dédaigner **de**	*to disdain (doing)*
défendre à qn **de** (= interdire à qn **de**)	*to forbid sb to*
défier qn **de**	*to challenge sb to*
dégoûter qn **de**	*to put sb off (doing)*
demander à qn **de**	*to ask sb to*
se dépêcher **de**	*to hurry and (do)*
se désaccoutumer **de**	*to break one's habit of*
désespérer **de**	*to despair/give up hope of (doing)*
déshabituer qn **de**	*to get sb out of the habit of (doing)*
se déshabituer **de**	*to get out of the habit of (doing)*
devoir à qn **de**	*to owe it to sb to*
se devoir **de**	*to owe it to oneself to*
différer **de**	*to postpone, to defer to*
dire à qn **de**	*to tell sb to*
dispenser qn **de**	*to exempt sb from (doing)*
se dispenser **de**	*to get out of/not to bother (doing)*
dissuader qn **de**	*to dissuade sb from (doing)*
douter **de**	*to doubt that*
écrire à qn **de**	*to write to sb to*
s'efforcer **de**	*to try hard/strive/endeavor to*
empêcher qn **de**	*to prevent sb from (doing)*
s'empêcher **de**	*to refrain from (doing)*
s'empresser **de**	*to hasten to*
endurer **de**	*to endure to, to put up with*
enrager **de**	*to be very angry about (doing)*
entreprendre **de**	*to undertake to*
envisager **de**	*to plan to*
épargner à qn **de**	*to spare sb the trouble of (doing)*
essayer **de**[3] (= tâcher **de**, tenter **de**)	*to try to*
s'étonner **de**	*to be surprised to*
éviter **de**	*to avoid (doing), to take care not to*
éviter à qn **de**	*to save sb from (doing)*

1. But: se décider / se résoudre **à**, être décidé / résolu **à** (see p. 246)
2. But: encourager qn **à** = *to encourage sb to*
3. But: s'essayer **à** = *to try one's hand at (doing)*

s'excuser **de**	*to apologize for (doing)*
excuser qn **de**	*to excuse sb for (doing/having done)*
exempter qn **de**	*to exempt sb from (doing)*
se fatiguer **de**	*to get tired of (doing)*
feindre **de**	*to pretend to*
féliciter qn **de**	*to congratulate sb on (doing)*
se féliciter **de**	*to be very pleased to*
finir **de**	*to finish (doing)*
se flatter **de**	*to pride oneself on (doing)*
frémir **de**	*to tremble at the thought of (doing)*
se garder **de**	*to be careful not to*
hasarder **de**[1]	*to risk (doing)*
se hâter **de**	*to hasten and (do)*
implorer qn **de**	*to implore sb to*
s'imposer **de**	*to make it a rule to*
s'indigner **de**	*to be outraged about (doing)*
s'inquiéter **de**	*to worry about (doing)*
inspirer à qn **de**	*to inspire sb to*
interdire à qn **de** (= défendre à qn **de**)	*to forbid/not allow sb to*
s'irriter **de**	*to get annoyed about (doing)*
jurer (à qn) **de**[2]	*to swear (to sb) to*
se jurer **de**	*to vow to*
se lamenter **de**	*to moan about (doing)*
se lasser **de**	*to get tired of (doing)*
louer qn **de**	*to praise sb for (doing)*
se louer **de**	*to congratulate oneself on (doing)*
manquer **de**[3]	*to almost (do), to fail to*
ne pas manquer **de**	*to be sure to, to not forget to*
méditer **de**	*to contemplate (doing)*
se mêler **de**	*to take it upon oneself to*
menacer (qn) **de**	*to threaten (sb) to*
mépriser qn **de**	*to despise sb for (doing)*
mériter **de**	*to deserve to*
se moquer **de**	*not to care less about (doing)*
négliger **de**	*to neglect to*

---

1. But: **se** hasarder **à** = *to venture to*
2. But: jurer + inf. = *to swear to* (see p. 248)
3. When followed by an infinitive, **manquer de** is always in the passé composé.
   J'*ai manqué* **de** m'évanouir. — *I almost fainted.*

obtenir **de**	*to manage to*
s'occuper **de**[1]	*to be in charge of (doing)*
offrir (à qn) **de**[2]	*to offer (sb) to*
omettre **de**	*to omit/neglect/fail to*
ordonner à qn **de**	*to order sb to*
oublier **de**	*to forget to*
pardonner à qn **de**	*to forgive sb for (having done)*
parler **de**	*to speak/talk about (doing)*
se passer **de**	*to do without ...-ing*
permettre à qn **de**	*to allow sb to*
se permettre **de**	*to take the liberty of (doing)*
persuader qn **de**	*to persuade sb to*
se plaindre **de**	*to complain about (doing)*
plaindre qn **de**	*to pity sb because*
prescrire à qn **de**	*to prescribe that sb (does)*
presser qn **de**	*to urge sb to*
se presser **de** (= se dépêcher **de**)	*to hurry to*
prévoir **de**	*to plan to*
prier qn **de**	*to ask/beg sb to*
projeter **de**	*to plan to*
promettre (à qn) **de**	*to promise (sb) to*
se promettre **de**	*to make up one's mind to*
proposer à qn **de**	*to propose to sb to/suggest that sb*
se proposer **de**	*to intend to*
punir qn **de**	*to punish sb for (having done)*
rappeler à qn **de**	*to remind sb to*
se rappeler **de**[3]	*to remember to*
réclamer **de**	*to demand to*
recommander à qn **de**	*to recommend to sb to*
redouter **de**	*to dread (doing)*
refuser **de**[4]	*to refuse to*
regretter **de**	*to regret to, to be sorry for (doing)*
se réjouir **de**	*to be happy to*
remercier qn **de**	*to thank sb for (doing/having done)*
se repentir **de**	*to repent/regret (having done)*
reprocher à qn **de**	*to reproach sb for (doing/having done)*
se reprocher **de**	*to blame oneself for (having done)*
requérir qn **de**	*to request/ask sb to*

---

1. But: être occupé **à** = *to be busy (doing)* [see p. 248]
2. But: s'offrir **à** = *to offer to, to volunteer to*
3. *se rappeler **de*** is followed by the *present infinitive* (see p. 249)
4. But: se refuser **à** = *to refuse to*

se réserver **de**	*to reserve the possibility of (doing)*
résoudre **de** (= décider **de**)	*to decide to*
retenir qn **de**	*to keep/stop sb from (doing)*
se retenir **de**	*to refrain from (doing), to try not to*
rêver **de**	*to dream of (doing)*
rire **de**	*to laugh about (doing)*
risquer **de**	*to risk/run the risk of (doing), to probably (do)*
se soucier **de**	*to care about (doing)*
souffrir **de**	*to suffer from (doing)*
souhaiter à qn **de**	*to wish sb to*
soupçonner qn **de**	*to suspect sb of (doing/having done)*
se souvenir **de**[1]	*to remember (doing)*
suggérer à qn **de**	*to suggest to sb to*
supplier qn **de**	*to beg sb to*
supporter **de**	*to bear/stand/endure to*
suspecter qn **de**	*to suspect sb of (doing/having done)*
tâcher **de** (= essayer **de**)	*to try to*
téléphoner à qn **de**	*to tell sb on the phone to*
tenter **de** (= essayer **de**)	*to try to*
trembler **de**	*to tremble (at the thought) of (doing)*
trouver (+ adj.)[2] **de**	*to find/deem it (+ adj.) to*
se vanter **de**	*to brag about/boast of (doing)*
venir **de**[3]	*to have just (done)*
en vouloir à qn **de**	*to be angry with sb for (doing)*
s'en vouloir **de**	*to be angry with oneself for (doing)*

Je m'*abstins* **de** lui répondre.	*I abstained from answering her.*
Acceptez-vous **de** devenir ma femme?	*Do you accept to become my wife?*
Il a *accepté* **de** venir.	*He agreed to come.*
On lui *accorda* **de** voir sa fille.	*They granted him permission to see his daughter.*
On m'a *accusé* **de** ne pas avoir été fidèle.	*They accused me of not having been faithful.*

---

1. **se souvenir de** is generally used with the *past infinitive* (= *avoir* or *être* + past participle).
   Je ne me souviens pas **d'**y *être allé.* — *I don't remember going there.*
2. bon, mauvais, drôle, etc.
3. **venir + de** + infinitive expresses the *passé récent.* (see p. 251)

Il *s'agit* **de** prendre la bonne décision.	*It is a question of making the right decision.*
J'*appréhende* **de** rentrer.	*I dread going home.*
Il n'a pas *arrêté* **de** pleuvoir. *Arrête* **de** dire des bêtises.	*It didn't stop raining.* *Stop talking nonsense.*
Attendez **de** voir le résultat.	*Wait till you see the result.*
Il m'a *averti* **de** ne pas faire ça.	*He warned me not to do that.*
Je *brûle* **de** vous revoir.	*I am longing to see you again.*
La situation ne *cesse* **d'**empirer.	*The situation keeps getting worse.*
On m'a *chargé* **d'**aller chercher de l'eau.	*They gave me the job of getting some water.*
Ils ont *choisi* **de** partir.	*They chose to leave.*
On lui a *conseillé* **de** se taire.	*They advised him to be silent.*
Il *continuera* **de** (or: **à**) travailler.	*He will continue to work.*
Il faut *convaincre* les électeurs **d'**aller voter.	*One must convince the voters to go to the polls.*
Nous avons *convenu* **de** nous voir tous les jours.	*We agreed to see each other every day.*
Il *craignait* **de** perdre ses facultés mentales.	*He was afraid of losing his mental capabilities.*
Ils ont *décidé* **de** se marier.	*They decided to get married.*
Il m'a *déconseillé* **de** prendre la route.	*He advised me not to drive.*
Le médecin m'a *défendu* **de** courir.	*The doctor has forbidden me to run.*
Nous vous *demandons* **de** ne plus fumer et **d'**attacher vos ceintures de sécurité.	*We ask you to stop smoking and to fasten your seatbelts.*
Dépêchez-vous **de** vous habiller.	*Hurry and get dressed.*
Il ne faut pas *désespérer* **de** guérir.	*One must not give up hope of getting well.*
Il *doit* à son père **d'**être devenu médecin.	*He owes it to his father to have become a doctor.*
Ne *différez* pas **de** lui téléphoner.	*Don't put off calling her.*
Je lui ai *dit* **de** rester.	*I told him to stay.*
On m'a *dispensé* **de** faire du sport.	*They exempted me from playing sports.*

Je me *dispenserai* **de** le saluer.	*I'll spare myself the trouble of greeting him.*
Elle *doute* **de** pouvoir le faire.	*She doubts that she can do it.*
Je lui ai *écrit* **de** venir.	*I wrote him to come.*
Le bruit m'*empêche* **de** dormir.	*The noise prevents me from sleeping.*
On donne des tétines aux enfants pour les *empêcher* **de** sucer leur pouce.	*One gives pacifiers to the children to prevent them from sucking their thumbs.*
J'*enrage* **d'**avoir perdu mes clés.	*I am very angry about having lost my keys.*
Il *envisage* **d'**aller vivre à l'étranger.	*He plans to go and live abroad.*
J'*essaie* toujours **de** faire de mon mieux.	*I always try to do my best.*
Je m'*étonne* **de** vous voir si déprimé.	*I am surprised to see you so depressed.*
J'*évite* **de** me mettre au soleil.	*I avoid exposing myself to the sun.*
Je m'*excuse* **de** vous avoir fait attendre.	*I apologize for having made you wait.*
Excusez-moi **d'**être en retard.	*Excuse me for being late.*
Il *se félicite* **d'**avoir gagné le procès.	*He is pleased to have won the trial.*
Il a *fini* **de** pleuvoir.	*It stopped raining.*
Elle *se flatte* **de** réussir.	*She prides herself on succeeding.*
Gardez-vous **de** patiner sur le lac.	*Be careful not to skate on the lake.*
Elle *implore* son père **de** lui pardonner.	*She begs her father to forgive her.*
Elle *s'est imposée* **de** ne jamais se mêler des affaires des autres.	*She made it a rule never to meddle in other people's affairs.*
Elle *s'inquiète* **de** ne pas l'avoir vu aujourd'hui.	*She is worried about not having seen him today.*
Je lui ai *interdit* **de** sortir.	*I didn't allow him to go out.*
Il a *juré* **de** le tuer.	*He vowed to kill him.*
Je *m'étais juré* **de** ne plus revenir.	*I had sworn to myself never to return.*
Il se *lamente* **d'**être cloué au lit.	*He moans about being confined to bed.*

Je *me loue* **de** l'avoir engagé.	*I congratulate myself on having hired him.*
Ne *manquez* pas **de** lui écrire.	*Be sure to write to him/her.*
Je ne *manquerai* pas **de** vous contacter.	*I will be sure to contact you.*
Il n'*a* pas *manqué* **de** célébrer.	*He didn't fail to celebrate.*
Il *méditait* **de** se venger.	*He contemplated taking revenge.*
Elle *se mêle* **de** corriger tout le monde.	*She takes it upon herself to correct everybody.*
Je le *méprise* **de** m'avoir poignardé dans le dos.	*I despise him for having stabbed me in the back.*
Il *mérite* **d'**être récompensé.	*He deserves to be rewarded.*
Il *se moque* **de** paraître ridicule.	*He couldn't care less about looking ridiculous.*
Elle a *négligé* **de** le[1] faire.	*She neglected to do it.*
Il a *obtenu* **d'**être nommé président.	*He managed to be named president.*
Il *s'occupe* **d'**aider les pauvres.	*He is in charge of helping the poor.*
Il m'a *offert* **de** me raccompagner.	*He offered to take me home.*
Ils ont *omis* **de** les[1] prévenir.	*They failed to inform them.*
Il a *ordonné* à la foule **de** reculer.	*He ordered the crowd to move back.*
Nous avons *oublié* **de** te faire la commission.	*We forgot to give you the message.*
N'*oubliez* pas **d'**avancer vos montres.	*Don't forget to set your watches ahead.*
Elle *parle* **de** se marier.	*She talks about getting married.*
Pardonnez-moi **de** vous appeler par votre prénom.	*Forgive me for calling you by your first name.*
Vous *vous passerez* **de** manger.	*You will do without eating.*
Permettez-moi **de** me présenter.	*Allow me to introduce myself.*
Je *me suis permis* **de** lui écrire.	*I took the liberty of writing to him.*
Il m'a *persuadé* **de** rester chez lui.	*He persuaded me to stay with him.*
Il se *plaint* **d'**être traité comme la cinquième roue du carrosse.	*He complains about being treated like the fifth wheel on the wagon.*

1. Note that the preposition **de** does *not* contract with **le** or **les** when *le* and *les* are object pronouns.

Le médecin m'a *prescrit* **de** faire de la marche.	*The doctor prescribed that I walk.*
Il me *pressait* **de** conclure ce marché.	*He urged me to conclude this deal.*
Tout le monde *se pressait* **de** rentrer.	*Everybody hurried to get home.*
Elle avait *prévu* **de** venir à Paris pour se faire soigner.	*She had made plans to come to Paris to get treated.*
Prévoyez **d'**apporter quelque chose à manger et à boire.	*Plan to bring something to eat and drink.*
Je vous *prie* **de** vous taire.[1]	*Will you please be quiet.*
Nous vous *prions* **de** passer à la salle à manger.[2]	*Will you please go to the dining room.*
Ils *projettent* **d'**avoir un enfant.	*They plan to have a child.*
Promettez-moi **d'**être sage.	*Promise me to be good.*
Je vous *propose* **d'**écouter.	*I suggest that you listen.*
Elle *s'est proposé* **de** passer une semaine à Paris.	*She intended to spend a week in Paris.*
Rappelez-moi **d'**acheter du pain.	*Remind me to buy some bread.*
Je vous *recommande* **de** prendre ce médicament.	*I recommend that you take this medication.*
Elle *redoute* **de** tomber malade.	*She dreads becoming ill.*
Je *refuse* **de** vous écouter.	*I refuse to listen to you.*
Ils ont *refusé* **de** se rendre.	*They refused to surrender.*
Je *regrette* **de** vous avoir réveillé.	*I am sorry that I woke you up.*
Je *me réjouis* **de** te rencontrer.	*I am happy to meet you.*
Je vous *remercie* **de** m'avoir aidé.	*I thank you for helping me.*
Ils se sont *repentis* **d'**avoir commis ce crime.	*They repented having committed this crime.*
Son mari lui a *reproché* **de** dépenser trop d'argent.	*Her husband reproached her for spending too much money.*
Il a *résolu* **d'**attendre.	*He decided to wait.*
Je n'ai pu me *retenir* **de** rire.	*I couldn't help laughing.*
La pitié me *retient* **de** le punir.	*Pity keeps me from punishing him.*
Elle *rêve* **de** devenir actrice.	*She dreams of becoming an actress.*

---

1. lit.: *I ask you to be quiet.*
2. lit.: *We ask you to go to the dining room.*

Nous avons *ri* **de** devoir nous comporter comme des guignols. — *We laughed about having to behave like fools.*

Vous *risquez* **de** vous faire écraser. — *You risk getting run over.*
La situation *risque* **d'**empirer. — *The situation may get worse.*
Ça ne *risque* pas **d'**arriver. — *That is not likely to happen.*

Je *souffre* **de** le voir malade. — *I suffer seeing him ill.*

Je ne *souhaite* à personne **d'**avoir à faire ça. — *I don't wish anybody to have to do that.*
Je te *souhaite* **de** trouver un emploi. — *I wish you to find a job.*

On les *soupçonne* **de** tricher. — *One suspects them of cheating.*

Je *me souviens* **de** vous avoir raconté l'histoire. — *I remember telling you the story.*

Je vous *supplie* **de** m'aider. — *I beg you to help me.*

Elle ne *supporte* pas **d'**attendre. — *She can't stand waiting.*

Je *tremble* **de** le rencontrer. — *I tremble at the thought of meeting him.*

Il a *trouvé* bon **de** s'absenter. — *He deemed it good to go away.*

Il *se vante* **d'**avoir gagné. — *He is bragging about winning.*

Je lui *en veux* **de** m'avoir menti. — *I am angry with him for having lied to me.*

Elle *vient* **de** partir. — *She just left.*

Idioms

Le livre vient **de** paraître. — *The book just came out.*
éclater **de** rire — *to burst out laughing*
pleurer **de** rire — *to shed tears with laughter*

• after the following expressions

avoir l'air **de** — *to seem, to appear, to look*
Vous n'avez pas l'air **de** comprendre. — *You don't seem to understand.*
Tu as l'air **d'**avoir faim. — *You look hungry.*

avoir l'âge **de** — *to be old enough to*
Elle a maintenant l'âge **de** se marier. — *She is now old enough to get married.*

avoir l'audace **de** — *to have the audacity/nerve to*
Elle a eu l'audace **de** dire cela. — *She had the audacity to say that.*

avoir besoin **de** — *to need to, to have to*
Tout le monde a besoin **de** manger. — *Everyone needs to eat.*

avoir le bonheur **de** — *to have the pleasure to*
J'ai le bonheur **de** vous annoncer nos fiançailles. — *I have the pleasure to announce our engagement to you.*

avoir pour but **de** — *to aim at (doing)*
Ces mesures ont pour but **de** baisser le chômage. — *These measures aim at lowering the unemployment.*

avoir la capacité **de** — *to have the ability to*
Il a la capacité **de** diriger cette entreprise. — *He has the ability to direct this business.*

avoir la certitude **de** — *to be certain of (doing)*
Nous avons la certitude **de** gagner. — *We are certain of winning.*

avoir (de) la chance **de** — *to be lucky/fortunate to*
J'ai la chance **de** pouvoir le faire. — *I am lucky to be able to do it.*

avoir des chances **de** — *to have a chance to*
Il a des chances **de** réussir. — *He has a chance to succeed.*
Ils ont de bonnes chances/de grandes chances/peu de chances **de** l'emporter. — *They have a good chance/a big chance/little chance to win.*

avoir le courage **de** — *to have the courage to*
Je n'ai pas le courage **de** parler en public. — *I don't have the courage to speak in public.*

avoir coutume **de** — *to be in the habit of (doing)*
Il a coutume **de** faire la sieste. — *He is in the habit of taking a nap.*
Elle avait coutume **de** dire... — *She used to say...*
Comme j'ai coutume **de** dire... — *As I usually say...*

avoir le culot **de** (fam.) — *to have the nerve to*
Elle a le culot **de** venir ici. — *She has the nerve to come here.*

avoir le devoir **de** — *to have the duty to*
Tu as le devoir **de** l'aider. — *You have the duty to help him.*

avoir le désir **de**	*to have the desire to*
Nous avons le désir **de** réussir.	*We have the desire to succeed.*
avoir le droit **de**	*to have the right to*
Est-ce qu'on a le droit **de** faire la grève?	*Does one have the right to go on strike?*
avoir envie **de**	*to feel like (doing), to want to*
Je n'ai pas envie **de** travailler.	*I don't feel like working.*
avoir l'espoir **de**	*to be hopeful of (doing)*
Il a l'espoir **de** guérir.	*He is hopeful of getting well.*
avoir la force **de**	*to have the strength to*
Elle n'a plus la force **de** marcher.	*She no longer has the strength to walk.*
avoir le front **de**	*to have the face/effrontery to*
Elle a eu le front **de** quitter la salle.	*She had the face to leave the room.*
avoir l'habitude **de**	*to be used to (doing)*
J'ai l'habitude **de** me lever tard.	*I am used to getting up late.*
avoir hâte **de**	*to be eager/anxious to*
J'ai hâte **de** revoir ma soeur.	*I cannot wait to see my sister again.*
avoir l'honneur **de**	*to have the honor of (doing)*
J'ai l'honneur **de** vous souhaiter la bienvenue.	*I have the honor of welcoming you.*
avoir honte **de**	*to be ashamed to*
J'ai honte **de** vous avoir menti.	*I am ashamed to have lied to you.*
avoir horreur **de**	*to detest (doing)*
Il a horreur **de** se coucher l'estomac plein.	*He hates going to bed with a full stomach.*
avoir l'idée **de**	*to have the idea to*
Il avait l'idée **de** leur rendre visite.	*He had the idea to visit them.*
avoir l'impression **de**	*to have the impression/feeling that, to feel that*
J'ai l'impression **de** l'avoir vu.	*I have the feeling that I saw him.*

avoir l'imprudence **de**	*to be foolish enough to*
Il a eu l'imprudence **de** contredire.	*He was foolish enough to contradict.*
avoir l'intention **de**	*to intend/have the intention to*
Nous avons l'intention/aucune intention **d'**accepter cette offre.	*We intend/have no intention to accept this offer.*
avoir la joie **de**	*to have the pleasure to/of (doing)*
J'ai la joie **de** vous annoncer la naissance de mon fils.	*I have the pleasure to announce the birth of my son to you.*
Quand aurai-je la joie **de** vous revoir?	*When will I have the pleasure of seeing you again?*
avoir la malchance/le malheur **de**	*to have the misfortune to*
J'ai eu le malheur **de** choisir cet hôtel.	*I had the misfortune to choose this hotel.*
en avoir assez/marre (fam.) **de**	*to be fed up with (doing)*
On en a marre **de** l'entendre.	*One is fed up with hearing it.*
(ne pas) avoir les moyens **de**	*(not) to be able to afford to*
Elle n'a pas les moyens **d'**acheter ce bijou.	*She cannot afford to buy this piece of jewelry.*
avoir l'occasion **de**	*to have the opportunity to*
Il a l'occasion **de** passer une année à Paris.	*He has the opportunity to spend a year in Paris.*
avoir la passion **de**	*to have a passion for (doing)*
Il a la passion **d'**écrire des poèmes.	*He has a passion for writing poems.*
avoir la patience **de**	*to have the patience to*
Il n'a pas la patience **d'**attendre.	*He doesn't have the patience to wait.*
avoir la pensée **de**	*to think of/about (doing)*
Je n'ai jamais eu la pensée **de** vendre ma maison.	*I never thought of selling my car.*
avoir/recevoir la permission **de**	*to have/get the permission to*
Je n'ai pas la permission **d'**y aller.	*I don't have permission to go there.*
avoir peur **de**	*to be afraid of (doing)*
J'ai peur **d'**attraper un PV.	*I am afraid of getting a (traffic) ticket.*

avoir le plaisir **de**	*to have the pleasure to*
J'ai le plaisir **de** vous annoncer que votre livre va être publié.	*I have the pleasure to announce to you that your book will be published.*
avoir la possibilité **de**	*to have the possibility to*
A-t-il eu la possibilité **d'**y aller?	*Did he have the possibility to go there?*
avoir le pouvoir **de**	*to have the power to*
Je n'ai pas le pouvoir **de** le gracier.	*I don't have the power to pardon him.*
avoir raison **de**	*to be right to*
Vous avez raison **de** vous plaindre.	*You are right to complain.*
avoir ses raisons **de**	*to have one's reasons to*
J'ai mes raisons/de bonnes raisons/ toutes les raisons **de** croire que...	*I have my reasons/good reasons/ every reason to believe that...*
n'avoir aucune raison **de**	*to have no reason to*
Tu n'as aucune raison **de** paniquer.	*You have no reason to panic.*
avoir le regret **de**	*to regret (doing)*
J'ai le regret **de** ne pouvoir vous aider.	*I regret not being able to help you.*
avoir la sensation **de**	*to have the feeling that*
J'ai eu la sensation **de** flotter.	*I had the feeling that I was floating.*
avoir le sentiment **de**	*to have the feeling that*
J'ai le sentiment **de** le connaître.	*I have the feeling that I know him.*
avoir la surprise **de**	*to be surprised to*
J'ai eu la bonne surprise **de** le voir.	*I was pleasantly surprised to see him.*
avoir le temps **de**	*to have the time to*
As-tu le temps **de** le faire?	*Do you have the time to do it?*
avoir tort **de**	*to be wrong to*
Vous avez tort **de** croire cela.	*You are wrong to believe that.*
avoir (de) la veine **de** (fam.)	*to be lucky to*
J'ai de la veine **d'**avoir trouvé un appartement.	*I am lucky to have found an apartment.*
avoir la volonté **de**	*to have the will to*
Il a la volonté **de** réussir.	*He has the will to succeed.*

donner envie/le goût à qn **de**	*to make sb want to*
Il faut donner envie aux enfants **d'**apprendre.	*One must make the children want to learn.*
Ça leur donne le goût **d'**apprendre.	*That makes them want to learn.*
donner l'impression **de**	*to give the impression of (doing)*
Cet article donne l'impression **d'**avoir été bâclé.	*This article gives the impression of having been dashed off.*
donner/recevoir l'ordre **de**	*to give/receive the order to*
Il nous a donné l'ordre **de** partir.	*He gave us the order to leave.*
se donner la peine **de**	*to take the trouble to*
Elle s'est donné la peine **de** m'aider.	*She took the trouble to help me.*
être à qn **de**	*to be sb's turn to, to be up to sb to*
C'est à Paul (moi, toi, lui...) **de** s'inscrire.[1]	*It's Paul's (my, your, his...) turn to register.*
C'est à eux **de** décider.	*It's up to them to decide.*
être dans l'impossibilité **de**	*to find it impossible to*
Il est dans l'impossibilité **d'**exprimer ses sentiments.	*He finds it impossible to express his feelings.*
être dans l'incapacité **de**	*to be unable to*
Nous sommes dans l'incapacité **de** finir ce travail.	*We are unable to finish this job.*
être dans l'obligation **de**	*to be under an obligation to*
Je suis dans l'obligation **de** le suivre.	*I am obliged to follow him.*
être en droit **de**	*to be entitled to*
Vous êtes en droit **de** réclamer une indemnité.	*You are entitled to demand a compensation.*
être en état **de**	*to be in a position of (doing)*
Il n'est pas en état **de** le faire.	*He is in no position to do it.*
être en mesure **de**	*to be able to/capable of (doing)*
Je ne suis pas en mesure **de** t'aider.	*I am unable to help you.*

---

1. Note that '*c'est*' can be omitted in this expression when a pronoun follows 'à'.
A *vous* **de** faire votre choix = *It's up to you to make your choice.*

être en train **de** — *to be in the process of (doing)*

Les élèves étaient en train **de** passer un examen quand la cloche a sonné. — *The students were in the process of taking an exam when the bell rang.*

être en voie **de** — *to be on the way to*

Ce chanteur est en voie **de** devenir une grande vedette. — *This singer is on the way to become a big star.*

être sur le point **de** — *to be about to*

J'étais sur le point **de** partir. — *I was about to leave.*

faire attention **de** (or: **à**) — *to pay attention/be careful to*

Faites attention **de** ne pas tomber. — *Be careful not to fall.*

faire bien **de** — *to do well to*

On a bien fait **de** réserver nos places à l'avance. — *We did well to reserve our seats in advance.*

faire exprès **de** — *to intentionally (do)*

Il a fait exprès **de** ne rien dire. — *He intentionally said nothing.*

se faire une joie/un plaisir **de** — *to look forward to (doing), to be delighted to do*

Je me ferai une joie **de** vous accueillir. — *I will be delighted to welcome you.*

faire mieux **de** — *to do better to*

Tu ferais mieux **de** te taire. — *You had better be silent.*

J'aurais mieux fait **de** raccompagner mon ami. — *It would have been better if I had taken my friend home.*

faire à qn le plaisir **de** — *to do sb the favor to*

Faites-moi le plaisir **d'**accepter mon invitation. — *Do me the favor of accepting/will you please accept my invitation.*

faire semblant **de** (= feindre **de**) — *to pretend to*

Il fait semblant **d'**être pauvre. — *He pretends to be poor.*

faire le serment **de** — *to make a solemn vow to*

Il a fait le serment **de** dire toute la vérité. — *He made a solemn vow to tell the whole truth.*

faire signe à qn **de** — *to signal/motion sb to*

Elle m'a fait signe **de** me taire. — *She signaled me to be silent.*

Il lui fait signe **de** s'asseoir. — *He signals him/her to sit down.*

faire (le) vœu **de**	*to vow to*
Il a fait (le) vœu **de** se venger.	*He vowed to take revenge.*
mettre qn au défi **de**	*to challenge sb to*
Je vous mets au défi **de** prouver le contraire.	*I challenge you to prove the contrary.*
ne pas pouvoir s'empêcher **de**	*not to be able to help (doing)*
Je ne peux pas m'empêcher **de** rire.	*I cannot help laughing.*
prendre l'habitude **de**	*to get into the habit of (doing)*
J'ai pris l'habitude **de** me lever tôt.	*I got into the habit of getting up early.*
prendre garde **de**	*to be careful not to*
Il faut prendre garde **de** n'accuser personne.	*One must be careful not to accuse anyone.*
Prenez garde **de** tomber.	*Be careful not to fall.*
prendre le parti **de**	*to decide to*
Il a pris le parti **de** s'installer à Paris.	*He decided to move to Paris.*
prendre la peine **de**	*to take the trouble to*
Il a quand même pris la peine **de** me remercier.	*He still took the trouble to thank me.*
Prenez la peine **d**'entrer!	*Please come in!*
prendre soin **de**	*to be careful to, to make sure to*
Prenez soin **de** ne pas réveiller les enfants.	*Be careful not to wake up the chidren.*
Prends soin **de** fermer les fenêtres.	*Make sure to close the windows.*
ne pas prendre soin **de**	*to fail to, to neglect to*
Nous n'avons pas pris soin **d**'éviter cette confrontation.	*We failed to avoid this confrontation.*
prendre sur soi **de**	*to take it upon oneself to*
J'ai pris sur moi **de** lui parler.	*I took it upon myself to speak to him.*
prendre le temps **de**	*to take the time to*
Prends le temps **de** te soigner.	*Take the time to take care of yourself.*
savoir gré à qn **de**	*to be grateful to sb for (doing)*
Il lui sait gré **de** l'avoir renseigné.	*He is grateful to him/her for having informed him.*

trouver moyen **de**	*to find a way to*
Le détenu a trouvé moyen **de** s'évader.	*The prisoner found a way to escape.*
valoir la peine **de**	*to be worth ...-ing*
La pièce vaut la peine **d'**être vue.	*The play is worth seeing.*

• after the following impersonal expressions[1]

il appartient à qn **de**	*it's up to sb to*
Il lui appartient **de** choisir un remède.	*It's up to him to choose a remedy.*
il (or: ça) arrive à qn **de**	*sb sometimes (does)*
Il lui arrive **de** se tromper.	*He is sometimes mistaken.*
Il m'arrive **d'**oublier.	*Occasionally I forget.*
Ça vous est déjà arrivé **d'**y penser?	*Did you ever think about that?*
il s'agit **de**	*it's a question of (doing)*
Il s'agit **de** trouver une solution.	*It's a question of finding a solution.*
il convient **de**	*it's advisable/proper to, one should/ought to*
Il convient **de** le faire.	*It's advisable to do it.*
il importe **de**	*it's important to*
Il importe **d'**arriver à temps.	*It's important to arrive in time.*
il me (te, lui...) plaît **de**	*I (you, he...) like(s) to*
Il me plaît **d'**agir ainsi.	*I like to act like that.*
il me répugne **de**	*I hate to, I am loath to*
Il me répugne **de** vous dire la vérité.	*I hate to tell you the truth.*
il (me, te, lui, vous...) suffit **de**	*all it takes is..., all I (you, he...) have (has) to do is...*
Il suffit **d'**appuyer sur le bouton.	*All you have to do is press the button.*
il me (te, lui...) tarde **de**	*I (you, he...) cannot wait to, I am (you are, he is...) anxious to*
Il me tarde **de** te revoir.	*I cannot wait to see you again.*

---

1. • Note that most *impersonal expressions* take **de** before a following infinitive. For exceptions, see p. 221 and p. 263-264.
   • For the use of **de** after impersonal expressions containing *nouns*, see p. 260-262.
   For the use of **de** after impersonal expressions containing *adjectives*, see p. 271-272.

il ne tient qu'à vous (lui...) **de**	*it's up to you (him...) to*
Il ne tient qu'à eux **de** vous accueillir.	*It's up to them to welcome you.*
il est/c'est mal vu **de**	*it's frowned upon to*
En France, c'est mal vu **de** parler d'argent.	*In France, it's frowned upon to talk about money.*

- **after cela (= ça) + verb** (usually if **ça + verb** refers to a *following* idea)

cela m'(t', nous...) amuse **de**	*I (you, we...) have fun (doing)*
Cela m'amuse **de** te taquiner.	*I have fun teasing you.*
ça console **de**	*it's a consolation to*
Ça console **de** savoir qu'il est en bonne santé.	*It's a consolation to know that he is healthy.*
cela coûte cher **de**	*it's expensive to*
Cela coûte cher **de** construire une maison.	*It's expensive to build a house.*
ça me dégoûte **de**	*it makes me sick to*
Ça me dégoûte **de** voir cela.	*It makes me sick to see that.*
ça me déplaît **de**	*I am sorry to*
Ça me déplaît **de** vous interrompre.	*I am sorry to interrupt you.*
ça ne me dérange pas **de**	*it doesn't bother me to*
Ça ne me dérange pas **d'**attendre.	*It doesn't bother me to wait.*
ça te dirait/plairait **de**	*would you like to*
Ça te dirait/plairait **d'**aller au zoo?	*Would you like to go to the zoo?*
ça me donne envie **de**	*that makes me want to*
Ça me donne envie **de** vomir.	*That makes me want to vomit.*
ça me fâche/me fatigue/ m'intéresse/m'irrite **de**	*it annoys me/tires me/interests me/irritates me to*
Ça m'irrite/m'agace **d'**entendre cela.	*It irritates me to hear that.*
Ça m'intéresse **de** participer.	*I am interested in participating.*
ça fait chaud au cœur **de**	*it's heartwarming to*
Ça fait chaud au cœur **de** voir cela.	*It's heartwarming to see that.*

cela (me, te, lui...) fait du bien **de**	*it does (me, you, him...) good to*
Cela fait du bien **de** se reposer.	*It does good to take a rest.*
Cela vous fera du bien **de** boire cela.	*It will do you good to drink that.*
cela (me, te, lui...) fait mal **de**	*it hurts (me, you, him...) to*
Cela me fait mal **de** la voir souffrir.	*It hurts me to see her suffer.*
Aïe, ça fait mal **de** marcher.	*Ouch, it hurts to walk.*
cela fait pitié **de**	*it's pitiful to*
Cela fait pitié **de** le voir dans cet état.	*It's pitiful to see him in that state.*
ça fait plaisir **de**	*it's fun to, it's a pleasure to*
Ça fait plaisir **de** jouer à ce jeu.	*It's fun to play this game.*
ça me (te, lui...) fait plaisir **de**	*it's a pleasure for me (you, him...) to, I (you, he...) enjoy(s) to*
Ça m'a fait plaisir **de** danser avec toi.	*I enjoyed dancing with you.*
ça me (te, lui...) plaît **de**	*I (you, he..) like(s) to*
Ça me plairait **de** le rencontrer.	*I would like to meet him.*
ça porte malheur **de**	*it brings bad luck to*
Les gens superstitieux croient que ça porte malheur **de** passer sous une échelle.	*Superstitious people think that it brings bad luck to walk under a ladder.*
ça ne rime à rien **de**	*it makes no sense to*
Ça ne rime à rien **de** faire cela.	*It makes no sense to do that.*
cela ne sert à rien **de**	*it's useless to*
Cela ne sert à rien **de** se plaindre.	*It's useless to complain.*
ça vaut la peine **de**	*it's worth (doing)*
Ça vaut la peine **d'**y aller.	*It's worth going there.*
ça ne me (te, lui...) vient (est venu, viendrait...) pas à l'esprit **de**	*it doesn't (didn't, wouldn't...) occur to me (you, him...) to*
Ça ne me viendrait pas à l'esprit **de** lui demander.	*It wouldn't occur to me to ask him.*
Ça ne nous serait jamais venu à l'esprit **de** faire la grève.	*It would have never occurred to us to go on strike.*

D. The preposition pour is required before the infinitive after the following expressions

être d'accord **pour**	*to be willing to, to agree to*
Seriez-vous d'accord **pour** signer la pétition?	*Would you be willing to sign the petition?*
Nous étions d'accord **pour** dire que...	*We agreed that...*
se mettre d'accord **pour**	*to agree to*
On s'était mis d'accord **pour** ne pas dépenser plus de 100 euros.	*We had agreed not to spend more than 100 euros.*
s'accorder **pour**	*to agree to*
Nous nous sommes accordés **pour** lui offrir ce travail.	*We agreed to offer him this job.*
s'arranger **pour**	*to make sure that*
Arrangez-vous **pour** être à l'heure.	*Make sure that you are on time.*
compter sur qn **pour**	*to count on sb (doing)*
Puis-je compter sur toi **pour** m'aider?	*Can I count on you helping me?*
se dévouer **pour**	*to devote/sacrifice oneself to*
Je me suis dévoué **pour** la soigner.	*I devoted myself to looking after her.*
se donner du mal **pour**	*to go to the trouble to*
Elle s'est donné beaucoup de mal **pour** écrire cet article.	*She went to a lot of trouble to write this article.*
donner le feu vert **pour**[1]	*to give permission to*
Il m'a donné le feu vert **pour** y aller.	*He gave me permission to go there.*
être bon **pour**	*to be good at (doing)*
Je ne suis pas très bon **pour** citer des livres.	*I am not very good at quoting books.*
être en retard **pour**	*to be late (doing)*
Il est en retard **pour** payer ses factures.	*He is late paying his bills.*
faire des difficultés **pour**[2]	*to raise objections about (doing)*
Ils ont fait des difficultés **pour** lui donner le certificat.	*They raised objections about giving him the certificate.*

1. lit.: *to give the green light (= the go-ahead) to*
2. But: avoir des difficultés **à** = *to have difficulty in (doing)*

faire un effort **pour**	*to try hard/make an effort to*
Il a fait de gros efforts **pour** réussir.	*He tried very hard to succeed.*
se faire prier **pour**	*to make sb beg oneself to*
Ne vous faites pas tant prier **pour** venir.	*Don't make me beg you so much to come.*
il faut/fallait/a fallu/faudra/faudrait [un certain temps] **pour**	*it takes/took/will take/would take* [+ time period] *to*
Il faut une semaine **pour** tout voir dans ce musée.	*It takes a week to see everything in this museum.*
Il a fallu trois jours **pour** aller à cet endroit.	*It took three days to go to this place.*
Il faudrait cinq ans **pour** tout reconstruire.	*It would take five years to rebuild everything.*
ne pas se gêner **pour**	*not to hesitate/mind (doing)*
Il ne s'est pas gêné **pour** le lui dire.	*He didn't mind telling him.*
insister **pour**	*to insist on (doing)*
Ils ont insisté **pour** obtenir une réponse.	*They insisted on getting an answer.*
se joindre à qn **pour**	*to join sb in (doing)*
Ma famille se joint à moi **pour** vous souhaiter une bonne année.	*My family joins me in wishing you a happy New Year.*
mettre [un certain temps] **pour**	*to take* [+ time period]
J'ai mis deux ans **pour** (or: **à**) écrire ce livre.	*It took me two years to write this book.*
tout mettre en œuvre **pour**	*to make every effort to*
Ils ont tout mis en œuvre **pour** réussir.	*They made every effort to succeed.*
se mettre en quatre **pour**	*to go out of one's way to*
Il s'est mis en quatre **pour** vous faire plaisir.	*He went out of his way to please you.*
se porter volontaire **pour**	*to volunteer to*
Il s'est porté volontaire **pour** les aider.	*He volunteered to help them.*
se proposer **pour**	*to offer to*
Elle s'est proposée **pour** porter le sac de la vieille dame.	*She offered to carry the bag of the old lady.*

punir qn **pour** + inf. passé	*to punish sb for (doing)*
Il a été puni **pour** avoir menti.	*He was punished for lying.*
se relayer **pour**	*to take turns (doing)*
Ils se sont relayés **pour** surveiller les enfants.	*They took turns watching the children.*

Note:

pour is also used before the infinitive after

- verb (mostly 'être') + assez/trop + adjective or adverb

Tu es assez grand **pour** comprendre cela.	*You are old enough to understand that.*
C'est trop tôt **pour** le dire.	*It's too early to say.*

- verb + assez/trop + de + noun

Il a trop de travail **pour** sortir avec nous.	*He has too much work to go out with us.*

- verb + assez/trop

Il boit trop **pour** réussir.	*He drinks too much to succeed.*

Do not confuse

♦ **aller** + *inf.*	*to go and (do)*
Va te laver les mains.	*Go and wash your hands.*
aller + *inf.* (expressing the close future)	*to be going to do sth*
Je vais vous téléphoner ce soir.	*I am going to call you tonight.*
Tu vas t'amuser.	*You are going to have fun.*
Il va y avoir un orage.	*There is going to be a storm.*
On va tirer au sort.	*We are going to draw lots.*
Vous allez tout gâcher.	*You are going to spoil everything.*
Il va aller en France.	*He is going to go to France.*
Tu vas me manquer.	*I am going to miss you.*
♦ **s'amuser *à*** + *inf.*	*to enjoy (doing)*
Il s'amuse **à** taquiner sa soeur.	*He enjoys teasing his sister.*
cela m'(t', l'...) **amuse *de*** + *inf.*	*it's fun for me (you, him...) to*
Cela m'amuse **de** plaisanter.	*It's fun for me to joke.*
♦ **arriver *à*** + *inf.*	*to manage to*
Je n'arrive pas **à** trouver son adresse.	*I can't manage to find his address.*
il m' (lui, nous...) **arrive *de*** + *inf.*	*it happens to me (him, us...) that, I (he, we...) sometimes...*
Il m'arrive rarement **de** perdre quelque chose.	*I rarely lose something.*

♦ **s'attendre** ***à*** + *inf.*	*to expect to*
Je m'attends **à** vous voir demain.	*I expect to see you tomorrow.*
attendre ***de*** + *inf.*	*to wait until*
Attends **d**'avoir les moyens avant d'acheter la voiture.	*Wait till you have the means/can afford to buy the car.*
♦ **commencer** ***à*** + *inf.*	*to begin* ***to****, to start* ***to***
Il commence **à** pleuvoir.	*It begins to rain.*
Commencez **à** vous y faire.	*Start to get used to it.*
commencer ***par*** + *inf.*	*to begin* ***by****, to start* ***out*** *(doing)*
Je vais commencer **par** vous donner une bibliographie.	*I will begin by giving you a bibliography.*
Commençons **par** lire et traduisons ensuite.	*Let us start out reading and then let's translate.*
♦ **compter** + *inf.*	*to plan to*
Quand comptez-vous partir?	*When do you plan to leave?*
compter sur qn ***pour*** + *inf.*	*to count on sb (doing)*
Je compte sur toi **pour** me le dire.	*I count on you telling me.*
♦ **décider**[1] qn ***à*** + *inf.*	*to persuade sb to*
Il faut le décider **à** partir.	*We must persuade him to leave.*
se décider / se résoudre ***à*** + *inf.*	*to decide/to make up one's mind to*
Elle s'est décidée/résolue **à** prendre le risque.	*She decided to take the risk.*
être décidé/être résolu ***à*** + *inf.*	*to be determined to*
Il est décidé/résolu **à** se battre.	*He is determined to fight.*
décider/résoudre ***de*** + *inf.*	*to decide to*
Il a décidé/résolu **de** vendre sa voiture.	*He decided to sell his car.*

---

1. The verb **décider** takes the preposition **à** before an infinitive in the expression **décider** qn ***à*** faire qch
   The verbs **décider** and **résoudre** take **à** before the infinitive
   - when used reflexively
   - when used as past participle after *être*

   Otherwise, **décider** and **résoudre** take **de** before an infinitive.

♦ **demander** *à* + *inf.*	*to ask/ask permission/request to*
Il demande **à** voir le gérant.	*He requests to see the manager.*
Les enfants n'ont pas demandé **à** venir au monde.	*The children did not ask to come into this world.*
Elle a demandé **à** échanger la robe contre une autre.	*She asked to exchange the dress for another.*
demander à qn ***de*** + *inf.*	*to ask sb to*
Les étudiants demandent au professeur **de** répéter la question.	*The students ask the teacher to repeat the question.*
♦ **devoir** + *inf.*	*to have to*
Je dois partir.	*I have to leave.*
devoir à qn ***de*** + *inf.*	*to owe it to sb to*
Je me dois **de** faire de mon mieux pour l'aider.	*I owe it to myself to do my best to help him.*
♦ **dire** + *inf.*	*to say that...*
Il dit ne rien comprendre.	*He says that he understands nothing.*
dire à qn ***de*** + *inf.*	*to tell sb to*
Dites-lui **de** m'attendre.	*Tell him to wait for me.*
♦ **être** à qn ***de*** + *inf.*	*to be somebody's turn to,* *to be up to sb to*
C'est à toi **de** juger.	*It's up to you to judge.*
Ce n'est pas à moi **de** le dire.	*It's not for me to say.*
être ***à*** + *inf.*	*to be + passive inf.*
Vous n'êtes pas **à** blâmer.	*You are not to be blamed.*
C'était **à** prévoir.	*That was predictable.* (= *to be foreseen*)
♦ **excuser** qn ***de*** + *inf.*	*to excuse sb for (doing)*
Excusez-moi **de** vous déranger.	*Excuse me for disturbing you.*
excuser qn ***pour*** + *past inf.*	*to excuse sb for (doing)*
Excuse-moi **pour** avoir été si long à te donner de mes nouvelles.	*Excuse me for taking so long to let you hear from me.*
s'excuser ***de*** + *inf.*	*to apologize for (doing/having done)*
Je m'excuse **de** vous importuner.	*I apologize for bothering you.*

♦ **finir** ***de*** + *inf.*	*to finish (doing)*
As-tu fini **de** travailler?	*Have you finished working?*
finir ***par*** + *inf.*	*to finally (do), to (do) in the end*
J'ai fini **par** trouver mon porte-monnaie.	*I finally found my wallet.*
Tout finira **par** s'arranger.	*Everything will be fine in the end.*
La vérité finira **par** éclater.	*The truth will come out in the end.*
♦ **forcer**/obliger/contraindre[1] qn ***à*** + *inf.*	*to force sb to*
Il m'a forcé/obligé/contraint **à** partir.	*He forced me to leave.*
être forcé/obligé/contraint[1] ***de*** + *inf.*	*to be forced to*
J'étais obligé/forcé/contraint **de** le punir.	*I was forced to punish him.*
♦ **jurer** + *inf.*	*to swear (= declare under oath) to*
Il jure être innocent.	*He swears to be innocent.*
jurer ***de*** + *inf.*	*to swear (= promise) to*
Ils ont juré **de** ne plus jamais mentir.	*They swore never to lie again.*
♦ **s'occuper** ***à*** + *inf.*	*to spend one's time (doing)*
Le week-end, il s'occupe **à** jardiner.	*On weekends, he spends his time gardening.*
être occupé ***à*** + *inf.*	*to be busy (doing)*
Chantal est occupée **à** faire la vaisselle.	*Chantal is busy washing the dishes.*
s'occuper ***de*** + *inf.*	*to be in charge of (doing), to take care of (doing)*
Je m'occuperai **de** vous trouver une chambre.	*I will take care of finding a room for you.*

---

1. The verbs *forcer, obliger* and *contraindre* take **à** before the following infinitive in the *active voice* and **de** in the *passive voice* (*être obligé/forcé/contraint* ***de***).

♦ **passer/perdre son temps *à*** + *inf.*	*to spend/waste one's time (doing)*
Je passe/perds mon temps **à** bricoler.	*I spend/waste my time tinkering about.*
avoir le temps ***de*** + *inf.*	*to have the time to*
Je n'ai pas le temps **de** vous accompagner.	*I don't have the time to accompany you.*
♦ **penser** + *inf.*	*to intend to, to plan to, to think that*
Elle pense aller en Europe.	*She plans to go to Europe.*
Je ne pense pas l'inviter.	*I don't intend to invite him.*
Il pense avoir fermé la porte.	*He thinks that he closed the door.*
penser ***à*** + *inf.*	*to think about (doing),* *to remember (= not to forget) to*
J'äi pensé **à** y vivre.	*I thought about living there.*
Il faut que je pense **à** acheter du lait.	*I must not forget to buy milk.*
As-tu pensé **à** poster la lettre?	*Did you remember to mail the letter?*
♦ **proposer** à qn ***de*** + *inf.*	*to suggest to sb to*
Je lui ai proposé **de** participer.	*I suggested to him to participate.*
se proposer ***de*** + *inf.*	*to intend to*
Elle s'est proposé de rester à Paris.	*She intended to stay in Paris.*
se proposer ***pour*** + *inf.*	*to offer to*
Il s'est proposé **pour** accompagner le malade à l'hôpital.	*He offered to accompany the patient to the hospital.*
♦ **se rappeler** + *past inf.*	*to remember (doing)*
Il se rappelle avoir passé des vacances avec eux.	*He remembers spending a vacation with them.*
se souvenir ***de*** + *past inf.*	*to remember (doing)*
Je me souviens **d'**avoir vu le film.	*I remember seeing the movie.*
se rappeler ***de*** + *inf.*	*to remember (= not to forget)*
Rappelez-vous **d'**apporter le livre.	*Remember to bring the book.*
se souvenir ***de*** + *inf.*	*to remember (= not to forget)*
Souviens-toi **d'**apporter ton appareil-photo.	*Remember to bring your camera.*

rappeler à qn ***de*** + *inf.*	*to remind sb to*
Rappelle-moi **de** te donner mon adresse.	*Remind me to give you my address.*
♦ **servir *à*** + *inf.*	*to be good for (doing)*
Cette machine sert **à** couper le bois.	*This machine is good for cutting wood.*
il/cela ne sert à rien *de* + *inf.*	*there is no point in (doing), it's useless to*
Cela ne sert à rien **de** mentir.	*There is no point in lying.*
♦ **souhaiter** + *inf.*	*to wish to*
Je souhaite réussir.	*I wish to succeed.*
souhaiter à qn ***de*** + *inf.*	*to wish sb to, to wish that sb*
Je vous souhaite **de** réussir.	*I wish you to succeed.*
♦ **suffire *à*** + *inf.*	*to suffice, to be enough to*
Ces arguments ont suffi **à** le persuader de rester.	*These arguments were enough to persuade him to stay.*
il suffit *de* + *inf.*	*it's enough to, all it takes is...*
Il suffit **de** lui faire des compliments pour la rendre heureuse.	*Giving her compliments is enough to make her happy.*
♦ **tarder *à***[1] + *inf.*	*to delay in, to be slow in (doing)*
ne pas tarder *à*	*to (do sth) soon*
Il ne tardera pas **à** vous répondre.	*He will answer you very soon.*
On ne va pas tarder **à** atterrir.	*We will land shortly.*
il me (te, lui...) **tarde *de*** + *inf.*	*I (you, he, she...) cannot wait to, I am (you are, he is...) anxious to*
Il me tarde **de** le revoir.	*I cannot wait to see him again.*
♦ **tenir *à*** + *inf.*	*to insist on (doing)*
Je *tiens* **à** vous renseigner.	*I insist on informing you.*
il ne tient qu'à vous (lui...) ***de*** + *inf.*	*it's up to you (him...) to*
Il ne tient qu'à toi **de** décider.	*It's up to you to decide.*

---

1. This expression is mostly used in its *negative* form '***ne pas tarder à***'.

♦ **trouver** ***à*** + *inf.*	*to find sth to*
Vous trouverez **à** manger dans le frigidaire.	*You will find (something) to eat in the refrigerator.*
trouver + adj. + **de** + *inf.*	*to find it + adj. + inf.*
J'ai trouvé bon **de** m'absenter.	*I found/considered it good to leave.*
♦ **venir** + *inf.*	*to come in order to (do)*
Je viens vous aider.	*I come (in order) to help you.*
venir ***de*** + *inf.*[1]	*to have* ***just*** *(done)*
Je viens **de** vous aider.	*I just helped you.*
venir ***à*** + *inf.*	*to happen to (do)*
Que feriez-vous s'il venait **à** pleuvoir?	*What would you do if it should (happen to) rain?*
en venir ***à*** + *inf.*	*to get to the point where*
J'**en** viens quelquefois **à** me demander s'il n'est pas fou.	*I sometimes get to the point where I wonder whether he is not crazy.*

Note:

The verbs and expressions listed in this chapter are grouped according to whether or not they take a preposition before a following **infinitive.** Sometimes, *no* preposition is required, sometimes **à**, sometimes **de**, and in a few instances **pour** are necessary. This does *not* mean that all these verbs add on a **noun** in the same manner. As the following examples show, the construction *verb +* ***noun*** frequently differs from the construction *verb +* ***infinitive***.[2]

Compare:

Verb + **infinitive**	Verb + **noun**
Il m'*aide* **à** préparer le dîner. *He helps me to cook dinner.*	Il *aide* sa mère. *He helps his mother.*
J'*apprends* **à** danser. *I learn to dance.*	J'*apprends* le latin. *I learn Latin.*

---

1. This construction expresses actions in the **recent past** (= le *passé récent*).
2. Note that not all verbs can take a noun object. Intransitive verbs like *hésiter, s'efforcer, aller, venir,* etc. can only be followed by an *infinitive.*

Verb + **infinitive**	Verb + **noun**
Je *commence* **à** m'ennuyer.[1] *I am beginning to get bored.*	Je *commence* le travail.[1] *I start/begin the work.*
Il *continue* **à** parler. *He continues to speak.*	Il *continue* son discours. *He continues his speech.*
Il *craint* **d'**être malade. *He is afraid to be ill.*	Il *craint* la mort. *He is afraid of death.*
Il me *demande* **de** l'aider. *He asks me to help him.*	Il *demande* **au** professeur. *He asks the teacher.* Il demande une explication. *He asks **for** an explanation.*
Elle leur *enseigne* **à** écrire.[2] *She teaches them to write.*	Elle *enseigne* le français. *She teaches French.*
Il *évite* **de** faire des fautes. *He avoids making mistakes.*	Il *évite* le danger. *He avoids the danger.*
J'*essaie* **de** vous aider. *I try to help you.*	J'*essaie* les chaussures. *I try on the shoes.*
Je vous *invite* **à** me suivre. *I invite you to follow me.*	J'*invite* mes amis. *I invite my friends.*
J'ai *oublié* **de** le faire. *I forgot to do it.*	J'ai *oublié* mon parapluie. *I forgot my umbrella.*
Je vous *permets* **de** sortir. *I allow you to go out.*	Je *permets* un verre de vin **à** mon fils. *I allow my son a glass of wine.*
Elle a *promis* **d'**être à l'heure. *She promised to be on time.*	Elle a *promis* un jouet **à** sa fille. *She promised her daughter a toy.*
Il a r*efusé* **d'**assister à son mariage. *He refused to attend her wedding.*	Il a *refusé* mon invitation. *He refused my invitation.*
Je vous *remercie* **de** me l'avoir dit.[3] *I thank you for telling me.*	Je *remercie* mes parents. *I thank my parents.*

---

1. See p. 254
2. See p. 254
3. See p. 254

Verb + **infinitive**	Verb + **noun**
Ils *réussissent* **à** bien prononcer. *They succeed in pronouncing well.*	Ils *réussissent* leur mariage. *They make their marriage work.*
Tu *risques* **de** tout perdre. *You risk losing everything.*	Tu *risques* ta vie. *You risk your life.*
Il *tient* **à** le faire. *He insists on doing it.*	Il *tient* sa promesse. *He keeps his promise.* Il *tient* **de** son père. *He takes after his father.*

There are however some verbs and expressions which take the *same* preposition before a *noun* and before an *infinitive*, such as:
s'attendre **à** *(to expect),* avoir besoin **de** *(to need),* avoir peur **de** *(to be afraid),* avoir envie **de** *(to feel like),* s'excuser **de** *(to apologize),* s'habituer **à** *(to get used to),* se souvenir **de** *(to remember)*

Il ne s'*attendait* pas **à** être réélu. *He didn't expect to be reelected.*	Il ne *s'attendait* pas **à** sa visite. *He didn't expect her visit.*
Tu n'*as* pas *besoin* **de** venir. *You don't need to come.*	J'*ai besoin* **de** ton aide. *I need your help.*
J'*ai peur* **de** tomber. *I am afraid to fall.*	J'*ai peur* **de** l'examen. *I am afraid of the exam.*
J'*ai envie* **de** partir. *I feel like leaving.*	J'*ai envie* **de** vacances. *I feel like a vacation.*
Il s'est *excusé* **de** lui avoir fait de la peine. *He apologized for having hurt her feelings.*	Il s'est *excusé* **de** sa conduite. *He apologized for his behavior.*
Elle *s'habitue* **à** vivre ici. *She gets used to living here.*	Elle *s'habitue* **au** climat. *She gets used to the climate.*
Je ne me *souviens* pas **d'**avoir dit ça. *I don't remember saying that.*	Je ne me *souviens* pas **de** son nom. *I don't remember his name.*

Some verbs take the same preposition before a noun and before an infinitive only before *certain* noun objects.

Il *apprend* **à** cuisiner. *He learns to cook.*	Il *apprend* la grammaire **aux** élèves. *He teaches the students grammar.*

Verb + **infinitive**

Il m'*enseigne* **à** patiner.
He teaches me to iceskate.

Je vous *remercie* **de** m'avoir appelé.
I thank you for calling me.

Il *réussit* **à** faire le travail.
He succeeds in doing the work.

Verb + **noun**

Il *enseigne* le grec **aux** étudiants.
He teaches the students Greek.

Il *remercie* son père **du** cadeau.
He thanks his father for the gift.

Il *réussit* **à** l'examen.
He passes the exam.

The verb 'commencer' takes the same preposition (**par**) before a *noun* and before an *infinitive* only when it means 'to begin **by** (doing)', and 'to begin **with** (sth)'

Je vais *commencer* **par** vous donner un exemple.
*I will begin **by** giving you an example.*

Il *commence* **par** une plaisanterie.
*He begins **with** a joke.*

The verb 'finir' takes the same preposition (**par**) before a *noun* and before an *infinitive* only when it means 'to **finally** (do)', 'to **end up** (doing)', to (do) **in the end**, and 'to end **in/with** (sth)'

Il a *fini* **par** tout avouer.
*He **finally** confessed everything.*

Ils ont *fini* **par** l'emporter.
*They **ended up** winning.*

Vous *finirez* **par** vous y habituer.
*You will get used to it **in the end**.*

Ce mot *finit* **par** une voyelle.
*This word ends **in** a vowel.*

Le spectacle a *fini* **par** un feu d'artifice.
*The performance ended **with** a fireworks display.*

Chapter 8

Prepositions in Noun[1] + Verb Constructions

A. The preposition de usually precedes the infinitive

attention **de**	*careful to*
Attention **de** ne pas vous brûler.	*Be careful not to burn yourself.*
défense/interdiction **de**[2]	*it is forbidden to*
Défense **d'**afficher.	*Post no bills.*
Défense **d'**entrer.	*Keep out! No admittance.*
Défense **de** stationner.	*No parking.*
merci **de**[3]	*thanks for...-ing*
Merci **d'**être venu.[4]	*Thanks for coming.*
Merci **de** me l'avoir dit.	*Thanks for telling me.*
Merci **de** fumer dehors.	*Thanks for smoking outside.*
mille excuses **de**	*apologies for*
Mille excuses **de** ne pas pouvoir rester.	*My apologies for not being able to stay.*
pardon **de**	*sorry to/for*
Pardon **d'**être en retard.	*Sorry to be late.*
Encore pardon **de** ne pas avoir écrit plus tôt.	*Sorry again for not having written earlier.*
prière **de**[2]	*please...*
Prière **de** ne pas fumer.	*No smoking please.*
Prière **de** préparer la monnaie.	*Please have the change ready.*
Prière **de** faire suivre.	*Please forward.*

---

1. For the use of prepositions before an infinitive after *verbal expressions* which contain **nouns**, see p. 219-221 (**à**), and p. 232-240 (**de**).
2. These expressions are found on signs.
3. For the use of prepositions between 'merci' and a following **noun**, see p. 79 #39.
4. Note that (contrary to English) 'merci' is often followed by the *past infinitive*.

le besoin **de**	*the need to*
J'éprouve le besoin **de** me reposer.	*I feel the need to take a rest.*
la chance/l'espoir **de**	*the chance/the hope to*
La chance **de** trouver des survivants s'amenuise.	*The chance to find survivors dwindles.*
le danger **de**[1]	*the danger of (doing)*
Le danger **de** tomber est écarté pour l'instant.	*The danger of falling is over for the time being.*
la difficulté **de**[2]	*the difficulty of (doing)*
Il connaît la difficulté **de** réussir.	*He knows the difficulty of succeeding.*
l'effort **de**	*the effort to*
Il a fait l'effort **de** rattraper le temps perdu.	*He made the effort to make up for lost time.*
l'étonnement **de**	*the surprise/astonishment to*
Son étonnement **de** me voir était grand.	*His surprise to see me was great.*
la facilité **de**	*the ease of (doing)*
La facilité **de** s'exprimer est une force.	*The ease of expressing oneself is a strength.*
la façon **de**	*the manner of, the way of (doing)*
Sa façon **de** conduire est dangereuse.	*The way he drives is dangerous.*
la faculté **de**	*the ability to*
Sa faculté **de** marcher est étonnante.	*Her ability to walk is amazing.*
le (seul) fait **de**	*the (mere) fact of (doing)*
Le (seul) fait **de** dire non ne signifie rien.	*The (mere) fact of saying no means nothing.*
l'incapacité **de**[3]	*the inability to*
L'incapacité **de** se concentrer est un handicap.	*The inability to concentrate is a handicap.*

---

1. But:

il y a (du) danger **à** faire qch	*there is danger in doing sth*
il n'y a aucun danger/pas de danger **à** faire qch	*there is no danger in doing sth*

2. But:
avoir de la (des) difficulté(s) ***à*** (see p. 219), *faire des difficultés* ***pour*** (see p. 243)
3. But: *l'incapacité/la capacité de qn* ***à*** (see p. 264)

la manière **de**	*the manner of, the way of (doing)*
La manière **de** vivre des Français est différente.	*The French way of life is different.*
C'est sa manière **de** peindre.	*It's his way of painting.*
l'occasion **de**	*the opportunity to*
Ne manquez pas l'occasion **de** participer.	*Don't miss the opportunity to participate.*
la perspective **de**	*the prospect of (doing)*
La perspective **de** le revoir me rend heureuse.	*The prospect of seeing him again makes me happy.*
le prétexte **de**	*the pretext/excuse for (doing)*
Quel est le prétexte **de** partir?	*What is the excuse for leaving?*
le projet **de**	*the plan to*
Le projet **de** construire ce pont se heurtera à de grandes difficultés.	*The plan to build this bridge will hit upon big difficulties.*
le refus **de**	*the refusal to*
Le refus **de** payer l'a conduit en prison.	*The refusal to pay led him to prison.*
le regret **de**	*the regret to*
Le regret **d'**avoir mal agi la tracassait.	*The regret to have acted badly worried her.*
le risque **de**	*the risk of (doing)*
Le risque **de** tomber m'a retenu de vous suivre.	*The risk of falling prevented me from following you.*
la surprise **de**	*the surprise to*
Il m'a fait la surprise **de** venir me voir.	*He made me the surprise to visit me.*
l'utilité **de**	*the use of (doing)*
Quelle est l'utilité **de** garder ces vieux jouets?	*What's the use of keeping these old toys?*

Expressions

drôle d'idée **de**	*(what a) funny idea to*
Drôle d'idée **de** faire une chose pareille.	*(What a) funny idea to do something like that.*

dans le dessein **de**	*with the intention of (doing)*
Il est venu dans le dessein **de** me parler.	*He came with the intention of talking to me.*
dans l'espoir **de**/sans espoir **de**	*with the/without any hope of*
Dans l'espoir **de** te lire bientôt, je...	*Hoping to hear from you soon, I...*
Ils cherchaient dans les décombres sans espoir **de** trouver des survivants.	*They searched in the rubble without any hope of finding survivors.*
dans l'intention **de**	*with the intention of (doing)*
Il a dit ça dans l'intention **de** vous choquer.	*He said that with the intention of shocking you.*
de peur/crainte **de**	*for fear of (doing)*
Il n'est pas venu de peur **de** rencontrer ses ennemis.	*He didn't come for fear of meeting his enemies.*
au point **de**	*to such extent/so much that*
Il a mangé au point **de** se rendre malade.	*He ate so much that he was sick.*
sous prétexte **de**	*on the pretext that*
Sous prétexte **de** vouloir changer de l'argent, il est arrivé à braquer la banque.	*On the pretext that he wanted to change money he succeeded in robbing the bank.*
au risque **de**	*at the risk of (doing)*
Il m'a sauvé au risque **de** perdre sa vie.	*He saved me at the risk of losing his life.*
le temps **de**	*by the time I (you, he...), I (you, he...) just need(s) to, just enough time to*
Le temps **de** me retourner, il n'était plus là.	*By the time I turned around, he no longer was there.*
Le temps **de** m'habiller et j'arrive.	*I just need to get dressed and I'll come.*

....

Especially

- after **ce + être + determiner + noun**
  (where the real subject of *être* + *noun* is the infinitive)

c'est une (grande) chance **de**	*it's (very) fortunate to*
C'est une chance **de** pouvoir voyager.	*It's fortunate to be able to travel.*

c'est un crève-cœur **de**	*it's heartbreaking to*
C'est un crève-cœur **de** voir ça.	*It's heartbreaking to see that.*
c'est un devoir **de**	*it's a duty to*
C'est un devoir **de** voter.	*It's a duty to vote.*
c'est une erreur **de**	*it's a mistake to*
C'est une erreur **de** croire cela.	*It's a mistake to believe that.*
ce n'est pas la façon **de**	*that's not the way to*
Ce n'est pas la façon **de** le faire.	*That's not the way to do it.*
c'est une folie **de**	*it's madness to*
C'est une folie **de** sortir par un temps pareil.	*It's madness to go out in this (bad) weather.*
c'est l'heure **de**	*it's time to*
C'est l'heure **d'**aller au lit.	*It's time to go to bed.*
c'est un (grand) honneur **de**	*it's a (big) honor to*
C'est un grand honneur pour moi **d'**être ici.	*It's a great honor for me to be here.*
c'est une honte **de**	*it's a disgrace to*
C'est une honte **de** mentir.	*It's a disgrace to lie.*
c'est une bonne idée **de**	*it's a good idea to*
C'est une bonne idée **de** faire cela.	*It's a good idea to do that.*
c'est une joie **de**	*it's a joy to*
C'est une joie **de** vous revoir.	*It's a joy to see you again.*
c'est la mode **de**	*it's fashionable to*
C'est la mode **de** voyager beaucoup.	*It's fashionable to travel a lot.*
c'est un/le seul moyen **de**	*it's a/the only way to*
C'est un moyen **de** connaître les gens.	*That's a way to get to know people.*
C'est le seul moyen **de** trouver sa trace.	*It's the only way to find his trace.*
c'est une occasion **de**	*that's an opportunity to*
C'est une occasion **d'**apprendre le français.	*That's an opportunity to learn French.*

c'est un plaisir **de**[1]	*it's a pleasure to*
C'est un plaisir **de** vous écouter.	*It's a pleasure to listen to you.*
c'est un régal **de**	*it's a treat/delight to*
C'est un régal **d'**entendre ce pianiste.	*It's a treat to hear this pianist.*
c'est le/au tour de qn **de**	*it's someone's turn to*
C'était le tour de Pierre **de** quitter la scène.	*It was Pierre's turn to leave the stage.*
C'est à votre tour **de** continuer.	*It's your turn to continue.*
c'est mon (ton, son...) tour **de**	*it's my (your, his...) turn to*
C'est mon (ton, son...) tour **de** parler.	*It's my (your, his...) turn to speak.*

Idioms

c'est/il est dommage **de**	*it's a shame to*
Ce serait dommage **de** perdre cet argent.	*It would be a shame to lose that money.*
c'est le moment **de**	*this is the time to*
C'est le moment **de** faire un vœu.	*This is the time to make a wish.*
Ce n'est pas le moment **de** parler.	*This is not the time to speak.*
ce n'est pas la peine **de**	*there is no need to/no point in (doing sth)*
Ce n'est pas la peine **de** parler si fort.	*There is no need to speak so loud.*
Ce n'est pas la peine **d'**aller voir ce film, il est nul.	*There is no point in going to see that movie, it is awful.*

- after **il + être + noun** (i.e. impersonal expressions introduced by *il est)*

il est d'usage **de**	*it's customary to*
Il est d'usage **d'**offrir un cadeau.	*It's customary to give a gift.*
il est (grand) temps **de**	*it's (about) time to*
Il est (grand) temps **de** le prendre au sérieux.	*It is (about) time to take him seriously.*

1. See p. 265

il est de bon ton **de**	*it's good manners to*
Il est de bon ton **de** dire cela.	*It's good manners (considered polite) to say that.*
il n'est pas besoin **de**	*there is no need to*
Il n'est pas besoin **d'**y aller.	*There is no need to go there.*
il est question **de**	*there is some talk about*
Il est question **de** construire un tunnel.	*There is some talk about building a tunnel.*
(il n'est) pas question **de**[1]	*it's out of the question to*
(Il n'est) pas question **d'**accepter.	*It's out of the question to accept.*
il est de règle **de**	*it's customary to*
Il est de règle **de** répondre.	*It's customary to answer.*

- when the English equivalent of **de + infinitive** is **of** +...**-ing**

L'idée **de** le quitter me fait peur.	*The idea **of** leav**ing** him frightens me.*
La pensée **de** devoir retourner me rend malade.	*The thought **of** hav**ing** to return makes me ill.*
Also:	
une façon **de** parler	*a manner **of** speak**ing***

- when the **noun** is seperated from the **infinitive** by (ce +) **être**

Le principal/l'essentiel, c'est **de** ne pas perdre patience.	*The main thing is not to lose patience.*
L'important, c'est **de** rester en bonne santé.	*The important thing is to stay healthy.*
Le mieux est **de** vous renseigner.	*The best (thing) is to get some information.*
La question, c'est **de** savoir si c'est vrai.	*The question is to know whether this is true.*
Ma tâche, c'est **d'**aider les autres.	*My task is to help others.*
Votre devoir est **de** faire tout votre possible.	*Your duty is to do your best.*

---

1. Synonym: *il est hors de question **de***

Le problème est **d'**empêcher une infection.	*The problem is preventing an infection.*
L'objectif, c'est **d'**abandonner le nucléaire.	*The goal is to get rid of nuclear power.*
L'idéal, ce serait **de** ne pas avoir de soucis.	*The ideal (situation) would be not to have any worries.*

- when the **noun** is part of the following *impersonal expressions*

il n'y a pas d'excuse **de**	*there is no excuse for*
Il n'y a pas d'excuse **de** ne pas y aller.	*There is no excuse for not going there.*
il y a lieu **de**	*there is reason to/for*
Il y a lieu **d'**être inquiet.	*There is reason to be worried.*
Il n'y a pas lieu **de** s'affoler.	*There is no reason to get upset.*
Il y a tout lieu **de** penser que nous allons gagner.	*There is good reason to believe that we are going to win.*
il n'y a pas moyen **de**	*there is no way to*
Il n'y a pas moyen **de** s'évader.	*There is no way to escape.*
il n'y a aucune/pas de raison **de**	*there is no reason to*
Il n'y a aucune raison **de** s'énerver.	*There is no reason to get upset.*
Il n'y avait pas de raison **d'**abattre tous ces animaux.	*There was no reason to kill all these animals.*
il me (te, lui...) prend l'envie **de**	*I (you, he...) feel(s) like, I (you, he...) have (has) the urge to*
Il me prend l'envie **de** sortir.	*I feel the urge to go out.*

B. The preposition à precedes the infinitive

- when the English equivalent of the French expression indicates that something must be done or is worth doing, or if the construction has a *passive meaning* in English

C'est un film **à** ne pas manquer.	*That's a movie one shouldn't miss.*
C'est une pièce de théâtre **à** voir.	*This play is worth seeing.*
C'est une faute **à** éviter.	*This is a mistake to avoid.*

une maison **à** vendre	*a house for sale (= to be sold)*
une chambre **à** louer	*a room for rent (= to be rented)*
des sandwichs **à** emporter	*sandwiches to go (= to be taken)*
une mission **à** accomplir	*a mission to accomplish (= to be accomplished)*
un exemple **à** ne pas suivre	*an example not to follow*

- when the infinitive expresses the *effect* or *consequence* of the noun on someone

des cris **à** faire peur	*frightening screams*
des soupirs **à** faire pitié	*moving sighs*
(Il fait) une chaleur **à** en mourir.	*(It's) a terrible heat.*

Sayings and expressions

Il fait un temps **à** ne pas laisser un chat dehors.[1]	*The weather is terrible.*
C'est un nom **à** coucher dehors.	*It's a bizarre/difficult name.*
une histoire **à** dormir debout[2]	*a far-fetched story, a totally improbable story*
une bonne **à** tout faire	*an all-around maid*

- after the *impersonal expression* **il y a**

il y a + noun + **à**	*there is...to, there are...to*
Il y a des progrès **à** faire.	*There is progress still to be made.*
Il y a du chemin **à** parcourir.	*There is a ways to go.*
Il y a tellement de choses **à** voir!	*There are so many things to see!*

il y a (du) danger **à**	*there is danger to*
Il y a (du) danger **à** s'aventurer sur la glace.	*There is danger to venture out on the ice.*

il n'y a aucun/pas de danger **à**	*there is no danger in (doing)*
Il n'y a aucun danger **à** camper ici.	*There is no danger in camping here.*

1. lit.: *It's a weather not to let a cat out.*
2. lit.: *a story to sleep standing up*

Idioms

il y a intérêt **à**	*it's advisable to*
Il y a intérêt **à** ne pas tarder.	*It's advisable not to delay.*
il y a urgence **à**	*it's urgent to, it's a matter of urgency to*
Il y a urgence **à** baisser la pression fiscale en France.	*It's urgent to lower taxes in France.*
il n'y a pas de mal **à**	*there is nothing wrong with*
Il n'y a pas de mal **à** boire une bière de temps en temps.	*There is nothing wrong with drinking a beer from time to time.*
il y a (là) matière **à**	*it's a matter of*
Il y a là matière **à** réfléchir.	*It's food for thought.*
Il n'y a pas là matière **à** se réjouir.	*It's no matter of rejoicing.*
Il n'y a pas matière **à** rire/plaisanter.	*It's no joking matter, there is nothing to laugh about.*

- after nouns such as

la capacité de qn **à**[1]	*the ability of sb to*
Il croit en notre capacité **à** construire un monde meilleur.	*He believes in our ability to build a better world.*
Ils doutent de sa capacité **à** tenir ses promesses.	*They doubt his ability to keep his promises.*
l'incapacité de qn **à**	*the inability of sb to*
L'incapacité de mon fils **à** se concentrer m'irrite un peu.	*My son's inability to concentrate irritates me a little.*
la détermination de qn **à**	*the determination of sb to*
Le président a réaffirmé sa détermination **à** lutter contre le terrorisme.	*The president reaffirmed his determination to fight against terrorism.*
la tendance **à**	*the tendency to*
Actuellement, on peut observer en France une tendance **à** décentraliser.	*Presently, one can observe in France a tendency to decentralize.*

1. But: avoir la capacité **de** faire qch — *to have the ability to do sth* (see p. 233)

Do not confuse

♦ avoir (de la) peine ***à***	*to have a hard time to*
J'ai (de la) peine **à** le croire.	*I find it hard to believe.*
J'ai eu beaucoup de peine **à** la trouver.	*I had a very hard time finding her.*
faire peine ***à***	*to be painful to*
Cela fait peine **à** voir.	*That's painful to see.*
ce n'est pas la peine ***de***	*there is no need to/no point in*
Ce n'est pas la peine **de** me le dire.	*There is no need to tell me this.*
valoir la peine ***de***	*to be worth* (doing)
Ce livre ne vaut pas la peine **d'**être lu.	*This book isn't worth reading.*
se donner/prendre la peine ***de***	*to take/go to the trouble to*
Je me suis donné la peine **de** faire ce détour pour vous faire plaisir.	*I went to the trouble of making this detour to please you.*
Il a pris la peine **de** venir.	*He took the trouble to come.*
Prenez la peine **de** vous asseoir!	*Please take a seat!*
♦ avoir/prendre/trouver (du) plaisir ***à***	*to take pleasure in* (doing)
J'ai/je prends/je trouve du plaisir **à** lire ce roman.	*I take pleasure in reading this novel.*
avoir le plaisir ***de***	*to have the pleasure to*
Vous allez avoir le plaisir **de** voir le président de la République.	*You are going to have the pleasure to see the French president.*
cela fait plaisir ***à***	*it's a pleasure to*
Ça fait plaisir **à** entendre.[1]	*That's a pleasure to hear.*
cela (me) fait (très) plaisir ***de***	*it's a (real) pleasure (for me) to*
Ça (m') a fait plaisir **de** vous voir.[2]	*It was a pleasure (for me) to see you.*
c'est un plaisir ***de***	*it's a pleasure to*
C'était un plaisir **de** vous connaître.	*It was a pleasure to meet you.*
faire à qn le plaisir ***de***	*to do sb the favor to*
Faites-moi le plaisir **de** venir.	*Do me the favor to come.*

1. When 'ça fait plaisir' refers to a *previously* made statement, **à** is used before the infinitive.
2. When 'ça fait plaisir' refers to a *following* idea (here: *to see you*), **de** is used before the infinitive.

se faire un plaisir ***de*** — *to be delighted to*

Je me ferai un plaisir **de** vous aider. — *I will be delighted to help you.*

Chapter 9

Prepositions in Adjective + Verb Constructions

A. The infinitive is preceded by de

- after the following **adjectives** and **past participles**[1]

être affligé **de**	*to be distressed to*
être aimable **de**	*to be nice to*
être avide **de**	*to be eager to*
être bête **de**	*to be stupid to*
être (in)capable **de**	*to be (un)able to*
être (in)certain **de**	*to be (un)sure to*
être chargé **de**	*to be in charge of (doing)*
être conscient **de**	*to be aware of (doing)*
être confus **de**	*to be embarrassed to*
être (mé)content **de**	*to be (dis)satisfied to*
être contraint **de**[2]	*to be forced to*
être convaincu **de**[2]	*to be convinced to*
être coupable **de**	*to be guilty of (doing)*
être courageux **de**	*to be courageous to*
être curieux **de**	*to be curious to*
être déçu **de**	*to be disappointed to*
être désireux **de**	*to be anxious/eager to*
être désolé **de**	*to be sorry to*
être (in)digne **de**	*to be (un)worthy of (doing)*
être enchanté **de** (= être ravi **de**)	*to be delighted to*
être étonné **de**	*to be astonished/amazed to*
être exempt **de**	*to be exempt from (doing)*
être fâché **de**	*to be angry to*
être fatigué **de**	*to be tired of (doing)*

---

1. Note that many of these adjectives and past participles express a feeling.
2. See footnote p. 269

être fier **de**	*to be proud to*
être forcé **de**[1]	*to be forced to*
être fou **de**	*to be crazy to*
être furieux **de**	*to be very angry to*
être gêné **de**	*to be embarrassed to*
être gentil **de**	*to be nice to*
être (mal)heureux **de**	*to be (un)happy to*
être inquiet **de**	*to be worried about (doing)*
être las **de**	*to be weary/tired of (doing)*
être libre **de**	*to be free to*
être méchant **de**	*to be vicious to*
être navré **de**	*to be very sorry to*
être obligé **de**[1]	*to be forced to*
être obligé à qn **de**	*to be obliged to sb for (doing)*
être oublieux **de**	*to be forgetful of (doing)*
être partisan **de**	*to be in favor of (doing)*
être (im)patient **de**	*to be (im)patient/anxious to*
être pressé **de**	*to be in a hurry to*
être prié **de**[1]	*to be (kindly) requested to*
être raisonnable **de**	*to be reasonable to*
être ravi **de** (= être enchanté **de**)	*to be delighted to*
être reconnaissant à qn **de**	*to be thankful to sb for (doing)*
être redevable à qn **de** (+ inf. passé)	*to be indebted to sb for (having done)*
être rusé **de**	*to be sly to*
être satisfait **de**	*to be satisfied to*
être soucieux **de**	*to be worried/concerned to*
être soulagé **de**	*to be relieved to*
être soupçonné **de**	*to be suspected of (doing)*
être stupéfait **de**	*to be astounded to*
être sûr **de**	*to be sure of (doing)*
être surpris **de**[1]	*to be surprised to*
(ne pas) être susceptible **de**	*to be (un)likely to*
être suspect **de**	*to be suspected of (having done)*
être suspecté **de**	*to be suspected of (having done)*
être tenté **de**[1]	*to be tempted to*
être tenu **de**	*to be obliged/forced to*
être triste **de**	*to be sad to*
être vexé **de**	*to be upset that*

---

1. See footnote p. 269

Je suis *affligé* **de** le voir dans cet état.	*I am distressed to see him in this state.*
Vous êtes bien *aimable* **de** me prévenir.	*You are very nice to inform me.*
Elle est *avide* **d'**apprendre.	*She is eager to learn.*
J'ai été *bête* **de** penser que...	*I was stupid to think that...*
Il est *incapable* **de** dire non.	*He is unable to say no.*
Tu es *certain* **de** ne pas les avoir vus?	*Are you sure that you didn't see them?*
Je suis *chargé* **de** surveiller la route.	*I am in charge of watching the road.*
Il est *content* **d'**avoir gagné le prix.	*He is happy to have won the prize.*
Je suis *curieux* **de** savoir si...	*I am curious to know whether...*
Ils sont *déçus* **d'**avoir perdu le match.	*They are disappointed to have lost the game.*
Je suis *désireux* **de** vous satisfaire.	*I am anxious to please you.*
Je suis *désolé* **de** vous avoir fait attendre.	*I am sorry I made you wait.*
Désolé **de** vous déranger/décevoir.	*Sorry to bother/to disappoint you.*
Il est *digne* **de** faire partie de notre club.	*He is worthy of belonging to our club.*
Je suis *enchanté* **de** faire votre connaissance.	*I am delighted to make your acquaintance.*
Il est *étonné* **d'**avoir été reçu à l'examen.	*He is amazed to have passed the exam.*
Je suis *fâché* **de** ne pas être invité.	*I am angry not to be invited.*
Je suis *fatigué* **de** faire la même faute.	*I am tired of making the same mistake.*
Elle est *fière* **de** recevoir la meilleure note.	*She is proud to receive the best grade.*
Elle est *folle* **d'**agir ainsi.	*She is crazy to act that way.*
Il est *furieux* **d'**avoir raté son train.	*He is furious to have missed his train.*
Tu es *gentil* **de** m'avoir appelé.	*You are nice to have called me.*
C'est *gentil* de votre part/de la part de votre sœur **de** m'avoir félicité.	*It's nice of you/of your sister to have congratulated me.*

---

1. Note that the past participle used as adjective generally takes the *same* preposition before an infinitive as the verb from which it stems

Il a tenté **de** s'enfuir.	*He tried to get away. (verb)*
Il est tenté **de** s'enfuir.	*He is tempted to get away. (past part. used as adjective)*

except *obligé, forcé, contraint* and *surpris*

Il m'a obligé (forcé, contraint) **à** rester.	*He forced me to stay. (verb)*
Il est obligé (forcé, contraint) **de** rester.	*He is forced to stay. (past part. used as adjective)*
J'ai surpris mon frère **à** fumer.	*I surprised (caught) my brother smoking. (verb)*
Je suis surpris **de** vous voir.	*I am surprised to see you. (past part. used as adjective)*

C'est *gentil* à vous **de** me l'avoir dit.	*It's nice of you to tell me.*
Tu seras *gentil* **de** fermer la fenêtre. (fam.)	*Would you please close the window?*
Très *heureux* **de** faire votre connaissance.	*(I am) very pleased to meet you.*
Je suis *impatient* **de** te voir.	*I can't wait to see you.*
Il est *inquiet* **de** ne pas avoir de leurs nouvelles.	*He is worried about not having any news from them.*
Elle était *lasse* **de** le répéter.	*She was tired of repeating it.*
Les femmes afghanes sont *libres* **de** ne pas porter le voile.	*The Afghan women are free not to wear the veil.*
Il était *obligé* **de** démissionner.	*He was forced to resign.*
Nous vous serions *obligés* **de** bien vouloir nous préciser la date de votre arrivée.	*We would appreciate if you could specify for us the date of your arrival.*
Ils sont *pressés* **de** rentrer chez eux.	*They are in a hurry to get home.*
Les passagers sont *priés* **de** se rendre à la porte 10.	*The passengers are kindly asked to go to gate 10.*
Je suis *ravi* **de** vous connaître.	*I am delighted to meet you.*
Je vous suis *reconnaissant* **de** m'avoir aidé.	*I am grateful to you for having helped me.*
Je lui suis *redevable* **d'**avoir fait ce travail.	*I am indebted to him for having done this job.*
Il est *soucieux* **de** vous plaire.	*He is anxious to please you.*
Je suis *soulagé* **de** vous voir sain et sauf.	*I am relieved to see you safe and sound.*
Il est *soupçonné* **d'**avoir tué l'enfant.	*He is supected of having killed the child.*
Il est *sûr* **de** gagner.	*He is sure of winning.*
Ces classes sont *susceptibles* **d'**être supprimées.	*These classes are likely to be cancelled.*
Il était *suspecté* **d'**avoir participé à ce hold-up.	*He was suspected of having participated in this hold-up.*
Je suis *tenté* **de** le gifler.	*I am tempted to slap him in the face.*
Les visiteurs sont *tenus* **d'**ôter leur chapeau.	*The visitors are obliged to take off their hats.*
Je suis *triste* **de** te voir partir.	*I am sad to see you leave.*
Ça aurait été *triste* **de** voir le monument disparaître.	*It would have been sad to see the monument vanish.*
Je suis *triste* **d'**apprendre cette mauvaise nouvelle.	*I am sad to learn these bad news.*
Il est *vexé* **de** s'être trompé.	*He is upset that he was wrong.*

Also after

juger/trouver (+ adjectif) **de**	*to consider it* (+ adjective) *to*
juger/trouver bon/mauvais **de**	*to consider it (a) good/bad (idea) to*
juger/trouver nécessaire/drôle...**de**	*to consider it necessary/funny...to*
Il a jugé/trouvé bon **de** se sauver.	*He considered it a good idea to run away.*

- after the impersonal pronoun **il*** + **être** + **adjective**

(In this case, the true subject of *être* + *adjective* is the infinitive, i.e. the impersonal expression **il est** + *adjective* refers to a *following* idea.)

il est avantageux **de**	*it is advantageous to*
il est (dés)agréable **de**	*it is (un)pleasant to*
il est amusant **de**	*it is amusing to*
il est bizarre **de**	*it is strange to*
il est bon **de**	*it is good to, it is right to*
il est commun/courant **de**	*it is common to*
il est (in)concevable **de**	*it is (in)conceivable to*
il est conseillé **de**	*it is advisable to*
il est convenable **de**	*it is proper to*
il est dangereux **de**	*it is dangerous to*
il est défendu **de**	*it is forbidden to*
il est demandé **de**	*it is asked to*
il est désirable **de**	*it is desirable to*
il est difficile (à qn) **de**	*it is difficult (for sb) to*
il est dur **de**	*it is hard to*
il est ennuyeux **de**	*it is boring to*
il est essentiel **de**	*it is essential to*
il est étonnant **de**	*it is amazing to*
il est étrange **de**	*it is strange to*
il est fâcheux **de**	*it is annoying/unfortunate to*
il est facile **de**	*it is easy to*
il est faux **de**	*it is false to*
il est formidable **de**	*it is fantastic to*
il est honteux **de**	*it is shameful/disgraceful to*
il est horrible **de**	*it is horrible to*
il est impératif **de**	*it is imperative to*
il est important **de**	*it is important to*

---

* Note that all impersonal expressions beginning with *il est* and followed by an adjective take **de** before the infinitive.

il est indifférent à qn **de**	*it makes no difference to sb to*
il est indispensable **de**	*it is indispensable to*
il est interdit **de**	*it is forbidden to*
il est intéressant **de**	*it is interesting to*
il est juste **de**	*it is fair/just to*
il est mal **de**	*it is bad to*
il est meilleur **de**	*it is better to*
il est merveilleux **de**	*it is marvellous to*
il est nécessaire **de**	*it is necessary to*
il est naturel **de**	*it is natural to*
il est normal **de**	*it is normal to*
il est obligatoire **de**	*it is mandatory to*
il est pénible **de**	*it is difficult/painful to*
il est (im)pensable **de**	*it is (un)thinkable to*
il est permis (à qn) **de**	*it is allowed (to sb) to*
il est (im)poli **de**	*it is (im)polite to*
il est (im)possible **de**	*it is (im)possible to*
il est préférable **de**	*it is preferable to*
il est raisonnable **de**	*it is reasonable to*
il est rare **de**	*it is rare to*
il est rassurant **de**	*it is reassuring/comforting to*
il est recommandé **de**	*it is recommended/advisable to*
il est regrettable **de**	*it is regrettable to*
il est ridicule **de**	*it is ridiculous to*
il est surprenant **de**	*it is surprising to*
il est terrible **de**	*it is terrible to*
il est triste **de**	*it is sad to*
il est (in)utile **de**	*it is useful (useless) to*

Il est *agréable* **d**'avoir des amis.	*It's pleasant to have friends.*
Par cette chaleur, il est *bon* **de** se plonger dans la piscine.	*In this heat, it's good to plunge into the swimming pool.*
Il est *conseillé* **de** boire beaucoup quand on a de la fièvre.	*It's advisable to drink a lot when one has a fever.*
Il est *dangereux* **de** s'arrêter ici.	*It's dangerous to stop here.*
Il est *défendu* **de** marcher sur la pelouse.	*It's forbidden to walk on the grass.*
Il (m') est *difficile* **de** le convaincre du contraire.	*It's difficult (for me) to convince him of the contrary.*
Il est *dur* **d**'apprendre une langue étrangère.	*It's hard to learn a foreign language.*

Il est *facile* **de** réparer cette voiture.	*It's easy to repair this car.*
Il serait *faux* **de** dire cela.	*It would be wrong to say that.*
Il est *honteux* **de** mentir.	*It's shameful to lie.*
Il est *impossible* **de** dire toujours la vérité.	*It's impossible to always tell the truth.*
Il m' (nous...leur) est *impossible* **de** faire mieux.	*It's impossible for me (us...them) to do better.*
Il m'est *indifférent* **de** rester ou **de** partir.	*It makes no difference to me to stay or to leave.*
Il est *interdit* **de** stationner ici.	*It's forbidden to park here.*
Il est *inutile* **de** marchander.	*It's useless to bargain.*
Il est *juste* **de** le punir.	*It's fair to punish him.*
Il est *mal* **de** gagner de l'argent en trichant.	*It's bad to earn money by cheating.*
Il n'était pas *nécessaire* **d'**aller voir ailleurs.	*It wasn't necessary to go and see elsewhere.*
Il est *obligatoire* **de** mettre la ceinture de sécurité.	*It's mandatory to put on a seatbelt.*
Il ne m'est pas *permis* **de** sortir.	*I am not allowed to go out.*
Il est *surprenant* **d'**apprendre que tu n'es pas au courant.	*It's surprising to learn that you are not informed.*
Il est *utile* **de** connaître cette personne.	*It's useful to know this person.*

Proverbs, sayings, and expressions

Il est bon **de** parler mais meilleur **de** se taire.	*It is good to speak but better to be silent.*
Il n'est pas facile **de** contenter tout le monde et son père.	*It's not easy to satisfy everybody and his brother.*
inutile **de** dire[1]	*needless to say*
Inutile **de** dire que je suis très content.	*Needless to say, I am very happy.*

1. Note that 'il est' is omitted in this expression.

Note:

- In the spoken language, **ce** + *être (+ adjective + de)* frequently replaces the impersonal **il** + *être* (+ *adjective + de)*

C'est *bon* **de** savoir qu'ils prient pour nous.	*It's good to know that they pray for us.*
C'est *défendu* **de** fumer.	*It's forbidden to smoke.*
C'est *dur* **de** plaire à tout le monde.	*It's hard to please everyone.*
Ce n'est pas *évident* **de** faire cela.	*It's not easy to do that.*
C'est *important* **de** manger.	*It's important to eat.*
C'était *génial* **de** vous écouter.	*It was great to listen to you.*
Est-ce que **c'**est *possible* **de** dire ça?	*Is it possible to say that?*

- **de** is also used before the infinitive after **c'est beaucoup**, **c'est trop**, **c'est peu** and **c'est assez**[1]

C'est beaucoup/assez/trop **d'**avoir dix enfants.	*It's much/enough/too much to have ten children.*

and after

c'est déjà beaucoup **de**...	*it's already quite something to...*
On n'a pas gagné le match, mais c'est déjà beaucoup **d'**avoir pu y participer.	*We didn't win the game, but it's already quite something to have been able to participate in it.*

Mistakes to avoid

Incorrect	*Correct*	*English meaning*
Il est possible ~~pour moi de~~ venir.	Je **peux** venir.	*It's possible for me to come.*
Il est ~~impossible pour moi de~~ venir.	Il **m'**est impossible de venir.	*It's impossible for me to come.*
C'est ~~nécessaire pour moi de~~ partir.	Je **dois** partir.	*It's necessary for me to leave.*

---

1. Note that *beaucoup, trop, peu* and *assez* are adverbs.

B. The infinitive following an adjective is preceded by à

- When the subject (noun or pronoun) *precedes* the infinitive[1]

Cette voiture est difficile **à** réparer.[2]	*This car is difficult to repair.*
Cette rose est facile **à** cultiver.	*This rose is easy to grow.*
Ce roman est agréable **à** lire.	*This novel is pleasant to read.*
Cette chaleur est difficile **à** supporter.	*This heat is difficult to endure.*
C'est une pilule dure **à** avaler.	*It's a bitter pill to swallow.*
Ce plat est lourd **à** digérer.	*This dish is heavy to digest.*
C'est une expresson utile **à** savoir.	*This expression is useful to know.*
C'est un numéro facile **à** retenir.	*This number is easy to remember.*
La décision n'était pas facile **à** prendre.	*The decision wasn't easy to make.*
L'eau du robinet est bonne **à** boire.	*Tap water is good to drink.*
Voilà un travail long **à** faire.	*Here is a job (that takes) long to do.*
L'argent est difficile **à** trouver.	*Money is difficult to find.*

Proverbs and idioms

Chagrin partagé est moins lourd **à** porter.[3]	*Two in distress make sorrow less.*
être facile/dur **à** vivre	*to be easy/hard to live with*
Il est facile **à** vivre.	*He is easy to live with.*

- When **ce + être + adjective** refers to a *previously* mentioned idea, i.e. is the speaker's reaction to what has already been said.

C'est bon **à** savoir.[4]	*That's good to know.*
C'est difficile/terrible **à** dire.	*That's difficult/terrible to say.*
C'est difficile **à** croire/**à** imaginer.	*That's hard to believe/to imagine.*

1. Here the infinitive has no complement and is usually at the end of the sentence.
2. But: **Il est** difficile **de** réparer cette voiture. *It's difficult to repair this car.*
3. lit.: *Shared pain is less heavy to carry.*
4. But: Il est / c'est bon **de** savoir que... *It's good to know that...*

Ce n'est pas facile **à** expliquer.	*That's not easy to explain.*
C'est impossible **à** prédire.	*That's impossible to predict.*
C'était facile **à** comprendre.	*That was easy to understand.*
C'est simple **à** faire.	*That's easy to do.*

Sayings

C'est plus facile **à** dire qu'**à** faire. — *It's easier said than done.*

Compare:

- C'est beau **de** voir les joueurs. — *It's wonderful to see the players.*

  [*C'est beau* refers to a *following* idea, namely seeing the players. Consequently, **de** is used before the infinitive]

  C'est beau **à** voir. — *That is wonderful to see.*

  [*C'est beau* refers to a *previously* made statement. Consequently, **à** is used before the infinitive.]

- Il/c'est impossible **de** résoudre ce problème. — *It's impossible to solve this problem.*

  [The infinitive + complement is the true subject of *être,* i. e. the impersonal 'il'+ être + adjective refers to a *following* idea, namely solving the problem. Consequently, **de** is used before the infinitive.]

  Ce problème est impossible **à** résoudre. — *This problem is impossible to solve.*

  [The subject (ce problème) *precedes* the infinitive. Consequently, **à** is used before the infinitive.]

- when the infinitive expresses the *effect* or *consequence* of the adjective on someone or something

Le bus est plein **à** craquer.	*The bus is full to bursting.*
Elle est belle **à** croquer. (fam.)	*She is as pretty as a picture.*
Je suis malade **à** devenir fou.[1]	*I am terribly ill.*
Il est fou **à** lier.[2]	*He is as crazy as a loon.*
Elle est maigre **à** faire pitié.	*She is pitifully thin.*
Elle est laide **à** faire peur.	*She is frightfully ugly.*
Cette conférence est ennuyeuse **à** mourir.	*This lecture is deadly boring.*

1. lit.: *I am ill to become crazy.*
2. lit.: *He is crazy to tie up.*

- when the infinitive is the object of one of the following adjectives and past participles

être allergique **à**	*to be allergic to*
être amené **à**[1]	*to be led to*
être apte **à**	*to be capable of/qualified for*
être attentif **à**	*to be careful to*
être autorisé **à**[1]	*to be authorized to*
être bon **à**	*to be good for* (doing)
être condamné **à**[1]	*to be condemned to*
être décidé **à**[1]	*to be decided/determined to*
être destiné **à**[1]	*to be intended/meant to*
être déterminé **à**[1]	*to be determined to*
être disposé **à**	*to be willing to*
être peu disposé **à**	*to be reluctant to*
être enclin **à**	*to be inclined/prone to*
être exact **à**	*to be exact/punctual in* (doing)
être expert **à**	*to be skilled in* (doing)
être habile **à**	*to be skillfull at* (doing)
être habitué **à**[1]	*to be used to* (doing)
être impuissant **à**	*to be powerless/helpless to*
être invité **à**[1]	*to be invited to*
être lent **à**	*to be slow in* (doing)
être long **à**	*to take a long time to*
être motivé **à**	*to be motivated to*
être occupé **à**	*to be busy* (doing)
être préparé **à**	*to be prepared to*
être préposé **à**	*to be in charge of* (doing)
être prêt **à**[2]	*to be ready/prepared to*

---

1. Note that the past participle used as adjective generally takes the *same* preposition before an infinitive as the verb from which it stems.

Je vous *invite* **à** me suivre.	*I invite you to follow me.* (verb)
Je suis *invité* **à** le suivre.	*I am invited to follow him.* (past part. used as adjective)
Elle *s'habitue* **à** vivre seule.	*She gets used to living alone.* (verb)
Elle est *habituée* **à** vivre seule.	*She is used to living alone.* (past part. used as adjective)

except *décider*

Elle *décide* **de** partir.	*She decides to leave.* (verb)
Elle est *décidée* **à** partir.	*She is determined to leave.* (past part. used as adjective)

2. Do not confuse **être prêt à** (*to be ready to*) and **être près de** (*to be about to*)

Il est toujours prêt **à** rendre service.	*He is always ready to help.*
Elle est près **de** réussir.	*She is about to succeed.*
Le problème n'est pas près **d'**être résolu.	*The problem is not about to be solved.*

être prompt **à**	*to be quick/prompt to*
être propre **à**	*to be suitable for* (doing)
être rapide **à**	*to be quick to*
être réduit **à**	*to be reduced to* (doing)
être résolu **à**	*to be decided to*
être réticent **à**	*to be hesitant/reluctant to*
être unanime **à**	*to be unanimous in* (doing)
être utile **à**	*to be useful to*

Je suis *amené* **à** croire que...	*I am led to believe that...*
Il faut être *attentif* **à** ne pas tout confondre.	*One must be careful not to confuse everything.*
Je suis *autorisé* **à** visiter cet endroit.	*I am authorized to visit this place.*
Est-ce que c'est *bon* **à** manger?	*Is this good to eat?*
Ils sont *condamnés* **à** vivre ensemble.	*They are condemned to live together.*
J'étais *décidé* **à** mener à bien cette tentative.	*I was determined to complete this project successfully.*
Il est *déterminé* **à** agir.	*He is determined to act.*
Je suis *disposé* **à** discuter.	*I am willing to discuss.*
Il est peu *enclin* **à** nous aider.	*He is little inclined to help us.*
Elle était toujours *exacte* **à** payer le loyer.	*She was always punctual in paying the rent.*
Il est *expert* **à** faire sauter les crêpes.	*He is skilled in tossing pancakes.*
Je suis *habitué* **à** travailler dur.	*I am used to working hard.*
Il est *impuissant* **à** maîtriser son émotion.	*He is powerless to control his emotion.*
Les passagers sont *invités* **à** se présenter à la porte 15.	*The passengers are asked to proceed to gate 15.*
Le taxi est *lent* **à** venir.	*The taxi is slow in coming.*
C'est *long* **à** faire.	*It takes a long time to do it.*
Ce serait trop *long* **à** expliquer.	*That would take too long to explain.*
Je suis désolé d'avoir été si *long* **à** te donner de mes nouvelles.	*I am sorry to have taken so long to write to you.*
Cette valise est *lourde* **à** soulever.	*This suitcase is heavy to lift.*
Elle est *occupée* **à** nettoyer la maison.	*She is busy cleaning the house.*
Les hôtels sont *prêts* **à** vous accueillir.	*The hotels are prepared to welcome you.*

Il est toujours *prompt* **à** se décider.	*He is always quick to decide.*
Cet exercice est *propre* **à** développer les muscles.	*This exercise is suitable for developing the muscles.*
Il est *réduit* **à** se taire.	*He is reduced to silence.*
Ils sont *unanimes* **à** condamner le terrorisme.	*They are unanimous in condemning terrorism.*

- after ***(le) seul, (la) seule, (les) seuls, (les) seules***

Vous êtes *le seul* **à** me comprendre.	*You are the only one who understands me.*
Elle n'est pas *la seule* **à** penser ainsi.	*She is not the only one who thinks like that.*
Jusqu'au 18e siècle, les Chinois étaient *les seuls* **à** connaître le secret de la porcelaine dure.	*Till the 18th century, the Chinese were the only ones who knew the secret of hard porcelaine.*
La France est *le seul* pays **à** avoir des fromages au lait cru.	*France is the only country which has cheeses made from raw milk.*
Il est *(le) seul* **à** avoir choisi cela.	*He is the only one who chose that.*

- after the adjective ***quitte*** in the expression ***quitte à*** (*at the risk of, even if*)

Je vais le faire *quitte à* perdre mon argent.	*I will do it at the risk of losing my money.*

- after an **ordinal number** ***(le premier, la première, les premiers, les premières, le/la deuxième,*** etc.*)* and after ***le dernier, la dernière, les derniers, les dernières*** with or without a following noun

Nous sommes *les premiers* **à** arriver et *les derniers* **à** partir.	*We are the first to arrive and the last to leave.*
Il a été *le premier* **à** le faire.	*He was the first to do it.*
En 1980, Marguerite Yourcenar devient *la première* femme **à** être admise à l'Académie française.	*In 1980, Marguerite Yourcenar becomes the first woman to be admitted to the French Academy.*
Je suis toujours *le dernier* **à** le savoir.	*I am always the last one to know.*

Il est l'une des *dernières* personnes **à** l'avoir vu.	*He is one of the last persons who saw him.*

- after ***être nombreux à*** *(to be numerous to)*[1]

Les gens *sont nombreux* **à** être inquiets.	*Numerous people are worried.*
Vous n'*êtes* pas très *nombreux* **à** avoir fait ce chemin.	*Not very many of you have taken this route.*
Ils étaient *nombreux* **à** s'abstenir.	*Many of them abstained.*

For the use of prepositions between *adjectives* and ***nouns***, see p. 50-51 (**de**), p. 48 (**à**), p. 148-149 (**avec**), and p. 160 (**contre**).

---

1. Also after *être* + **cardinal number***

Ils *seraient* plus de *10.000* **à** franchir la frontière chaque année.	*More than 10,000 of them supposedly cross the border each year.*
Ils *étaient quatre* **à** postuler.	*Four of them applied.*

* Note that cardinal numbers are adverbs.

Chapter 10

The Use of Prepositions with Geographical Names

In order to choose the correct preposition before geographical expressions (English *in* and *to* can be translated with *à, au, aux, en* or *dans le,* and English *from* can be translated with *de*, *du* or *des*) one must know the gender (masculine or feminine) and number (singular or plural) of these names and whether they are used with the definite article or without.

- Unlike English, French generally uses the definite article before geographical names

L'Espagne est un beau pays.	*Spain is a beautiful country.*
As-tu déjà visité **l'**Asie?	*Have you already visited Asia?*
J'aime beaucoup **la** Corse.	*I like Corsica a lot.*

except

Andorre (*Andorra*), Bahreïn (*Bahrein*), Chypre (*Cyprus*), Cuba, Djibouti, Haïti, Hong-Kong, Israël, Madagascar, Monaco, Oman, Singapour, Taïwan, Terre-Neuve (*Newfoundland*)[1]

Je connais bien Israël.	*I know Israel well.*

The definite article is also *not* used when referring to a **city**

Paris est une belle ville.	*Paris is a beautiful city.*

unless it is part of the city name

La Rochelle, **La** Nouvelle Orléans (*New Orleans*), **La** Havane (*Havana*), **La** Haye (*The Hague*), **La** Mecque (*Mecca*), **La** Baule, **Le** Bourget, **Le** Mans, **Le** Havre, **Le** Caire (*Cairo*), **Les** Baux-de-Provence, **Les** Sables-d'Olonne

or when the city name is modified

le Paris du 19e siècle	*19th century Paris*

---

1. For islands used without the definite article see p. 291.

- Geographical names can be masculine *(le Maroc),* feminine *(la France)* or plural *(les Philippines)*.

  Continents, countries, regions, French provinces, American states and Canadian provinces which end in **-e** are feminine

  except

  l'Arctique, l'Antarctique, **le** Bélize, **le** Cachemire, **le** Cambodge, **le** Caucase, **le** Dauphiné, **le** Maine, **le** Mexique, **le** Mozambique, **le** Nouveau Mexique, **le** Tennessee, **le** Zaïre, **le** Zimbabwe

  All countries, regions, French and Canadian provinces and American states which do *not* end in **-e** are masculine

  except
  la Saskatchewan

A. The use of prepositions with cities

With cities, **à** expresses 'in'[1] and 'to', **de** expresses 'from'

Elle habite **à** Papeete [papɛt].	*She lives **in** Papeete.*
Il se rend **à** Marseille.	*He is going **to** Marseilles.*
Ils vivent **à** la Nouvelle Orléans.	*They live **in** New Orleans.*
L'avion part **de** Paris.	*The plane leaves **from** Paris.*
Je suis **de** Bordeaux.	*I am **from** Bordeaux.*

Contractions (à + le = **au**; à + les = **aux**; de + le = **du**; de + les = **des**) occur when 'le' or 'les' is part of the city name[2]

Ils habitent **au** Havre.	*They live **in** Le Havre.*
Nous allons **aux** Baux-de-Provence.	*We go **to** Les Baux-de-Provence.*
Il vient **du** Caire.	*He comes **from** Cairo.*

B. The use of prepositions with continents, countries, islands, regions, French regions, provinces and departments, American states and Canadian provinces

The use of prepositions before these geographical expressions will be discussed following each list of their names.

---

1. For the use of 'dans' to express 'in' with city names, see p. 19 and p. 122.
2. See also p. 281 and footnote p. 52.

1. Continents

All continents end in **-e** and are (with the exception of two) feminine.

French name of the continent	*English equivalent*	*Adjective*
l'Afrique[1]	*Africa*	africain,e
l'Amérique[2]	*America*	américain,e
l'Arctique (m)	*the Arctic*	arctique
l'Antarctique (m)	*Antarctica*	antarctique
l'Asie	*Asia*	asiatique
l'Australie	*Australia*	australien,ne
l'Europe[3]	*Europe*	européen,ne

Since most continents are feminine and all start with a vowel, **en** expresses 'in' and 'to', **de** (d') expresses 'from' with all of them.[4]

Il vit **en** Afrique.	*He lives* ***in*** *Africa.*
Elle vient **d'**Europe.	*She comes* ***from*** *Europe.*

But:

If the continent if modified, **dans l'** is used to express *'in'* [5]

dans l'Afrique subsaharienne — ***in*** *sub-Saharian Africa*

2. Countries

French name of the country	*English equivalent*	*Adjective*[6]
l'Afghanistan (m)	*Afghanistan*	afghan,e
l'Albanie (f)	*Albania*	albanais,e

---

1. | | | |
|---|---|---|
| l'Afrique du Nord | *North Africa* | nord-africain,e |
| l'Afrique australe | *Southern Africa* | sud-africain,e |

2. | | | |
|---|---|---|
| l'Amérique du Nord | *North America* | nord-américain,e |
| l'Amérique du Sud | *South America* | sud-américain,e |
| l'Amérique centrale | *Central America* | centraméricain,e |
| l'Amérique latine | *Latin America* | latino-américain,e |

3. | | | |
|---|---|---|
| l'Europe de l'Ouest | *Western Europe* | ouest-européen,ne |
| l'Europe de l'Est | *Eastern Europe* | est-européen,ne |

4. See also p. 85 (**en**), and p. 52 (**de**)
5. See also p. 85 and p. 121
6. • In French, adjectives of nationality are *not* capitalized: une voiture **i**talienne.
   • The inhabitant of a country or region has the same form as the adjective but is capitalized (un **A**nglais sympathique = a nice Englishman), except after *être* (Il *est* **a**nglais. = He is an Englishman.)

French name of the country	*English equivalent*	*Adjective*[1]
l'Algérie (f)	*Algeria*	algérien,ne
l'Allemagne (f)[2]	*Germany*	allemand,e
Andorre (f)	*Andorra*	andorran,e
l'Angleterre (f)	*England*	anglais,e
l'Angola (m)	*Angola*	angolais,e
l'Arabie Saoudite (f)	*Saudi Arabia*	saoudien,ne[3]
l'Argentine (f)	*Argentina*	argentin,e
l'Arménie (f)	*Armenia*	arménien,ne
l'Autriche (f)	*Austria*	autrichien,ne
l'Azerbaïdjan (m)	*Azerbaijan*	azerbaïdjanais,e
Bahreïn (m)	*Bahrain*	bahreïni,e
le Bangladesh	*Bangladesh*	bangladais,e
la Belgique	*Belgium*	belge
le Bélize	*Belize*	bélizien,ne
la Biélorussie	*Byelorussia*	biélorusse
le Bénin	*Benin*	béninois,e
la Birmanie	*Burma*	birman,e
la Bolivie	*Bolivia*	bolivien,ne
la Bosnie	*Bosnia*	bosniaque
le Botswana	*Botswana*	botswanais,e
le Brésil	*Brazil*	brésilien,ne
la Bulgarie	*Bulgaria*	bulgare
le Burkina Faso[4]	*Burkina Faso*	burkinabé,e
le Burundi	*Burundi*	burundais,e
le Cambodge	*Cambodia*	cambodgien,ne
le Cameroun	*Cameroon*	camerounais,e
le Canada	*Canada*	canadien,ne
le Chili	*Chile*	chilien,ne
la Chine	*China*	chinois,e
Chypre	*Cyprus*	chypriote
la Colombie	*Colombia*	colombien,ne

---

1. In order to express the **language** of a country, one generally uses the masculine form of the adjective preceded by *le*. All languages are masculine and *not* capitalized.
   Elle apprend **le** portugais. — *She learns Portuguese.*
   Le russe est une langue difficile. — *Russian is a difficult language.*
2. or: la République Fédérale d'Allemagne — *the Federal Republic of Germany*
3. The language spoken in Saudi-Arabia is **l'arabe** (*Arabic*).
4. today's name of the former **Haute Volta**

French name of the country	*English equivalent*	*Adjective*
le Congo	*the Congo*	congolais,e
la Corée	*Korea*	coréen,ne
la Corée du Nord	*North Korea*	nord-coréen,ne
la Corée du Sud	*South Korea*	sud-coréen,ne
le Costa Rica	*Costa Rica*	costaricain,e
la Côte d'Ivoire	*Ivory Coast*	ivoirien,ne
la Croatie	*Croatia*	croate
Cuba	*Cuba*	cubain,e
la Dalmatie	*Dalmatia*	dalmate
le Danemark	*Denmark*	danois,e
Djibouti	*Djibouti*	djiboutien,ne
l'Ecosse (f)	*Scotland*	écossais,e
l'Egypte (f)	*Egypt*	égyptien,ne
les Emirats arabes unis (m)	*the United Arab Emirates*	arabe
l'Equateur (m)	*Ecuador*	équatorien,ne
l'Espagne (f)	*Spain*	espagnol,e
l'Estonie (f)	*Estonia*	estonien,ne
les Etats-Unis (m) (d'Amérique)	*the United States (of America)*	américain,e
l'Ethiopie (f)	*Ethiopia*	éthiopien,ne
la Finlande	*Finland*	finlandais,e[1]
la France	*France*	français,e
le Gabon	*Gabon*	gabonais,e
la Gambie	*Gambia*	gambien,ne
la Géorgie	*Georgia*	géorgien,ne
le Ghana	*Ghana*	ghanéen,ne
la Grande-Bretagne	*Great Britain*	britannique
la Grèce	*Greece*	grec, grecque
le Groenland	*Greenland*	groenlandais,e
le Guatemala	*Guatemala*	guatémaltèque
la Guinée	*Guinea*	guinéen,ne
la Guyane (française)	*(French) Guyana*	guyanais,e
Haïti	*Haiti*	haïtien,ne
la Hollande	*Holland*	hollandais,e

1. The language spoken in Finland is **le finnois**.

French name of the country	*English equivalent*	*Adjective*
le Honduras	*Honduras*	hondurien,ne
la Hongrie	*Hungary*	hongrois,e
l'Inde (f)	*India*	indien,ne
l'Indonésie (f)	*Indonesia*	indonésien,ne
l'Irak (or: l'Iraq) (m)	*Iraq*	irakien,ne
l'Iran (m)	*Iran*	iranien,ne[1]
l'Irlande (f)	*Ireland*	irlandais,e
l'Irlande du Nord	*Northern Ireland*[2]	
l'Islande (f)	*Iceland*	islandais,e
Israël (m)	*Israel*	israëlien,ne[3]
l'Italie (f)	*Italy*	italien,ne
le Japon	*Japan*	japonais,e
la Jordanie	*Jordan*	jordanien,ne
le Kazakhstan	*Kazakhstan*	kazakh
le Kénya	*Kenya*	kényan,e
le Koweït	*Kuwait*	kowaïtien,ne
le Laos	*Laos*	laotien,ne
la Lettonie	*Latvia*	letton,e
le Liban	*Lebanon*	libanais,e
le Liberia	*Liberia*	libérien,ne
la Libye	*Libya*	libyen,ne
le Liechtenstein	*Liechtenstein*	liechtensteinois,e
la Lituanie	*Lithuania*	lituanien,ne
le Luxembourg[4]	*Luxembourg*	luxembourgeois,e
la Macédoine	*Macedonia*	macédonien,ne
Madagascar (m)	*Madagascar*	malgache
la Malaisie	*Malaysia*	malais,e
le Malawi	*Malawi*	malawien,ne

---

1. The language spoken in Iran is **le persan** (*Persian*).
2. or: Ulster
3. The language spoken in Israel is **l'hébreu** (*Hebrew*).
   Jewish = juif, juive
4. Note that ***le*** *Luxembourg (Luxembourg)*, ***au*** *Luxembourg (in/to Luxembourg)* and ***du*** *Luxembourg (from Luxembourg)* refer to the country;
   Luxembourg (Luxembourg), ***à*** *Luxembourg (in/to Luxembourg)* and
   de *Luxembourg (from Luxembourg)* refer to the city.

French name of the country	*English equivalent*	*Adjective*
le Mali	*Mali*	malien,ne
le Maroc	*Morocco*	marocain,e
la Mauritanie	*Mauritania*	mauritanien,ne
le Mexique[1]	*Mexico*	mexicain,e
la Moldavie	*Moldova*	moldave
Monaco	*Monaco*	monégasque
la Mongolie	*Mongolia*	mongol,e
le Monténégro	*Montenegro*	monténégrin,e
le Mozambique	*Mozambique*	mozambicain,e
la Namibie	*Namibia*	namibien,ne
le Népal	*Nepal*	népalais,e
le Nicaragua	*Nicaragua*	nicaraguayen,ne
le Niger	*Niger*	nigérien,ne
le Nigeria	*Nigeria*	nigérian,e
la Nouvelle Zélande	*New Zealand*	néo-zélandais,e
la Norvège	*Norway*	norvégien,ne
Oman (m)	*Oman*	omanais,e
l'Ouganda (m)	*Uganda*	ougandais,e
l'Ouzbékistan	*Uzbekistan*	ousbek, ousbèke
le Pakistan	*Pakistan*	pakistanais,e
le Panama	*Panama*	panaméen,ne
la Papouasie-Nouvelle-Guinée	*Papua New Guinea*	papouan-néo-guinéen,ne
le Paraguay	*Paraguay*	paraguayen,ne
les Pays-Bas	*the Netherlands*	néerlandais,e
le pays de Galles	*Wales*	gallois,e[2]
le Pérou	*Peru*	péruvien,ne
la Perse[3]	*Persia*	persan,e
les Philippines (f)	*the Philippines*	philippin,e
la Pologne	*Poland*	polonais,e
le Portugal	*Portugal*	portugais,e
la Prusse[4]	*Prussia*	prussien,ne

---

1. Note that ***le** Mexique* (*Mexico*), ***au** Mexique* (*in/to Mexico*) and ***du** Mexique* (*from Mexico*) refer to the country; *Mexico, **à** Mexico* and ***de** Mexico* refer to *Mexico City*.
2. Do not confuse 'g**al**lois' (*Welsh*) with 'g**au**lois' (*Celtic*).
3. The Persian Empire took the name of **Iran** in 1935.
4. former German state

French name of the country	*English equivalent*	*Adjective*
le Qatar	Qatar	qatari,e[1]
la République centrafricaine	*the Central African Republic*	centrafricain,e
la République démocratique du Congo	*the Democratic Republic of Congo*	congolais,e
la République dominicaine	*the Dominican Republic*	dominicain,e
la République d'Afrique du Sud	*the Republic of South Africa*	sudafricain,e
la République tchèque[2] (or: la Tchequie)	*the Czech Republic*	tchèque
la Roumanie	*Romania*	roumain,e
le Royaume Uni	*the United Kingdom*	anglais,e
la Russie	*Russia*	russe
le Rwanda (or: le Rouanda)	*Rwanda*	rwandais,e
le Salvador	*El Salvador*	salvadorien,ne
le Sénégal	*Senegal*	sénégalais,e
la Serbie	*Serbia*	serbe
la Sierra Leone	*Sierra Leone*	sierra-léonais,e
Singapour	*Singapore*	singapourien,ne
la Slovaquie[2]	*Slovakia*	slovaque
la Slovénie	*Slovenia*	slovène
la Somalie	*Somalia*	somalien,ne
le Soudan	*Sudan*	soudanais,e
le Sri Lanka	*Sri Lanka*	sri-lankais,e
la Suède	*Sweden*	suédois,e
la Suisse	*Switzerland*	suisse[3]
le Surinam(e)	*Surinam*	surinamien,ne
le Swaziland	*Swaziland*	swazi,e
la Syrie	*Syria*	syrien,ne
le Tadjikistan	*Tajikistan*	tadjik,e
Taïwan	*Taiwan*	taïwanais,e
la Tanzanie	*Tanzania*	tanzanien,ne

---

1. the inhabitants of Qatar: **les Qatariens**
2. This country is a part of *former Czechoslovakia* [= l'ex-Tchecoslovaquie (f)]
3. The female inhabitant of Switzerland is **la Suissesse**. The languages spoken in Switzerland are: **l'allemand**, **le français**, **l'italien**, and **le romanche**.

French name of the country	*English equivalent*	*Adjective*
la Tasmanie	*Tasmania*	tasmanien,ne
le Tchad	*Chad*	tchadien,ne
la Tchétchénie	*Chechnya*	tchétchène
la Thaïlande	*Thailand*	thaïlandais,e [1]
le Togo	*Togo*	togolais,e
la Tunisie	*Tunisia*	tunisien,ne
le Turkménistan	*Turkmenistan*	turkmène
la Turquie	*Turkey*	turc, turque
l'Ukraine (f)	*Ukraine*	ukrainien,ne
l'Uruguay (m)	*Uruguay*	uruguayen,ne
les U.S.A.	*the USA*	américain,e
le Venezuela	*Venezuela*	vénézuélien,ne
le Vietnam (Viêt-nam)	*Vietnam*	vietnamien,ne
le Yémen	*Yemen*	yéménite
la Yougoslavie	*Yugoslavia*	yougoslave
le Zaïre [2]	*Zaire*	zaïrois,e
la Zambie	*Zambia*	zambien,ne
le Zimbabwe	*Zimbabwe*	zimbabwéen,ne

- When the country name is *masculine* singular and does *not* begin with a vowel or mute *h*, **au** expresses 'in' and 'to', **du** expresses 'from'

J'habite **au** Portugal.	*I live **in** Portugal.*
Je n'ai jamais été **au** Japon.	*I have never been **to** Japan.*
Elle est **du** Canada.	*She is **from** Canada.*
Il revient **du** Danemark.	*He comes back **from** Denmark.*

But:

dans (+ definite article) is used to express 'in' and 'to' with *modified* masculine countries.[3]

dans le Pérou moderne — ***in** modern Peru*

---

1. The language spoken in Thailand is **le thaï**.
2. Since 1997 this country is called **la République démocratique du Congo**.
3. See also p. 121

- When the name of the country is *feminine* (or masculine beginning with a vowel or mute *h*)[1] **en** expresses 'in' and 'to' **de** (d') expresses 'from'. The definite article is *not* used.

Je vais **en** Arabie Saoudite.	*I am going **to** Saudi Arabia.*
Téhéran est **en** Iran.	*Teheran is **in** Iran.*
Il vient **de** Norvège.	*He comes **from** Norway.*
Elles arrivent **d'**Afghanistan.	*They arrive **from** Afghanistan.*

But:

dans (+ definite article) is used to express 'in' with *modified* feminine countries.[2]

dans la France d'aujourd'hui	***in** today's France*

- When the country name does *not* have an article and does *not* begin with a vowel or mute *h*, **à** expresses 'in' and 'to', **de** expresses 'from'

à Bahreïn	***in/to** Bahrein*
de Bahreïn	***from** Bahrein*
à Chypre	***in/to** Cyprus*
de Chypre	***from** Cyprus*
à Cuba	***in/to** Cuba*
de Cuba	***from** Cuba*
à Djibouti	***in/to** Djibouti*
de Djibouti	***from** Djibouti*
à Madagascar	***in/to** Madagascar*
de Madagascar	***from** Madagascar*
à Monaco	***in/to** Monaco*
de Monaco	***from** Monaco*
à Porto Rico	***in/to** Puerto Rico*
de Porto Rico	***from** Puerto Rico*
à Singapour	***in/to** Singapore*
de Singapour	***from** Singapore*
à Taïwan	***in/to** Taiwan*
de Taïwan	***from** Taiwan*

---

1. See also p. 85
2. See also p. 121

But:

en Andorre	***in/to*** *Andorra*
d'Andorre	***from*** *Andorra*
en Haïti	***in/to*** *Haiti*
d'Haïti	***from*** *Haiti*
en Israël	***in/to*** *Israel*
d'Israël	***from*** *Israel*
en Oman	***in/to*** *Oman*
d'Oman	***from*** *Oman*

- When the name of the country is *plural*, **aux** expresses 'in' and 'to', **des** expresses 'from'[1]

Nous voyageons **aux** Etats-Unis.	*We travel* ***in*** *the United States.*
Il est originaire **des** Philippines.	*He is* ***from*** *the Philippines.*

3. Islands

- Islands without an article

French name of the island	*English equivalent*
Bornéo	*Borneo*
Ceylan	*Ceylon*
Chypre	*Cyprus*
Cuba	*Cuba*
Hawaï	*Hawaii*
Madagascar	*Madagascar*
Majorque	*Majorca*
Malte	*Malta*
Mayotte	*Mayotte*
Porto Rico	*Puerto Rico*
Sainte-Hélène	*Saint Helena*
Tahiti	*Tahiti*
Ténérif(f)e	*Teneriffa*
Terre-Neuve	*Newfoundland*

Before islands that are *not* preceded by an article, **à** generally expresses 'in/on' and 'to', **de** expresses 'from'

Napoléon mourut **à** Saint-Hélène.	*Napoleon died* ***on*** *Saint Helena.*
Il revient **de** Tahiti.	*He comes back* ***from*** *Tahiti.*

1. See also p. 20 (**aux**), and p. 53 (**des**).

- Islands with a feminine singular definite article[1]

French name of the island	*English equivalent*	*Adjective*
la Corse	*Corsica*	corse
la Crète	*Crete*	crétois,e
la Guadeloupe[2]	*Guadeloupe*	guadeloupéen,ne
la Jamaïque	*Jamaica*	jamaïcain,e
la Martinique[2]	*Martinique*	martiniquais,e
la Nouvelle Calédonie[3]	*New Caledonia*	néo-calédonien,ne
la Nouvelle Guinée	*New Guinea*	néoguinéen,ne
la Réunion[2]	*Reunion Island*	réunionnais,e
la Sardaigne	*Sardinia*	sarde
la Sicile	*Sicily*	sicilien, ne

Small *feminine singular* islands generally use **à la** to express 'in/on' and 'to', **de la** to express 'from'

Je vais **à la** Réunion.	*I go **to** Reunion Island.*
Il habite **à la** Guadeloupe.	*He lives **on** Guadeloupe.*
Joséphine vient **de la** Martinique.	*Josephine comes **from** Martinique.*

Bigger *feminine singular* islands use **en** to express 'in/on' and 'to', **de** to express 'from'

(aller, habiter) **en** Corse, **en** Crète, **en** Jamaïque, **en** Sardaigne, **en** Nouvelle Calédonie, **en** Sicile, **en** Nouvelle Guinée

(venir) **de** Corse, **de** Crète, **de** Jamaïque, **de** Sicile, **de** Sardaigne, etc.

---

1. Note that with all islands mentioned above, whether an article is part of their name or not, it is also correct to say **sur l'île de** (or: **dans l'île de**) + name of the island to express 'on'.
   Ils habitent **sur l'île de** Cuba. — *They live **on** the island of Cuba.*
   Il est né **sur l'île de** la Réunion. — *He was born **on** Reunion Island.*

2. Note that **la Réunion, la Martinique** and **la Guadeloupe** (as well as *la Guyane française*) are French *overseas departments* [= départements d'outre-mer], i.e. they have the same statute as the departments in France, and the citizens of these places are French.

3. **La Nouvelle Calédonie** belongs to France's *overseas territories* [= territoires d'outre-mer]. These territories also include *la Polynésie française, Saint-Pierre et Miquelon* and *Wallis-et-Futuna.*

   The acronym **DOM-TOM** is frequently used to refer to France's overseas departments and territories.

- Islands with a plural definite article

French name of the islands	*English equivalent*
les Antilles	*the West Indies*
les Açores	*the Azores*
les (îles) Bahamas	*the Bahamas*
les (îles) Baléares	*the Balearic Islands*
les Bermudes	*the Bermudas*
les (îles) Canaries	*the Canary Islands*
les Caraïbes	*the Caribbean*
les (îles) Comores	*the Comoros*
les (îles) Fidji	*the Fiji Islands*
les (îles) Galapagos	*the Galapagos Islands*
les (îles) Maldives	*the Maldive Islands*
les (îles) Malouines	*the Falklands*
les (îles) Marquises	*the Marquesas Islands*
les Nouvelles Hybrides	*the New Hebrides*
les Seychelles	*the Seychelles*
les îles de la Société	*the Society Islands*
les îles anglo-normandes	*the Channel Islands*

Before islands that are preceded by a plural article, **aux** generally expresses 'in/on' and 'to', **des** expresses 'from'

(aller, habiter) **aux** Antilles, **aux** Bahamas, **aux** Baléares, **aux** Maldives, **aux** (îles) Canaries, **aux** Seychelles, **aux** îles de la Société, **aux** Açores, **aux** (or: dans les) Caraïbes, etc.

(venir) **des** Caraïbes, **des** Comores, **des** (îles) Fidji, **des** Marquises, etc.

- Smaller islands that use *'l'île de'* + name of the island

French name of the island	*English equivalent*
l'île du Diable	*Devil's Island*
l'île d'Elbe	*Elba*
l'île Maurice	*Mauritius*
l'île de Ré	*the Island of Ré*

With these islands, **à**, **sur** or **dans** express 'in/on' and 'to', **de** expresses 'from'

(aller, habiter) **à** l'île d'Elbe, **sur** l'île Maurice, **dans** l'île de Ré

(venir) **de** l'île Maurice, **de** l'île de Ré, **de** l'île du Diable

4. Regions

French name of the region	*English equivalent*
l'Amazonie (f)	*the Amazon*
l'Andalousie (f)	*Andalusia*
l'Asie Mineure (f)	*Asia Minor*
les Balkans	*the Balkans*
la Bande de Gaza	*the Gaza Strip*
la Bavière	*Bavaria*
le Bengale	*Bengal*
la Bohème	*Bohemia*
le Cachemire	*Kashmir*
la Catalogne	*Catalonia*
la Castille	*Castile*
le Caucase	*the Caucasus*
la Cisjordanie	*the West Bank* (of Jordan)
l'Indochine	*Indochina*
le Kosovo	*Kosovo*
le Kurdistan	*Kurdistan*
le Labrador	*Labrador*
la Laponie	*Lapland*
le Maghreb[1]	*the Maghreb*
la Mandchourie	*Manchuria*
le Midi	*the South of France*
la Mongolie	*Mongolia*
la Nouvelle Angleterre	*New England*
la Nouvelle Calédonie	*New Caledonia*
l'Occident (m)	*the West*
l'Orient (m)	*the East*
l'Extrême Orient (m)	*the Far East*
le Moyen Orient (m)	*the Middle East*
le Proche-Orient (m)	*the Near East*
la Palestine	*Palestine*
les pays baltes	*the Baltic States*
la Polynésie	*Polynesia*
la Rhénanie	*the Rhineland*
la Scandinavie	*Scandinavia*

---

1. Includes Morocco, Algeria and Tunisia. The word comes from an Arab expression which means '*land where the sun sets*'.

French name of the region	*English equivalent*
la Sibérie	*Siberia*
la Terre Sainte	*the Holy Land*
le Tibet	*Tibet*
le Tyrol	*Tyrol*
la Wallonie	*Walloon area* (of Belgium)

With regions (as with countries and continents), French uses

- **en** to express 'in' and 'to', **de** to express 'from' when the region is *feminine* (or *masculine* starting with a vowel)

  (aller, habiter) **en** Cisjordanie, **en** Polynésie, **en** Extrême Orient, **en** Terre Sainte, **en** Nouvelle-Calédonie, etc.

  (venir) **de** Palestine, **de** Bohème, etc.

- **au** to express 'in' and 'to', **du** to express 'from' when the region is *masculine*

  (aller, habiter) **au** Tibet, **au** Proche Orient, **au** Maghreb, etc.

  (venir) **du** Labrador, **du** Midi, **du** Tibet, etc.

But:

dans la Bande de Gaza = *in the Gaza Strip*
dans le Tyrol = *in/to Tyrol*
dans le Caucase = *in the Caucasus*
dans les Balkans = *in/to the Balkans*
dans les pays baltes = *in the Baltics*

5. French provinces and regions

French name of the region	*English equivalent*	*Adjective*
l'Alsace (f)	*Alsace*	alsacien,ne
l'Anjou (m)	*Anjou*	angevin,e
l'Aquitaine (f)	*Aquitaine*	aquitain,e
l'Auvergne (f)	*Auvergne*	auvergnat,e
le Béarn	*Bearn*	béarnais,e
le Berry	*Berry*	berrichon, ne
la Bourgogne	*Burgundy*	bourguignon,ne
la Bretagne	*Britanny*	breton,ne
la Camargue	*Camargue*	camarguais,e
la Champagne	*Champagne*	champenois,e

French name of the region	*English equivalent*	*Adjective*
le Dauphiné	*Dauphine*	dauphinois,e
la Dordogne	*Dordogne*	dordognais,e
la Flandre	*Flanders*	flamand,e
la Franche-Comté	*Franche-Comte*	franche-comtois,e
la Gascogne	*Gascony*	gascon,ne
l'Ile-de-France (f)	*Ile-de-France*	francilien,ne
le Languedoc	*Languedoc*	languedocien,ne
le Limousin	*Limousin*	limousin,e
la Lorraine	*Lorraine*	lorrain,e
la Normandie	*Normandy*	normand,e
le pays basque	*the Basque country*	basque, basquaise
le Périgord	*Perigord*	périgourdin,e
la Picardie	*Picardy*	picard,e
le Poïtou	*Poitou*	poitevin,e
la Provence	*Provence*	provençal,e
le Roussillon	*Roussillon*	roussillonnais,e
la Savoie	*Savoy*	savoyard,e
la Sologne	*Sologne*	solognot,e
la Touraine	*Touraine*	tourangeau, elle

- With French provinces and regions which are *feminine* or *masculine* beginning with a vowel, one uses **en** (without article) to express 'in' and 'to', **de** (d') to express 'from'

en Alsace	***in/to*** *Alsace*	**en** Anjou	***in/to*** *Anjou*
en Savoie	***in/to*** *Savoy*	**en** Dordogne	***in/to*** *Dordogne*
d'Auvergne	***from*** *Auvergne*	**d'**Aquitaine	***from*** *Aquitaine*
de Provence	***from*** *Provence*	**de** Normandie	***from*** *Normandy*

- With *masculine* French provinces and regions beginning with a consonant, one uses **dans le** to express 'in' and 'to', **du** to express 'from'

dans le Béarn	***in/to*** *Bearn*
dans le Languedoc	***in/to*** *Languedoc*
dans le Berry	***in/to*** *Berry*
dans le pays basque	***in/to*** *the Basque Country*

du Berry ***from*** *Berry* **du** Périgord ***from*** *Perigord*

6. French departments (administrative areas)

01 l'Ain (m)
02 l'Aisne (m)
03 l'Allier (m)
04 les Alpes de Haute-Provence
05 les Hautes-Alpes
06 les Alpes-Maritimes
07 l'Ardèche (f)
08 les Ardennes (f)
09 l'Ariège (f)
10 l'Aube (f)
11 l'Aude (f)
12 l'Aveyron (m)
13 les Bouches-du-Rhône
14 le Calvados
15 le Cantal
16 la Charente
17 la Charente-Maritime
18 le Cher
19 la Corrèze
20 la Corse (la Corse-du-Sud, la Haute-Corse)
21 la Côte-d'Or
22 les Côtes-d'Armor
23 la Creuse
24 la Dordogne
25 le Doubs
26 la Drôme
27 l'Eure (f)
28 l'Eure-et-Loir (f)
29 **le** Finistère
30 le Gard
31 la Haute-Garonne
32 le Gers
33 la Gironde
34 l'Hérault (m)
35 l'Ille-et-Vilaine (f)
36 l'Indre (m)
37 l'Indre-et-Loire (m)
38 l'Isère (f)
39 le Jura
40 les Landes
41 le Loir-et-Cher
42 la Loire
43 la Haute-Loire
44 la Loire-Atlantique

45 le Loiret
46 le Lot
47 le Lot-et-Garonne
48 la Lozère
49 le Maine-et-Loire
50 la Manche
51 la Marne
52 la Haute-Marne
53 la Mayenne
54 la Meurthe-et-Moselle
55 la Meuse
56 le Morbihan
57 la Moselle
58 la Nièvre
59 le Nord
60 l'Oise (f)
61 l'Orne (f)
62 le Pas-de-Calais
63 le Puy-de-Dôme
64 les Pyrénées-Atlantiques
65 les Hautes-Pyrénées
66 les Pyrénées-Orientales
67 le Bas-Rhin
68 le Haut-Rhin
69 **le** Rhône
70 la Haute-Saône
71 la Saône-et-Loire
72 la Sarthe
73 la Savoie
74 la Haute-Savoie
75 Paris
76 la Seine-Maritime
77 la Seine-et-Marne
78 les Yvelines
79 les Deux-Sèvres
80 la Somme
81 le Tarn
82 le Tarn-et-Garonne
83 le Var
84 **le** Vaucluse
85 la Vendée
86 la Vienne
87 la Haute-Vienne
88 les Vosges
89 l'Yonne (f)
90 le Territoire de Belfort
91 l'Essonne (f)

92 les Hauts-de-Seine
93 la Seine-Saint-Denis
94 le Val-de-Marne
95 le Val-d'Oise

- With *masculine* French departments **dans le** (dans l') is used to express 'in' and 'to', **du** (de l') is used to express 'from'

(aller, habiter)

dans l'Ain	**dans le** Cher	**dans le** Lot
dans l'Aisne	**dans le** Gers	**dans le** Rhône
dans le Calvados	**dans l'**Hérault	**dans le** Var
dans le Cantal	**dans l'**Indre	**dans le** Vaucluse

(venir)

du Bas-Rhin	**de l'**Hérault	**du** Jura

- With *feminine* French departments the use of prepositions varies

  - **dans la** (dans l') is generally used to express 'in' and 'to', **de la** (de l') is used to express 'from' in the following cases

(aller, habiter)

dans l'Ariège	**dans la** (Haute-)Loire	**dans l'**Orne
dans l'Aude	**dans la** Lozère	**dans la** Sarthe
dans la Creuse	**dans la** Manche	**dans la** Somme
dans la Drôme	**dans la** (Haute-)Marne	**dans la** Vienne
dans l'Essonne	**dans la** Meuse	**dans l'**Yonne
dans l'Eure(-et-Loir)	**dans la** Nièvre	
dans l'Isère	**dans l'**Oise	

(venir)

de l'Eure	**de la** Lozère	**de la** Vienne

  - **en** is generally used to express 'in' and 'to', **de** (d') is used to express 'from' in the following instances

(aller, habiter)

en Ardèche	**en** Haute-Garonne	**en** Saône-et-Loire
en Charente(-Maritime)	**en** Haute-Saône	**en** (Haute-)Savoie
en Corrèze	**en** Ille-et-Vilaine	**en** Seine-Maritime
en Côte-d'Or	**en** Loire-Atlantique	**en** Seine-et-Marne
en Dordogne	**en** Mayenne	**en** Seine-Saint-Denis
en Gironde	**en** Moselle	**en** Vendée

(venir)

de Dordogne	**d'** Ille-et-Vilaine	**de** Savoie

- With *plural* French departments **dans les** is used to express 'in' and 'to', **des** is used to express 'from'

(aller, habiter)

dans les Alpes-Maritimes
dans les Landes
dans les Hautes-Pyrénées
dans les Yvelines

(venir)

des Bouches-du-Rhône
des Hauts-de-Seine
des Landes
des Yvelines

Note:

dans le département de [+ article + name of department] can be used with *any* department to express 'in' and 'to'

Il vit **dans le départment *du*** Lot.
Nous sommes allés **dans le départment *de la*** Creuse et **dans le département *de l'*** Isère.

7. American States

l'Alabama (m)
l'Alaska (m)
l'Arizona (m)
l'Arkansas (m)
la Californie
la Caroline du Nord
la Caroline du Sud
le Colorado
le Connecticut
le Dakota du Nord
le Dakota du Sud
le Delaware
la Floride
la Géorgie
Hawaï (m) [= les îles Hawaï]
l'Idaho (m)
l'Illinois (m)
l'Indiana (m)
l'Iowa (m)
le Kansas
le Kentucky
la Louisiane
le Maine
le Maryland
le Massachusetts
le Michigan
le Minnesota
le Mississippi
le Missouri
le Montana
le Nebraska
le Nevada
le New Hampshire
le New Jersey
le Nouveau Mexique
l'état de New York (m)
l'Ohio (m)
l'Oklahoma (m)
l'Oregon (m)
la Pennsylvanie
le Rhode Island
le Tennessee
le Texas
l'Utah (m)
le Vermont
la Virginie
la Virginie Occidentale
le Washington
le Wisconsin
le Wyoming

- When the French name of the American state is *feminine*, or when it *begins with a vowel*, **en** is used to translate 'in' and 'to', **de** (d') is used to translate 'from'

en Californie	***in/to** California*	**en** Alaska	***in/to** Alaska*
de Californie	***from** California*	**d'**Alaska	***from** Alaska*

- When the French name of the American state is *masculine* and does not begin with a vowel, **dans le** is used to translate 'in' and 'to'[1], **du** is used to translate 'from'

dans le Tennessee	***in/to** Tennessee*
dans le Michigan	***in/to** Michigan*
du Colorado	***from** Colorado*
du Nouveau Mexique	***from** New Mexico*
du Texas	***from** Texas*

Note:

♦ **dans l'état de** (d') [+ name of state without an article] can be used with *any* American state to express 'in' and 'to'

dans l'état de Montana	***in/to** Montana*
dans l'état d'Alaska	***in/to** Alaska*
dans l'état de Floride	***in/to** Florida*

de l'état de (d') [+ name of state without an article] can be used with *any* American state to express 'from'

de l'état de Pennsylvanie	***from** Pennsylvania*
de l'état d'Arizona	***from** Arizona*

♦ Since *Hawaï* is an island, **à** is used to express 'in' and 'to', **d'** is used to express 'from'

Je suis allé **à** Hawaï (or: **aux îles** Hawaï).	*I went **to** Hawaii.*
Elle vient **d'**Hawaï (or: **des** îles Hawaï).	*She comes **from** Hawaii.*

♦ *New York, **à** New York* and ***de** New York* refer to the city; ***dans/de l'état de** New York* refer to the state of New York.

♦ *Washington, **à** Washington* and ***de** Washington* refer to the city of Washington; ***le*** Washington, ***dans le** Washington* and ***du** Washington* refer to the state of Washington.

---

1. Except: **au** Texas (*in/to Texas*), **au** Nouveau Mexique (*in/to New Mexico*)

8. Canadian provinces and territories

French name of the Canadian province	*English equivalent*
l'Alberta (m)	*Alberta*
la Colombie Britannique	*British Columbia*
l'Ile du Prince-Edouard (f)	*Prince Edward Island*
le Manitoba	*Manitoba*
le Nouveau-Brunswick	*New Brunswick*
la Nouvelle-Ecosse	*Nova Scotia*
l'Ontario (m)	*Ontario*
le Québec	*Quebec*
la Saskatchewan	*Saskatchewan*
Terre-Neuve (f)	*Newfoundland*
les Territoires du Nord-Ouest (m)	*the Northwest Territories*
le (Territoire du)Yukon	*the Yukon (Territory)*

- When the French name of the Canadian province is *feminine*, or when it *begins with a vowel*, **en** is used to translate 'in' and 'to'[1], **de** (d') is used to translate 'from'[2]

  (aller, habiter)
  en Alberta, **en** Saskatchewan, **en** Colombie Britannique, **en** Ontario

  (venir)
  d'Ontario, **de** Nouvelle Ecosse, **d'**Alberta, **de** Terre-Neuve

- When the French name of the Canadian province is *masculine* and does not begin with a vowel, **au** is used to translate 'in' and 'to', **du** is used to translate 'from'

  (aller, habiter)
  au Manitoba, **au** Québec, **au** Nouveau-Brunswick

  (venir)
  du Manitoba, **du** Québec, **du** Nouveau Brunswick

---

1. But: **à** Terre-Neuve (*in/to Newfoundland*) since it is an island,
   sur l'Ile du Prince-Edouard (or: **dans** l'Ile du Prince-Edouard)
2. But: **de l'**Ile du Prince-Edouard

- With the territories, 'in/to' and 'from' is expressed the following way

  (aller, habiter)
  dans les Territoires du Nord-Ouest, **dans le** (Territoire du) Yukon

  (venir)
  des Territoires du Nord-Ouest, **du** (Territoire du) Yukon

Note:

- **dans la province de** (d') [+ name of province without an article] can be used with *any* Canadian province to express 'in' and 'to'

dans la province de Manitoba	*in/to Manitoba*
dans la province d'Ontario	*in/to Ontario*

  de la province de (d') [+ name of province without an article] can be used with *any* Canadian province to express 'from'

de la province de Québec	*from Quebec*
de la province d'Alberta	*from Alberta*

- *Québec, **à** Québec* and ***de** Québec* refer to the city of Québec; ***le** Québec, **au** Québec* and ***du** Québec* refer to the province.

Expressions with geographical words

filer **à l'anglaise**	*to take a French leave*
marcher **en** file **indienne**	*to walk in single file*
C'est **de l'hébreu/du chinois** pour moi.	*It's Greek to me.*
bâtir des châteaux **en Espagne**	*to build castles in the air*
travailler **pour** le roi de **Prusse**	*to work for nothing*
renvoyer qch **aux** calendes **grecques**	*to postpone sth till much later*
Ce n'est pas **le Pérou**.	*It's not a fortune.*

Index